The Old Fictions and the New

By Richard Kostelanetz

BOOKS OF FICTION
In the Beginning (1971)
Ad Infinitum (1973)
Short Fictions (1974)
Come Here (1975)
Extrapolate (1975)
Modulations (1975)
Openings & Closings (1975)
Constructs (1976)
Numbers: Poems & Stories (1976)
One Night Stood (1977)
Foreshortenings (1978)
Constructs Two (1978)
Tabula Rasa (1978)
Inexistences (1978)
And So Forth (1979)
Exhaustive Parallel Intervals
  (1979)
More Short Fictions (1980)
Reincarnations (1981)
Epiphanies (1983)

AUDIOTAPES OF FICTION
Openings & Closings (1975)
Experimental Prose (1976)
Foreshortenings & Other Stories (1977)
Monotapes (1978)
Seductions (1981)
Conversations/Dialogues (1984)
Audio Writing (1984)

CRITICISM OF FICTION
The End of Intelligent Writing (1974)
Grants & the Future of Literature (1978)
Twenties in the Sixties (1979)

ANTHOLOGIES WITH FICTION
Twelve from the Sixties (1967)
The Young American Writers (1967)
Future's Fictions (1971)
In Youth (1972)
Breakthrough Fictioneers (1973)
The Yale Gertrude Stein (1980)

The Old Fictions and the New

Richard Kostelanetz

McFarland & Company, Inc., Publishers
Jefferson, North Carolina, and London

Library of Congress Cataloguing-in-Publication Data

Kostelanetz, Richard.
 The old fictions and the new.

 Includes index.
 1. American fiction — 20th century — History and
criticism. 2. French fiction — 20th century — History
and criticism. 3. Fiction. 4. Avant-garde (Aesthetics)
I. Title.
PS379.K66   1987   813'.54'09   85-43581

 ISBN 0-89950-208-3 (acid-free natural paper) ∞

Printed in the United States of America.

McFarland   Box 611   Jefferson NC 28640

to Sasha Newborn

Table of Contents

Acknowledgments ix
Preface xi
Fictions in My History (1985) 1
Inventory of Fictions (1985) 13

THE OLD FICTIONS

New American Fiction (1965) 21
The American Absurd Novel (1965) 52
"New American Fiction" Reconsidered (1967) 58
Short Story Anthologies and a History (1966) 72
Notes on the American Short Story Today (1967) 76
Ralph Ellison (1969) 86
Leslie A. Fiedler (1972) 103
Interchangeable Parts (1975) 106
"The Fiction Collective" Again (1978) 108
Avant-Garde Past (1981) 110

THE NEW FICTIONS

Dada and the Future of Fiction (1968) 117
Gertrude Stein (1975) 128
Jack Kerouac (1980) 141
Innovations in Fiction (1973) 151
New Fiction in America (1974) 157
Michel Butor (1963) 171
Jean-François Bory (1974) 173
Tom Phillips (1976, 1985) 176
Richard Grayson (1981) 180
Twenty-Five Fictional Hypotheses (1969) 182
Constructivist Fictions (1974) 186
And So Forth (1978) 191
On Symmetries: My Visual Novel (1985) 192
Epiphanies (1983) 196
Retrospect on My Fictions (1985) 197
Index 199

Acknowledgments

The chapters of *The Old Fictions and the New* first appeared in the following publications:

Bambu: "Epiphanies (1983)"
Books: "Addendum 1967"
Chicago Review: "Short Stories Anthologies and a History (1966)"
Contemporary Novelists: "Leslie A. Fiedler (1972)," "Addendum 1971" (Irvin Faust)
Cumberland Journal: "Richard Grayson (1981)"
Denver Review: "New Fiction in America (1974)"
Hollins Critic: "Gertrude Stein (1975)"
The Listener: "The American Absurd Novel (1965)"
Margins: "Interchangeable Parts (1975)," "Jean-François Bory (1974)," "Tom Phillips (1976)"
Minnesota Review: "Notes on the American Short Story Today (1967)"
New York Arts Journal: "Jack Kerouac (1980)"
New York Times Book Review: "The American Absurd Novel (1965)"
Panache: "Twenty-Five Fictional Hypotheses (1969)"
Partisan Review: "Avant-Garde Past (1981)"
Pulpsmith: "Retrospect on My Fiction (1985)"
Ramparts: "The New American Fiction (1965)"
Shenandoah: "Ralph Ellison (1969)"
Tracks: "Constructivist Fictions (1974)"
Tri-Quarterly: " 'New American Fiction' Reconsidered (1967)"
Twenties in the Sixties (Assembling-Greenwood, 1979): "Michel Butor (1963)"
El Urogallo: "Innovations in Fiction (1973)"
Washington Review of the Arts: " 'The Fiction Collective' Again (1978)"
Wordsand (Gallery of Simon Fraser University-RK Editions, 1978): "And So Forth (1978)"
Works: "Dada and the Future of Fiction (1968)"

Every effort has been made to identify the sources of original publication of these essays and make full acknowledgment of their use. If any error or omission has occurred, it will be rectified in future editions, provided that appropriate notification is submitted in writing to the publisher or author (P.O. Box 73, Canal Street, New York, NY 10013).

Preface

Several years ago Donald Hall invited me to gather my fugitive essays on poetry into a book for his "Poets on Poetry" series. This collection, titled "The Old Poetries and the New," appeared under the University of Michigan Press's imprint in 1981 in a series that also included comparable compilations by Robert Bly, Galway Kinnell, Louis Simpson, Diane Wakoski, among many others of similar repute and persuasions. There was no doubt about it. I was the odd man out, probably included to expand the parameters of the series. Instead, the book fell outside it, selling perceptibly less than all the others. There was no doubt that I had, in the essays, taken a position far outside established poetic discourse, as well as poetic business in this country—not just in my poetry, but in my ideas about poetry and the poets I chose to discuss.

Another fact distinguishing me from the others in Hall's canon is that I do a lot of fiction, in similarly unusual forms needless to say, and had written much about fiction. It seemed appropriate for me to make a companion book of my essays about fiction. However, there is no series comparable to Hall's for American fictioners—a fact that may or may not be significant, and so this book appears by itself, fortunately in immediate competition with nothing.

Its theme is an extension of its title (and, beyond that, of the division within the book)—that there is a distinct difference between the established modes of post–1960 American fiction and truly avant-garde work. It is not for nothing that most of the "New Fiction" discussed in the second part of this volume was not reviewed, has not been discussed by other fiction critics, and is not now taught.

The following essays were written for a variety of publications, for a variety of reasons (as well as rates of pay), and this circumstance accounts for variations in diction and cultural pitch. Were I to write about "The Old Fictions and the New" from scratch, it might be a more unified book, but I doubt if it would be a livelier one. This book differs from others of its kind in being not a collection of judgments and or attitudes but in staking a definite critical position that I take to be unique.

I repaired some stylistic clumsiness and thought often about expunging repetitions of theme and example before deciding that, since my ideas were so unfashionable and, alas, easily misunderstood, they are generally worth repeating (and incidentally give this collection a spatial coherence). Most of these essays are fairly conventional in expository style, which perhaps explains why some readers seem to prefer them to my fiction; but given the exploratory premises of my fiction, that discrepancy in appreciation should scarcely be surprising. The truth is I long ago made a decision to write about avant-garde art in the common language, in an accessible (unavant garde) way. Now that I have moved further into unfamiliar territory in my creative work, I have had occasion to reconsider that earlier decision, but insufficient reasons to repudiate it.

Richard Kostelanetz
New York, New York
May 14, 1986

Post–World War II America has witnessed the development of two dominant types of critic: the writer-critic and the scholar-critic. The writer-critic's apprenticeship is an extension of the traditional Grub Street or newspaper city-room route to criticism. Beginning by writing and publishing poems, novels, stories and essays in little magazines or the underground press, he progresses to criticism to defend a new literary charter or a rising generation, or to make his reputation. Hence the writer-critic tends to begin by writing reviews. — Grant Webster, *The Republic of Letters* (1979).

What is fictitious in a novel is not so much the story but the method by which thought develops into action, a method which never occurs in daily life. — Alain, as quoted by E.M. Forster, *Aspects of the Novel* (1927).

Every art that greatly differs from its predecessors involves a transformation of taste and this is often the point of departure for further changes. — André Malraux, *The Imaginary Museum* (1953).

The novel must exist outside of the life it deals with; it is not an imitation. The novel is an invention, something that is made; it is not the expression of "self"; it does not mirror reality. ... It is the novel, of itself, that must have form, and if it be honestly made, we find, not the meaning of life, but a revelation of its actuality. We are not told what to think, but are instead directed to an essence, the observation of which leads to the freeing of our imagination and our arrival at the only "truth" that fiction possesses. The flash, the instant or cluster of meaning, must be extrapolated from "the pageless actual" and presented in its imaginative qualities. The achievement of this makes a novel which is art: the rest is pastime. — Gilbert Sorrentino, " 'The Various Isolated': W.C. Williams' Prose," *New American Review* (1972).

Fictions in My History (1985)

The great artist, in this view, is essentially a revolutionary
spirit who remakes his art, disclosing ever new forms. The
accomplishment of the past ceases to be a closed tradition
of noble content or absolute perfection, but a model of in-
dividuality, of history-making effort through continual self-
transformation. Far from being the destroyers of eternal
values, as their opponents said, the new artists believed
themselves to be the true bearers of a great tradition of
creativeness. Movement and novelty, the working out of latent possibilities, were, they supposed, the essence of
history. In this, as well as in the beauty of his work, lay the
artist's dignity. The movement of modern art had therefore
an ethical content; artistic integrity required a permanent
concern with self-development and the evolution of art. —
Meyer Schapiro, "The Introduction of Modern Art in
America" (1952).

As a child, I read less fiction than history, which may or may not be
significant; but among the former were sequences of boys' books, including
some pre-war gems I had inherited from a cousin. My recollection is that
my absolute favorite was Jules Verne's *Twenty Thousand Leagues Under the
Sea*. In high school, the first novelist to capture my imagination was Sinclair
Lewis, to whom I devoted a ninth-grade paper that was written with more
enthusiasm than any other work for school. The first imaginative publications to appear under my name were satires that reflected his influence. The
next fiction to strike me as special, if not the most important I had read so
far, was Jean-Paul Sartre's "The Wall," and most every other fiction that
came my way during high school was critically compared to it. Another
detail that may or may not be significant is that in college aptitude tests my
"quantitative" score exceeded my verbal (and that discrepancy reappeared
when I took the Graduate Record Examinations at the end of college).

For better and perhaps worse, I never had any taste for trash fictions
(e.g., best-sellers, mysteries, romances) or for Hollywood movies (which
were "zoned out" of the suburban community where we lived). My favorite
kinds of pop culture were (and still are) sports, comedies, and folk songs.

Though I have always thought myself eccentric and underprivileged, my upbringing was basically unexceptional with continuous schooling for twenty years, my own room first in a large apartment and then in a detached house, parents who stayed married to each other, steady girlfriends, and enough allowance to keep me out of trouble.

By the time I got to college, I knew I would be a writer. In my freshman year, I took a prose-writing workshop whose teacher, now a famous novelist, assured me that I "had no talent for prose." (Perhaps he wrote scholastic aptitude tests in his spare time.) Since I majored not in English but "American Civilization," as it was called at Brown, I read the standard American classics, in addition to continental fiction in translation. English literature scarcely captured me. By the time I turned twenty, I overcame my teenage insomnia by reading through the night, every night, preferring fiction to poetry (without quite understanding why or how), and before long read (and owned) more literary novels than anyone else at school, because I (and everyone else) knew that, aside from whether I ever became a writer, I would be at minimum a professional reader of prose. I became a junior editor of the official undergraduate literary magazine and then co-editor of an off-campus alternative. About that time, I discovered for myself two works that were not taught then — Ralph Ellison's *Invisible Man* and the multivolumed saga of Henry Miller. I did my A.B. honors thesis on Miller (which was returned to me with an "A," but no notes on its pages, because the professor could not comment on what was not yet academic), as well as a long "independent study" on the image of the city in American fiction. Even though my interest in fiction was then more scholarly than creative, from time to time I outlined and even began, outside of "workshops," several fictions that, on second thought, dangerously resembled Nathanael West's *The Day of the Locust*.

Once I got to graduate school, not in literature but American History, I extended my way of reading *Invisible Man*, as a fictional interpretation of black political history, back into earlier fictions by Richard Wright, W.E.B. DuBois and James Weldon Johnson and then portrayed these political fictions as implicitly commenting on each other. In the library of Columbia University is my 1966 M.A. thesis on *Politics in the Negro Novel in America* — on literature as intellectual history, perhaps indicating that at the time my taste for fiction exceeded my commitment to conventional historiography. Even though all its chapters, except the introduction, appeared in literary and scholarly magazines, they have yet to become a coherent book.

At university I regarded fiction primarily as grist for some kind of scholarly mill; during summer vacations, in the early '60s, I began to read and think about fiction as fiction. Among the then-recent books I came to treasure as my own were John Barth's *The Sot-Weed Factor*, Joseph Heller's *Catch-22*, Irvin Faust's *Roar, Lion Roar*, William Burroughs' *Naked Lunch*.

Toward the end of college, I also began reading literary criticism in earnest, and decided that writing such essays would be an interesting thing for me to do. Since no one else at the time was discussing these new enthusiasms of mine, they became the subjects of my first extended critical essays on fiction: "The New American Fiction" (1965) and "The American Absurd Novel" (1965).

Around this time, I also edited a Dell paperback anthology of new stories by such certifiably emerging talents as Saul Bellow, Bernard Malamud, Thomas Pynchon, and James Purdy, among others. *Twelve from the Sixties*, as this book was called, was introduced by my first extended essay in formalist criticism in which an uninflected flat form was identified as the principal new structure of short fiction (superceding both the arc-form of the classic story and then the post–Joycean epiphany form). As recently as 1976, that essay became the concluding chapter of Charles E. May's anthology of *Short Story Theories*, and it may still represent an advanced edge of reprintable thinking about the subject. Back in the middle sixties, I also from time to time reviewed new fiction, which some review editors thought to be my critical specialty. Since I was writing mostly about books that were commercially published, I became a favorite of not just puffing publicists who wanted me to review their latest produce but paperback editors desiring my free advice on what they should reprint.

In 1965, the Pulitzer Prize committee gave me a Fellowship in Critical Writing especially for studies in the nonliterary arts, and out of this research initially came my book on *The Theatre of Mixed Means* (1968), which was my term for the nonliterary theater of "happenings," environments and other mixed-means events. I also began to write the extended essays on new developments in sculpture, painting, music and dance, as well as the new intermedia arts, that were eventually collected in *Metamorphosis in the Arts* (1980). The more deeply I studied the nonliterary arts, the more sure I became in my commitment to the importance and integrity of formal achievements. When I got back to considering fiction, my initial critical interest, I found myself less impressed by my enthusiasms of a few years before — they seemed esthetically too conventional and too compromised by commercial considerations. Instead, I became more interested in fiction that was as different from those works (and their like) as the mixed-means theater was from conventional theater.

The first reflection of this departure in my literary taste was the anthology *Future's Fictions* which began as a special issue of the literary magazine *Panache* (1981). With full 8½" by 11" pages, this book favored kinds of fictions (and people) who were *not* in the previous anthology — visual narratives by Jochen Gerz, Jean-Francois Bory and Tom Phillips, as well as unusual prose by Dick Higgins and Madeline Gins, among others. Prefacing this selection was my aphoristic "Twenty-Five Fictional Hypotheses" which turned out to be at once so radical and so agreeable that I reused it a decade later to preface my own second collection of *More Short Fictions* (1980). It suggests, among other notions, that anything can be used to tell a story, not only nonsyntactic language but visual materials, and then that fiction differs from poetry in creating not a concentration of image and effect but a world of related sequential activities. *Future's Fictions* represented such a great leap beyond my earlier thinking about fiction that few critics and colleagues have acknowledged its existence, and I still have (and occasionally sell) copies of its original edition of only a thousand. One way I knew for sure that I had done something radical was that neither publicity managers nor paperback editors bothered me again.

Future's Fictions became a prelude to a yet more compendious anthology, *Breakthrough Fictioneers* (1973), that in its 384 pages contains a variety of alternatives (visual fiction, skeletal fiction, multipath fiction, experiments in style and typography) from over a hundred people, including Jamake Highwater (in his earlier incarnation as "J Marks"), Eleanor Antin, Tom Ahern, Alain Arias-Mísson, Kenneth Gangemi, M.D. Elevitch, Carol Emshwiller, Jackson Mac Low, John Mella, Alan Sondheim, Robert Smithson, Ruth Krauss, Emmett Williams, Stanley Berne and Arlene Zekowski among others whose fiction is rarely, if ever, anthologized elsewhere. Even now, it can be said that, as an exploration of radical innovation in fiction, this book has never been surpassed. Future literary historians may someday note that in *Breakthrough Fictioneers* is the only American publication of certain great European texts, such as Dieter Rot's "Hänsel und Gretel," M. Vaughn-James' "Scythes in the Night," and an excerpt from Hans G. Helms's *Fa:m Ahniesgwow*.

At the time *Breakthrough Fictioneers* appeared, serious critics of fiction should have reviewed it with another anthology with a similar theme that appeared from a commercial publisher the year before—Jerome Klinkowitz and John Somer's *Innovative Fiction* (1972). One superficial index of the divisive difference between the two books is that only one author appeared in both collections—John Barth; but his contribution to my book, unlike that in the other, had *not* been reprinted by Barth himself in any of his own collections (meaning either that he had repudiated it or that it came to represent something foreign to his definitive tastes). To my mind, the editors of the other anthology were extending the territory mapped in my *Twelve from the Sixties*—developments within the traditions of contemporary fiction—whereas my anthology favored those fictions that, to my taste, resembled avant-garde art. (To this day, whenever my name is paired with Klinkowitz's as prophets of a similar new—most recently by Richard Ohmann in *Critical Inquiry*—such linkage indicates to me that the commentator is unaware of the genuine issues dividing us and, beyond that, of profound general differences between the books each of us likes). Another reflection of this new taste of mine was the long critical essay on "Innovations in Fiction" that appeared in my 1974 book on literary politics in America.

II

It is through Art, and through Art only, that we realize our
perfection; through Art and Art only that we can shield
ourselves from the sordid perils of actual existence. — Oscar
Wilde.

Around the time my taste in fiction was changing, I began to write my
own narratives, remembering my observation, made long before, that
critics predisposed to innovation are more likely than conservatives to produce creative work as well. Given what I had already written, I knew I had
to begin with extremely radical premises that would generate work
necessarily different from what I had been taught to do, or would have done
only a few years before. My first story, "One Night Stood," had no more
than two words to a paragraph. Not unlike later fictions of mine, it told a
story of a boy meeting a girl and, as the point of view regularly alternated
between them, of the resulting complications. With alternate lines in-
dented, this text also appeared in *Panache*. A later story, "Milestones in a
Life," portrayed a bourgeois existence in terms of the most important event
to happen in each year, running from "O Birth" to "77 Death." For "Excelsior," I adopted a yet more severe constraint of single-word paragraphs
to narrate again a heterosexual encounter.

By the end of the decade, I also began to produce my own fictions of
images in sequence. The first, "Accounting," was an enlarging progression
of pyramids composed entirely of an incremental sequence of numerals —
one 1, two 2s, three 3s, etc. — that concluded, like all good accounting procedures, with a bottom row of zeros that, in this context, had ironic implications. Other visual fictions extended the initial strategy of my poetry, which
had words visually arranged; but instead of being individual word-images
(poems), these new works were sequences, such as the alphabet in my
novella *In the Beginning* (1981) or "Goods" that appeared in *Short Fictions*
(1974). One quality of the latter piece is that the meanings of words change
through the introduction not just of different words but different nonverbal
shapes. For another story, fictitious names and professions were displayed
in the outline of a family tree, thereby compressing an extended narrative
into a single page.

In yet another story, a vertical rectangle, whose corners are connected
by an X shape, is subjected to a series of changes that lowers its top, while
enlarging its sides, until it becomes a horizontal rectangle of approximately
similar dimensions (and proportions). To my mind, this can be called an
abstract story, whose narrative comes from shifts of lines alone; as an abstract
story, it stands to representational literature much as abstract painting
stands to representational.

From this sort of reductionism came yet another alternative strategy, the single-sentence story, either the openings of hypothetical stories, or the closings of stories that may have come before. Once complete, this appeared as a book, *Openings & Closings* (1975), with all the openings in italic type and the closings in roman. One radical ambition implicit in both compression and extension was radically redoing the traditional scales of fiction.

When *Short Fictions* was ready, I decided to explore other kinds of experiments, both visual and verbal. I returned to numbers as a language neglected by Art, and tried to tell stories with them alone. In "Times Perceived: A Working Day" is a sequence of digital times from the early morning to the middle of the night. As the title suggests, they document the moments when a person looks at the clock during the course of a normal working day. When he or she registers "8:55, 8:58, 9:00" in the morning, we imagine that someone might be rushing to work; and when long periods of time elapse, we similarly assume the protagonist is preoccupied with activities other than looking at the clock. At other times the life suggested by the data is less clear. Every minute between 8:00 and 8:07 in the evening is observed, for reasons we are free to imagine. "Times Perceived" initially appeared, along with other numerical fictions of mine, in a tabloid-sized newsprint book, *Numbers: Poems & Stories* (1976). *Exhaustive Parallel Intervals* (1979) is a more difficult work, perhaps a novel, about a kind of magic diamond, whose component numerals relate to each other in exactly similar ways, even though their positions in the diamond exchange exhaustively during the course of the sequence. One ideal in my mind when I wrote this was the complexity of serial music or *Finnegans Wake*.

"Constructive Fictions" became my generic term for visual narratives of four-sided symmetries that metamorphose in some sort of systemic sequence. One goal here was fictions as pure as constructivist paintings are pure — images in sequence referring only to themselves, offering narrative pleasures undistracted by the vulgarities of content. In the simplest example, a square is progressively quartered to become equal fourths, sixteenths, sixty-fourths, etc. of the initial whole. In other examples, the units are more complex geometric figures, manipulated in more complicated ways. *Constructs* (1975) was the first collection of such work; *Constructs Two* (1978) was the second. At least two more collections, as well as two sustained book-length narratives (novels?), remain unpublished.

I also did circular stories, in which words set in a pattern much like hands on a clock flow from one to the next, but have neither beginning nor end; and a modular fiction (a novel?), *And So Forth* (1979), of geometric line-drawings whose shapes assume different sizes and places within a continuous square, whose positions in the narrative are interchangeable and whose pages in sequence nonetheless suggest stories. For *Reincarnations* (1981), I took a single photograph of myself, cut it apart into 80 squares, and then recomposed 64 sets of eighty chips into 64 different images that, since they portray no existence in fact, must be fictions.

The idea of a modular structure of a fiction's elements was extended in *Foreshortenings & Other Stories* (1978) to a narrative of eighty-four simple sentences (likewise about boy-meets-girl) that are initially foreshortened (omitting alternate sentences from beginning to end) until, after several degenerations, only the opening sentence remains. In the "Other Stories," these initial eighty-four sentences are then systematically recomposed in six other ways ("Shifting," "Revising," "Displacing," "Leaping," "Reversing," "Mirroring") to generate different emphases of the same words or gestures, if not radically different stories. For another story, "Seductions," I took sixteen different seduction narratives and interwove them, one sentence at a time, as continuous prose set in sixteen different typefaces, each unique to one of the stories, in sum portraying both verbally and visually fictional variety within narrative unity. Here and elsewhere, it should be clear, I choose to portray heterosexual encounters not because I claim profound insight into them but because a familiar, transparent subject better exposes my technical concerns.

Beginning in 1975, I began to think seriously about media, first publishing some of these fictions in unusual book-formats, such as my novella *Modulations* (1975), which is a Constructivist Fiction in the form of a ladderbook (3 ¾" high, 84" long) whose twenty-seven images can be read in either direction (being about such abstract-art themes as the progression from images opening outwards to images closing inwards, and vice versa). In *Extrapolate* (1975), another ladderbook with slightly larger pages, the progress of the pattern is more subtle, but it too can be read sequentially in either direction. When colleagues, aware of the unclear status of the epithet "novella," ask me how long mine is, I simply hold one end of the book high and let the other fall a full seven feet to the floor.

"One Night Stood" was published in 1977 in two formats, one a small paperback with one paragraph (of no more than two words) to a page, the other a tabloid-sized newspaper with several paragraphs on each of its twenty-four pages. My concern here was discovering whether the exact same text could generate different reading experiences in bookish media so physically different. *And So Forth*, mentioned before, appeared as a looseleaf book whose 100-plus 8½" by 11" pages were gathered in an envelope. These unconventional books were included in many group exhibitions of "Artists' Books," as well as a traveling one-man "Book Art" exhibition that began in 1978 at PS 1 in New York.

In that year I also produced two volumes of ostensibly blank books, one twice the dimensions of the other—the larger, *Tabula Rasa* subtitled "A Constructivist Novel"; the second, *Inexistences* subtitled "Constructivist Fictions." To give further context to the whitest paper I could find, the first had on its sole printed page the following epigraph from Ulises Carrion: "The most beautiful and perfect book in the world is a book with only blank pages, in the same way that the most complete language is that which lies beyond all that the words of a man can say." For the smaller book, I had another epigraph from Carrion: "Every book of the new art is searching after that book of absolute whiteness, in the same way that every poem searches for silence." Unlike other book-art books of mine, these two could not be publicly exhibited, because pages so white cannot be fingered.

Around this time, I also began to explore media other than printed pages for publishing my stories. The first alternative was audiotape. For the single-word paragraphs of "Excelsior," I put the male lines on one side of the stereophony and the female lines on the other; for "Milestones in a Life," my words were subjected to increasing reverberation. The openings of *Openings & Closings* were read on one side of a stereo tape; the closings, on the other. For *Foreshortenings & Other Stories*, I read solo in alternation with a multitracked quartet of myself. For "Seductions," the sixteen narratives, read in sixteen different amplifications of my voice, were cut into individual sentences which were then interwoven one at a time into a single continuous narrative that leaped among sixteen voices. For "Dialogues," the German words for Yes, No and Sure were processed through a Fairlight Computer Music Instrument to produce three dozen variations of two voices engaging, as well as disengaging, each other.

One step ahead of me now would be the creation of sound fiction, which is to say stories whose principal means of narrative enhancement would be acoustic, whose ultimate realization would be on audiotape (whatever printed text becoming the equivalent of a musical score). A suggestive example in my mind is Naoya Uchimura's *Marathon* (1958), in which, to quote Mark Ensign Cory:

> The plot is carried by two micro-durational or rhythmic figures: the anapest of [the runner's] breathing and the iambus of his footsteps. Each can be extremely effective, as in the moment when the steady rhythm of [the runner's] controlled breathing begins to falter, or when the clean beat of his footsteps becomes uncertain and then is momentarily obscured by a passing competitor.

In addition to producing representational sound fictions, with scenes as specific as this, I would also like to realize stories exclusively of less definite, if not abstract sounds that would, much like the visual abstractions of my constructivist fictions, metamorphose in a narrative way. These would, of course, approach the narrative lines of music; but the crucial difference in my own mind is that, in both scoring and performance, my sounds would not be particular pitches but fiction-suggestive noises. (It would then be interesting to discover if a tape of these fictions could be played backwards, much as the images of, say, *Modulations* can be read backwards.) If short stories in these modes turned out to be successful, I would try to extend this latter principle to the acoustic equivalent of novelistic lengths. The musical model in my mind for this last sort of fiction would be Bach's *Art of Fugue*.

In my own actual, as distinct from projected, history, next came videotape. For "Excelsior," I created a dark abstract oval shape for the male and a light oval shape for the female, and had them appear on the small screen in different sizes and proportions in rough accompaniment to their voices on the soundtrack. For "Plateaux," with its single-word paragraphs, each relating a different stage (or plateaux) in the development of a love affair, we used video feedback to create a kaleidoscopic moiré pattern that changes slowly in no particular direction, complementing visually the pointless, ultimately circular development of the fiction's plot. For my video *Openings & Closings*, I read the stories continuously, while instructing the studio crew to make each new image clearly different from the one before. Just as all openings in print were italic, here they were all in color; the closings, in print roman, were on videotape all black-white. By these techniques, I wanted to realize visually the leaps of time and space that characterize the discontinuous prose text. "Constructivist Fictions" I cast into film, shooting them in negative (so that my original black lines on a white field became white lines on the film's black field). While I respected the ordering of the initial images, I also used techniques more possible in film than in books, such as echoing previous images in the course of moving ahead, or generating pixilated patterns between images.

III

Every art translates all content into the means of expression
more suitable to the medium of representation. — Rudolf
Arnheim, *Radio: An Art of Sound* (1937).

Epiphanies, my principal fiction project for the 1980s, reflects several strains of earlier work. It began as a text of single-sentence stories, each meant to represent the most luminous moment — an epiphany in the Joycean sense — of otherwise unwritten stories that had no relation to each other. Over two thousand of these were written, initially on small cards. Even though each story had no connection to any other, they were typed continuously on manuscript pages that were then offered to editors of literary periodicals, who were invited to choose which ones they liked and then to publish those selections in any order they wished. For some, this invitation posed more problems to their editorial competence than one would have supposed. A few asked to publish continuous pages as I typed them, while others returned the text to me as "unedited and therefore unfinished." Even in late 1984, an elder fictioner wrote me, "Although I consider myself a demon editor, ready to cut and slash, I still prefer for writers to write their own stories." Nonetheless, over two dozen selections from the text have appeared in American literary magazines. I would also like to see *Epiphanies* appear as a book, with the sentences in largish type, scattered over two-page spreads, much like headlines in a newspaper. (Literariches Colloquium Berlin published in 1983 a selection of German translations in a small-format book.)

Given my recent thinking, it is scarcely surprising that from the beginning I considered publishing these *Epiphanies* in media other than print. They were typed on over two thousand cards, 4" by 6", for distribution over a gallery space. They were also offered to theatre directors to excerpt their tastes, distributing the selected lines to as many readers as they wished. For the first production, at the University of North Dakota, these lines were elegantly read by four readers distributed along a circumference around an audience gathered in the middle. For the second production, at Vassar College, three times as many lines were distributed to three times as many readers, who often read in chorus and thus, oddly, took just as much time as the first production — forty-five minutes; these performers were scattered throughout an art gallery in which other works of mine were exhibited.

In 1982, I also recorded fifty speakers declaiming individual *Epiphanies* for a tape that, after editing and processing, will be several hours long (and may later be divided into, say, fifty-two very short programs for distribution to public radio here, as a sort of nonserial serial). When I was offered free use of a video character-generator (an electronic letter-making machine), I put the words for the stories on a screen in various typographical arrays, producing a videotape that, because it is composed entirely of words, must be *read* to be "seen."

To make a film *Epiphanies*, I decided not to shoot my own footage — the camera style would be too consistent, contrary to my purposes — but, instead, to solicit other filmmakers' outtakes and from them select passages that visually had this epiphanic quality. I could not use much from one source, because crosss-referencing would also be contrary to my purposes. By 1981, I edited perhaps a hundred parts into a film 28 minutes long from which a silent print was made. For screenings of this version, I used first an audiotape of the North Dakota performance and then parts of the new tape-in-progress. The following year, I made a 20-minute version for German television, with a German soundtrack and a 70-minute version with 290 excerpts (that has not yet been printed). On one hand, I want to make a very long film that will probably be shown in nonstandard venues, where spectators can come and go as they wish, seeing only bits at a time — such as the waiting room of a bus station. On another hand, I also imagine making a number of very short films, perhaps fifty-two, each about five minutes in length, that could be screened in a conventional theater as a sort of nonserial serial, a pre-film film with a new installment every week.

Two major questions still unanswered in my mind are which of these media might be the most propitious for publishing, for making public, my fiction *Epiphanies* and whether the whole might be more significant than the sum of its parts?

IV

I'm obsessive about [defining my work through
manifestoes]. I am continually reading, writing notes to
myself on how to proceed because I'm always afraid when I
wake up tomorrow I won't know how to proceed. — Richard
Foreman, in an interview (1981).

While continuing to write fiction criticism, I approached new novels
and stories with a different intelligence, now informed by creative practice;
and especially in a series of short essays on the alternative, developing purposes of my own fiction, my remarks became more general than specific.
I have continued to edit anthologies filled with fiction, such as *The Yale Gertrude Stein* (1980), typically favoring more experimental, more audacious,
more distinguished work. If there has been any progress in this history, it
comes I think not from making better fictions or from reading them better,
but in understanding the essence of fiction (and what makes it different from
poetry on one side and history on the other). What has also improved, I'd
like to believe, is the quality of my ambition. One reason why I write so little
fiction nowadays is that I know full well what I do not want to do, while only
the very best plans are worth pursuing.

As some of my principles have been radical, my fiction is rarely reviewed. Even though my stories are not obscure or difficult, once their
premises are understood, no book of them has sold more than a few hundred
copies. Precisely because these stories are so different, they cannot be easily
merchandized (which ought to be a critical virtue, though perhaps not for
current fiction critics umbilically tied to flacks). My fiction is never anthologized (unlike my poetry, which is reprinted quite often); nor (again unlike
my poetry) is it mentioned in critical surveys of contemporary literature.
There have been no commercial (or even semi-commercial) contracts; no
grants for writing fiction; no offers to teach the writing of fiction. (The one
prize, to reprint "Milestones in a Life" in a local Sunday newspaper, came
from an art museum in western Canada!) There has not even been journalistic acknowledgment of the basic fact that no one else in America today
was making fiction in these ways. Two reasons for this critical neglect might
be that literate, intelligent people who have learned easily to accept abstraction and minimalism in visual art have considerable difficulty accepting
similar premises in fiction and that I never published any conventional
fiction (and thus could not be portrayed as, or credited with, departing
dramatically beyond it!). While I would not claim to have made a revolution in the concept of fiction, I would, to be frank, be disappointed, profoundly disappointed, if no one, absolutely no one, thought I had.

On the personal level, fiction is only one of several creative interests,
while the creation of it nowadays blends into my interest in media. (In my

professional life, I do not do one art or another as much as *work*, as an encompassing category, all the time.) It seems to me that my creative sensibility is more fictional than poetic, and less visual than musical, and that my creative work at its best reflects these linear preferences. (Others may disagree.) I do not read as much fiction as I used to, perhaps because I once read so much (and have at home whole walls of shelves filled exclusively with fiction), but also because I tend nowadays to learn more from other arts. Nonetheless, I continue to write it, and write about it, when I feel inspired to do so, out of the sense, perhaps naïve, that what I am doing is important. (1985)

Inventory of Fictions (1985)

Printed Formats

In the Beginning. 64 pp., 5½" × 8½", perfectbound. The initial visual novella, based upon the alphabet incrementally enhanced, in a pyramidal form, through two-dozen-plus images. Somerville, MA: Abyss, 1971. ISBN: 911856-05-6. Designed and drawn, with an afterword, by the author. Dedicated to John Furnival. Printed in an edition of one thousand copies by Gerard Dombrowski. Twenty-six copies were signed and lettered by the author.

Ad Infinitum: A Fiction. 16 pp., 3" × 4¼", saddlestitched. A second alphabet novella. [Friedrichsfehn, West Germany]: International Artists' Cooperation, n.d. [1972]. Designed, typeset and bound by the author. Printed by Klaus Groh in Friedrichsfehn, West Germany.

Accounting. 28 pp., 4¼" × 5¼", sidestitched. The initial numerical fiction whose enlarging image concludes with a row of zeros (superseding an earlier defective edition, announced and printed by Edizioni Amodulo, Milanino sul Garda, Italy). [Sacramento, CA]: PN Books, 1973. Dedicated to J.F. Bory. Printed by Wally Depew.

Short Fictions. 64 pp., 7" × 10", perfectbound (back to back with *I Articulations*). The initial collection of visual fictions with Entree, Goods, Arising, Ashes-Dust, Framing, Histories, Amplify, Obliterate, Counterpoints, X & Y, Annihilate, Shrink, Development. New York: Kulchur Foundation, 1974. Designed and drawn, with an afterword, by the author. Dedicated to Mina, Marian and Andre. Printed by Harry Gantt, New York, in an edition of one thousand softcover copies and one hundred hardcover copies bound in plastic boards. Thirteen hardback copies were signed and lettered A/B to Y/Z by the author.

Metamorphosis. One card, 4½" × 5¼". A succinct visual fiction within a single image. Milwaukee, WI: Membrane, 1974. Designed and typeset by the author. Printed by Karl Young.

Obliterate. Sixteen sheets, 2¾" × 2", in a folded cardstock case. A dissected image. [Sacramento, CA]: Ironwhorsebook, 1974. Printed, cut and assembled by Wally Depew.

Openings & Closings. 96 pp., 7" × 10", perfectbound. Single-sentence fictions that are either the openings of stories that hypothetically follow, or the closings of stories that might have come before. New York: D'Arc Press, 1975. Designed by the author. Dedicated to Kenneth Gangemi. Typeset by Carl Martyn, Academy Typesetting, New York. Printed in an edition of one thousand copies by Zaccar Offset, New York. Twenty-six copies were signed and lettered by the author.

Constructs. 112 pp., 8¼" × 8⅛", perfectbound. The initial collection of symmetrical line-drawings in systematic sequence, including Introduction, Tensions, Supersede, Stretch Out, Trajectory, Incision, Curvature, Partitions, Coincide, Metagenesis, Reflective Quadrants, Frame, Path. Reno, NV: West Coast Poetry Review, 1975. Designed and drawn, with a foreword, by the author. Dedicated to Sytske A.D.E.O. Negatives by the Print Center, Inc., Brooklyn, NY. Printed in Reno in an edition of five hundred copies with gray covers and twenty-six copies in black covers that were signed and lettered by the author.

Come Here. 20 pp., 5" × 7", saddlestitched. An erotic visual fiction that the U.S. copyright office refused to accept on the grounds that it "lacks copyrightable artistic expression." Brooklyn, NY: Assembling; Des Moines, IA: Cookie, 1975. Designed by the author. Dedicated to JoAnne Akalaitis. Typeset and printed in an edition of two hundred fifty copies by Fred Truck, Des Moines. Twenty-six copies were signed and lettered by the author.

Modulations. 28 images, 3" × 3¼", accordion book. A constructivist novella that can be read from one end to the other and back again. [Brooklyn, NY:] Assembling, 1975. Designed and drawn by the author. Printed by Bob Heman at the Print Center, Inc., Brooklyn, NY, in an edition of three hundred copies on yellow cardstock. Twenty-six copies were signed and lettered by the author.

Extrapolate. 24 images, 3¾" × 3¾", accordion book. A second constructivist novella, in a similar format, that can likewise be read in either direction. [Brooklyn, NY:] Assembling; [Des Moines, IA:] Cookie, 1975. Designed and drawn by the author. Printed by Fred Truck, Des Moines, in an edition of four hundred copies on white stock and twelve copies in brown stock, signed and lettered by the author.

Numbers: Poems & Stories. 24 pp., 11½" × 16", folded newsprint. The initial collection of numerical literature, including Short Fiction, Times Perceived, Multiples, Combinational Rotations, 202–505, Olympian Progress and Numerations, as well as several numerical poems. Brooklyn, NY: Assembling, 1976. Dedicated to Milton Babbitt. Printed in an edition of one thousand copies by Fred Truck, Des Moines, IA. Twenty-six copies were signed and lettered by the author.

Three Places in New Inkland [with two other authors]. 33 pp. [for RK], 8½" × 11", perfectbound. Three constructivist fictions: Displacements, Ripening, Transit. New York: Zartscorp, 1977. Designed by Lynn Hurwitz Zelevansky. Drawn by the author. Printed by Edwards Bros., Inc., Ann Arbor, MI, in an edition of five hundred copies.

Milestones in a Life. Lethbridge, Alberta: Lethbridge Herald, 1978. Newsprint poster, 15" × 22¾". A four-color realization of a skeletal fiction — winner of an international contest, organized by the Southern Alberta Art Gallery, for a work of art to appear in the local Sunday newspaper. Also, Pittsburgh: Carnegie-Mellon University Press, 1979–80. A bus placard, 28" × 11". A five-color realization, likewise a contest winner, for Pittsburgh Public Transportation.

One Night Stood. 175 pp., 5⅜" × 4", perfectbound; & 24 pp., 11" × 17", folded newsprint. A minimal fiction, with no more than two words to a paragraph, in two radically different book formats. New York: Future Press, 1977. Dedicated to Wendy Bartlett. The bound version was printed by the Print Center, Inc., Brooklyn, NY, in an edition of one thousand softcover copies and one hundred sets of folded and gathered sheets that were bound between boards by the Center for Book Arts, Inc., New York. Twenty-six hardback copies were signed and lettered by the author. The newsprint version was printed in an edition of one thousand copies by Expedie Printing, Inc., New York. Twenty-six of these newsprint copies were also signed and lettered by the author.

Foreshortenings and Other Stories. 32 pp., 5½" × 8½", saddlestitched. An ur-text of eighty-four different sentence-modules, alternately male and female, rearranged systemically in seven ways: Foreshortenings, Shifting, Revising, Displacing, Leaping, Reversing, Mirroring. Berkeley, CA: Tuumba, 1978. Dedicated to Loris Essary. Printed with a letterpress by Lyn Hejinian, Berkeley, in an edition of 450 copies.

Constructs Two. 80 pp., 4¼" × 5½". The second collection of symmetrical line-drawings in systemic sequence: Paradigm, Passage, Flare, Disseminate, Dispersion, Atrophy, Ripening. Milwaukee, WI: Membrane, 1978. Designed and drawn by the author. Dedicated to Manfred Mohr. Printed in an edition of one thousand copies by Karl Young. Twenty-six copies were signed and lettered by the author.

Tabula Rasa: A Constructivist Novel. Approx. 1,000 pages, 8" × 8". A very thick book, blank with the exception of the printed title page from which subsequent content can be inferred. New York: RK Editions, 1978. Dedicated to Richard Minsky, Twelve copies, bound at the Center for Book Arts, New York, were signed and lettered by the author.

Inexistences: Constructivist Fictions. Approx. 667 pages, 4" × 4". A collection of stories, likewise blank with the exception of the title page from which subsequent contents can be inferred. New York: RK Editions, 1978. Dedicated by Evelyn Kaykoff. Twenty-six copies were bound at the Center for Book Arts, New York. All were signed and lettered from A to Z by the author.

And So Forth. Approx. 105 pp., 8½" × 11", gathered loose in an envelope. Related geometric drawings that form modular narratives from page to page and can be read in any order, to any number. New York: Future Press, 1979. Drawn, designed and prefaced by the author. Dedicated by Judith Hoffberg. The pages were printed at Gallery Photocopy, Inc., New York; the envelopes were printed in an edition of seventy-five copies at Milner Bros., New York. Ten complete sets were individually initialed and numbered by the author.

Exhaustive Parallel Intervals. 160 pp., 6" × 9", perfectbound. A book-length narrative, perhaps a novel, with sequences of four increasingly larger diamond-shaped arrays of intricately related numbers whose positions in the shape change in systematic sequence. New York: Future Press, 1979. Designed, with an afterword, by the author. Dedicated to Karen Wright (Campbell). Printed in an edition of five hundred paperbound copies and one hundred hardbound copies by Thomson-Shore, Dexter, MI. Twenty-six of the latter were signed and lettered by the author.

More Short Fictions. 192 pp., perfectbound. A second collection of short fictions, other than Constructivist Fictions, this containing stories both visual and verbal, including Apertures, Plateaux, Confluence, Replicate, eight untitled circular stories, an untitled abstract with interwoven loops, Exponential, Seductions, Acquisitions, Great-Greater-Greatest, Ingrowth, Around, Scale, Milestones in a Life, Metamorphosis, Enrichments, Plus-Minus, an untitled abstract with tiny circles, Transforms, Dialogues, Progeny, Research, fourteen handwritten single-sentence stories, Choking, Return, a maze fiction, Temperatures of Life's Decades, Untitled, Communication, Retreat-Retire, The End and the Beginning, Squares Squared, Biography, Excelsior, Pyramid, 120-Yard High Hurdles, Recapitulate, Revelation, On Fortune and Fate. New York: Assembling, 1980. Designed and drawn, with an afterword, by the author. New typesetting by Edward J. Hogan, Aspect Communication, Cambridge, MA; Sharon Skeeter, Enkidu, Watertown, MA; and Fred Truck, Des Moines, IA. Dedicated to Paul Zelevansky. Printed in an edition of nine hundred paperback copies and one hundred hardback copies by Thomson-Shore, Dexter, MI. Twenty-six of the latter were signed and lettered from A to Z by the author.

Reincarnations. 64 pp., 5" × 7", saddlestitched. An extended fiction, perhaps a novella, composed entirely of altered photographs of the author. NY: Future, 1981. Designed, with an afterword, by the author. Dedicated to Scott Hyde. Printed in an edition of one thousand copies by Braun-Brumfield, Ann Arbor, MI. Twenty-six were lettered by the author.

Epiphanies (1983). 48 pp., 4⅛" × 5⅞", perfectbound. A selection of single-sentence stories, translated into German. West Berlin: Literarisches Colloquium Berlin, 1983. Designed by the author, in collaboration with Nicolaus Ott + Bernard Stein. Typeset by Nagel Fototype, West Berlin. Printed in an edition of five hundred copies by Karl Holste, West Berlin.

Audiotapes

Experimental Prose. Forty-minute stereo audiocassette. The initial collection of audio realizations by various techniques, including, among other works, Dialogue [in three different realizations], Plateaux, Milestones in a Life, Excelsior. Brooklyn, NY: Assembling Press, 1976. Read almost entirely by the author. Engineered by David Dial, to whom it is dedicated, at wxxi-fm, Rochester, NY. Mastered and produced by Ashley-Skull, Huntington, NY, in an edition of three hundred copies.

Openings & Closings. Sixty-minute stereo audiocassette. A stereo audio rendition of the book text, read entirely by the author. New York: RK Editions, 1977. Engineered by David Dial and John Gaines at wxxi-fm, Rochester, NY.

Foreshortenings and Other Stories. Sixty-minute stereo audiocassette, with two different renditions of the complete text: RK in a duet with a chorus of RKs; RK and John P. Morgan. New York: RK Editions, 1977. Engineered by David Dial at wxxi-fm, Rochester, NY.

Monotapes. 30' audiocassette. A collection of new works, including Plateaux [in a new, different audio realization], Times Perceived: A Working Day and One Night Stood, among other pieces. New York: RK Editions, 1978. Read almost entirely by the author. Engineered by Ceil Muller, to whom it is dedicated.

Audio Art. A 45' retrospective with commentary, commissioned by Australian Broadcasting, with Milestones in a Life, Foreshortenings [only] and Excelsior, among other pieces. New York: RK Editions, 1977.

Seductions. 60' audiocassette [backed with *Relationships*, an erotic memoir.] Sixteen seduction stories told by sixteen different amplifications of the same voice and interwoven, one sentence at a time, into a continuous, albeit spatial, narrative. New York: RK Editions, 1981. Read entirely by the author. Engineered by William Brunson at the Electronic Music Studio of Stockholm.

Conversations/Dialogues. 60' audiocassette. Skeletal, implicitly erotic conversations between two voices saying only three German words—Jah, Nein, Doch (yes, no, sure)—in respectively twenty-seven and a dozen different, suggestive ways. New York: RK Editions, 1983. Read by Rita Dove and Fred Viebahn. Engineered by Alex Noyes on a Fairlight CMI at Public Access Synthesizer Studio, New York, NY.

Audio Writing. 91' audiocassette. A new retrospective with commentary, including, among other pieces, Excelsior, Milestones in a Life and Plateaux, in addition to excerpts from Openings & Closings, Seductions, Foreshortenings, Conversations and Epiphanies (both for speakers and for music by Bruce Kushnick). New York: RK Editions, 1984. Dedicated to Charles Dodge. Engineered by Skip Brunner at the Center for Computer Music at Brooklyn College.

Videotapes

Three Prose Pieces. 22", color, on ¾" cassette and ½" tape. Video realizations of three texts, including Excelsior and Plateaux. New York: RK Editions, 1975. Directed and read (almost entirely) by the author. Produced at Synapse, Syracuse, NY.

Openings & Closings. 55", color, on ¾" cassette and ½" tape. A sustained video realization of the author reading the book's text, with a different visual setting for each story. New York: RK Editions, 1976. Directed and read by the author. Produced by Synapse, Syracuse, NY.

Literary Video. 12', black-white, on a ¾" cassette. Fictional texts, including Milestones in a Life, Dialogue [in three versions] and Plateaux, read by the author, with only parts of his face visible. New York: RK Editions, 1977. Produced by Joanne Caring, to whom it is dedicated.

Epiphanies. 31', black-white, on a ¾" cassette. Realizations of the single-sentence texts exclusively by means of a character-generator (an electronic letter-making machine). New York: Davidson Gigliotti, 1980. Typeset by the author, in the studio of the producer, to whom it is dedicated.

Epiphanies. 20', color, on a ¾" cassette. The surviving video copy of a film version, no longer extant, made especially for broadcast over the North German Television Network. Directed by the author, with sixteen readers. West Berlin: Sender Freies Berlin, 1983.

Films

Constructivist Fictions. 16 mm, black-white, 7'. Negative cinematic realizations of certain sequential drawings, made in collaboration with Peter Longauer. New York: RK Editions, 1977.

Openings & Closings. 16 mm, black-white, 22'. The typography of the book on screen, with the closings in negative, the openings in positive, made in collaboration with Bart Weiss. New York: RK Editions, 1978.

Epiphanies. 16 mm, color, 28', silent. The first print of a film currently in progress (customarily screened along with an acoustically processed audiotape of declamations of the text, also still in progress). New York: RK Editions, 1981.

The Old Fictions

New American Fiction (1965)

Let us finish with a positive assurance that the stories that
we offer today will be absolutely new and in no way em-
broideries of known sources. This quality is of some merit
in an age when everything appears to have been done. —
Marquis de Sade, "Essay on the Novel" (1800).

In retrospect, we see that Sade's contemporaries were naïve to think
that writers had milked dry all of fiction's possible resources, even if, as Sade
then put it, "The exhausted imagination of authors [of his time] seems no
longer able to create anything new." In literature, as well as in science, in-
capacity is no proof of impossibility, and the future showed literature what
it continually demonstrates to all arts: that everything has *not* been done.
In fact, the major revolutions in fiction took place in the last quarter of the
nineteenth century, as thinkers and writers began to explore with increasing insight the subtle realities of consciousness and the complex nature of
society — in intellectual thought, Nietzsche and Freud, Weber and Marx;
and in fiction, Dostoevsky and Zola. Thus, just as Sade himself, who in the
above quotation was introducing his own fiction, added new dimensions to
that underground tradition of prose literature which is more concerned
with recording a personal fantasy than with accurately depicting external
reality; so his own work in this direction was, in turn, surpassed by more
extreme fantasies — Poe's stories, Apollinaire's *The Debauched Hospodar*,
Kafka's fiction and Jean Genet's *Our Lady of the Flowers*. In the same fashion,
just as the proclamations of some contemporary critics and thinkers that
nothing new could happen in the post–Joycean, –Gidean, and –Faulknerian novel are, with each passing year, more decisively repudiated,
we can now securely judge that equally irrelevant are the oft-heard claims
that the "New French Novel," our lump-name for a variety of trends,
represents the end of fiction. The point is that an achieved originality
always inspires, not stifles, further invention. As Sade's fiction led to, and
was superseded by, artworks possessed of a distinctly different originality,
so the literature of modernism's major phase — the 1920s — has by 1964
become a segment of the total literary tradition upon which contemporary
writers selectively draw. As the possibilities of life have changed and
esthetic ideas in the other arts have been assimilated by novelists, fiction

has been similarly transformed; and in decisive respects, the books that comprise the new American fiction move beyond the literature of this modern period, as well as beyond the post–World War II phase of American fiction, to chart in form and content new directions in both mainstreams, the sociological and the psychological, of modern fiction.

I

What might first suggest that there *is* no new American fiction is the widespread opinion that *nearly all* the promising novelists of 1946–58 have not, as of mid–1964, equalled their earlier pieces. The grotesque novelists, whose big splash in the late 1940s has smoothed out to a faint ripple in our literary history, have all but ceased imaginative writing; and their few later books, such as Carson McCullers' *Clock Without Hands* (1961), are disappointing. The recent fiction of their most promising, albeit eccentric heir, the late Flannery O'Connor, does not match her previous achievements. James Agee, Isaac Rosenfeld, and John Horne Burns all died in the mid-fifties, just as they were finally gaining control of their promising talents. J.D. Salinger remains silent after the debacle of *Seymour: An Introduction* (1959), though his admirers have high hopes for his long-germinating next book. Robert Penn Warren, despite his immense talent and sophistication, sinks with each novel deeper and deeper into the groove of high-handed, semi–Christian romance; and both Mary McCarthy and James Jones exhibit similar failures of narrow range and repetition, the former offering in "The Fact in Fiction" a ridiculous defense of nineteenth-century principles as contemporary ideals. With each new novel, Wright Morris predictably creates another colorless microcosm of modern sterility, and Louis Auchincloss another portrait of moral ambivalence in upper-class, old-line America.

Few would defend, to list several sets of recent disappointments as opposed to previous achievements, William Styron's *Set This House on Fire* (1961) as better than his brilliant *Lie Down in Darkness* (1951), J.F. Powers' *Morte D'Urban* (1962) against *The Prince of Darkness* (1947), Delmore Schwartz's *Successful Love* (1961) against the more successful stories of *The World Is a Wedding* (1948), Herbert Gold's *Salt* (1963) against the similar "Love and Like" (1958), Frederick Buechner's unread *The Return of Ansel Gibbs* (1958) against his much-heralded but hardly read *A Long Day's Dying* (1949), Leo E. Litwak's *To the Hanging Gardens* (1964) against "The Solitary Life of Man" (1959), or Nelson Algren's recent work against his *Man with the Golden Arm* (1949); and even fewer would favor J.P. Donleavy's *The Singular Man* (1963) against *The Ginger Man* (1955). Alas, even Herman Wouk and Leon Uris have declined. Andrew Lytle, whose unduly neglected *The Velvet Horn* (1957) was the best work of his long novelistic career, has not published a book since assuming the editorship of *The*

Sewanee Review, nor has Robie Macauley, author of the well-realized *The Disguises of Love* (1952), published long fiction since becoming editor of *Kenyon Review*. Whatever hope Jack Kerouac and those trailing behind him ever offered American fiction has, by 1964, thoroughly evaporated. Norman Mailer's fiction career, which became more interesting as he moved away from the naturalism of his first novel to the more mythic fictional universe of *The Deer Park* (1955), abruptly stalled around 1957 when he began concentrating his immense energies on essays; and the story "The Time of Her Time" (1959) and *The American Dream* (1964) are less realized achievements than public warm-ups for future work.

On the other hand, some writers of that generation born in the early 1920s have matured. Vance Bourjaily, for one, records with increasingly accurate realism the typical experiences of our time; no American novel I know has such a convincing portrait of life at an American men's college as his *Confessions of a Spent Youth* (1959). Evan S. Connell, Jr., for another, after writing a series of rather realistic and conventional stories, collected as *The Anatomy Lesson* (1957), and novels, *Mrs. Bridge* (1959) and *The Patriot* (1960)—each book more ambitious than its predecessor—created in *Notes from a Bottle Found on the Beach at Carmel* (1963) a collage of images of the decline of modern civilization, all told through notes left behind by a quest hero. A third, James Baldwin, wrote his most honest and, despite disintegrating structure, his best novel in *Another Country* (1962), an eloquently written protest fiction on behalf of Negroes *and* homosexuals that is a vital complement to his polemical writing. In any event, but for Connell, none of these writers, in my opinion, has recently, even in his less successful work, done anything decisively new in fiction.

In our time "new" has become so honorific a word, particularly in the non-literary arts, that even in literary criticism it is applied with such cheapening indiscriminateness that it verges on joining "great," "wonderful," and "exciting" in the dustbin of platitudes. This is unfortunate, for the epithet must be used with extreme precision if it is to be used at all. I do not, for instance, find anything truly new in most of Bernard Malamud's fiction, though I think him one of the most accomplished storytellers of our time. His moral concerns and fictional style, derived it seems largely from Gogol and Yiddish fiction, strike those of us who have come of age in the sixties as, like Isaac Bashevis Singer's work, more an archaic remnant than a contemporary voice. The prime exception, of course, is his *The Natural* (1952), his most original work, in which, however, absurd details fail to create an absurd vision. The young and over-praised John Updike, despite his gift for language, continually overblows the trivial and skips over the significant until his fiction becomes lumpy, bloated and artsy-craftsy. The fiction of an older novelist, George P. Elliott, is wildly uneven, particularly falling off, I find, once his religious impulses overtake his fictional sense.

As a general rule, I would say that writers who emphasize their ability to render the external details of life today, rather than create a vision of existence, penetrate the human psyche, or achieve a formal originality do not belong among the new American novelists. This judgment includes, to mention several young novelists, Philip Roth, whose ability to reproduce in detail contemporary mannerisms and idiom is extraordinary; Warren Miller, whose ersatz-sociological study of divorcée culture, *The Way We Live Now* (1958), fulfills its limited, almost reportorial intentions, as does Richard Yates' portrait of young suburbia, *The Revolutionary Road* (1961); John Knowles, whose two well-crafted novels, *A Separate Peace* (1959) and *Morning in Antibes* (1962), seem a trifle too pat; Clancy Sigal, whose *Going Away* (1962) in its realism, linguistic energy and obsessive self-concern greatly echoed Thomas Wolfe's writings much as Sigal's earlier *Weekend in Dinlock* (1961) echoed George Orwell's *The Road to Wigan Pier* (1937); John Rechy, whose field in *City of Night* (1963) is male prostitution and whose style is awful; and Wallace Markfield, whose satirical, mildly comic novel *To an Early Grave* (1964) propagates the theme that New York Jewish intellectuals find mass culture more enjoyable than high art.

Those pretenders to newness whose admirers base their claim on esthetic criteria can usually make a stronger case, though sometimes not a convincing one. John Hawkes, for instance, has since 1948 regularly published a kind of dream fiction in which usually, if not predictably, a group of grotesque characters pass through strongly visual, bizarre images, all rendered with a precise rhetoric filled with odd, jarring metaphors. These stylistic gimmicks, serviced by a disjointed narrative, produce a sense of vague nightmare; but just because Hawkes is the only novelist doggedly exploiting this surreal style does not, as some of his admirers think, make him a new and/or important writer. To my taste, his fictional style was more successfully realized, with greater thematic resonance, in Djuna Barnes' *Nightwood* (published way back in 1936); and Hawkes in his later novels, *The Lime Twig* (1961) and *Second Skin* (1964), seems to debase his formula by introducing elements, such as a more cohesive narrative, that make his recent work more accessible to the larger public. Susan Sontag, who exchanges admiring words with Hawkes, wrote in *The Benefactor* (1963) a depressingly dull, oddly written, thoroughly ironic novel about a decrepit man's unfulfilled love-life, the irony being doubled by an inverted Albertine strategy—that "male" narrator seems to be a woman in disguise.

Several other writers, hailed here and there as "new," likewise seem on second examination to use their predecessors' techniques with less success. Terry Southern, whose satirical technique in *Flash and Filigree* (1958) and *The Magic Christian* (1960) eschews the creation of sympathetic characters to contrast with those he mocks, strikes me as essentially imitating what Nathanael West achieved in *The Day of the Locust* twenty years before, as do the stories in John Anthony West's *Call Out the Malicia* (1963). While Jerome

Charyn in *Once Upon a Droshky* (1964) and Grace Paley in the best stories in *The Little Disturbances of Man* (1959) have not fully enough emancipated themselves from Isaac Babel's example, Elliott Baker's funny but trivial *A Fine Madness* (1964), Stanley Elkin's mildly comic *Boswell* (1964), and Thomas Berger's intellectually interesting but fictionally soporific *Crazy in Berlin* (1958) and *Reinhart in Love* (1962) seem spun wholecloth out of Ellison, Bellow and the fifties' picaresque. The same failure — derivativeness — is characteristic of two other remarkable writers, Tillie Olsen and John F. Gilgun, both of whom published in *New World Writing #16* (1960), respectively, the intensely moving "Tell Me A Riddle" and "A Penny for the Ferryman," stream-of-consciousness short stories that excessively reflect the influence of William Faulkner (of *The Sound and the Fury* and *The Bear*) without achieving, particularly in Gilgun's case, the master's breadth and depth. Faulkner of *As I Lay Dying*, along with Gide and the other great modern practitioners of the multiple point-of-view, seems the omnipresent guide behind promising books by other young writers who have learned their lessons well: William Melvin Kelley's uneven *A Different Drummer* (1962); Peter Sourian's *Miri* (1957), a neat demonstration of how to create three convincing narrators; Benjamin DeMott's obtuse *The Body's Cage* (1959), Norman Fruchter's intelligent *Coat Upon a Stick* (1963), to which are added dashes of Malamud and Robbe-Grillet; and Charles Haldeman's impressive *The Sun's Attendant* (1964), an ambitious novel with a flighty point-of-view that fails to keep all its weighty political baggage from dragging.

Other interesting, but hard-to-classify, new novelists include the critic Leslie A. Fiedler, whose novella *Nude Croquet* (1957) is the most realized application I know of Westian satirical technique to another social milieu and who created in *The Second Stone* (1963) a rather suggestive, ironic and befuddling novel; John Yount, whose superbly comic, deeply moral tale, "The Scattering," in *Contact* (July, 1963), displayed both command and style; Arno Karlen and Ivan Gold, two younger writers whose mastery of the resonant symbolist tale, as in Karlen's "The Clown" (1957) and the latter's "The Nickel Miseries of George Washington Carver Brown" (1960), marks remarkable, if so far limited, achievement; and Jack Gelber, more noted for his play *The Connection*, whose *On Ice* (1964) appears, I think, to be an ambitious attempt to pattern a novel after the structures of vanguard music. Perhaps because most contemporary minds do not retain and reorganize fictional motifs as easily as they can those of music, the novel seems, at least to this reader, disintegrating and dull. But possibly, in the hands of another writer, the same attempt could be better realized; and in any case, *On Ice* establishes Gelber as capable of producing fiction as experimental in intent as his plays.

Of course, not all attempts for true originality are even faintly successful. William Gaddis' *The Recognitions* (1956), which many fervently admire, strikes me as incoherent for any two of its 956 pages, as do the much shorter, potentially more interesting, supposedly subliminal writings of Arlene Zekowski, *Concertions* (1962) and *Abraxas* (1964), and Stanley Berne, *The Dialogues* (1962). Richard Stern's *Golk* (1960), despite blurbs, did not jell as a satire of television, capitalism or even the semi-cultured sons of rich men. Alan Harrington's *The Revelations of Doctor Modesto* (1955), a satire of conformity, sank into all its over-intellectualized trappings; while Douglas Woolf's dullness, exhibited all through his two novels, rivals that of nearly all the contributors (Hubert Selby and Michael Rumaker excepted) to LeRoi Jones's collection of late-beat "New [Prose] Writing in America," *The Moderns* (1963). Against this background of declining older writers and the heralded prophets of the pseudo-new, the derivative and the pretentious — against the waves of novels that flow out of New York each September — what little that is new and worthwhile in recent fiction collects in an isolated eddy to attract a following slowly but, in all cases, surely.

Of the older writers, the two who seem most likely to hurdle the barrier of 1959 noted before — if not the two most significant of that generation now about fifty — Ralph Ellison and Saul Bellow have each been working on a novel for several years. The sections of Ellison's work I have seen in print, especially the breath-taking "And Hickman Arrives," in *Noble Savage #1*, and those I have heard him read aloud, suggest it will be a superior novel, resembling perhaps the absurd fiction of recent years. Bellow's oft-announced and much-postponed *Herzog*, which finally appeared in the autumn of 1964, is a disappointment. In attempting to portray a deranged man as hero, Bellow compromised both efforts, creating a character whose derangement is too mild to disturb and whose heroism consists largely of tilting with windmills.

The one older writer who has successfully bucked the trend, Vladimir Nabokov, was probably saved by the singularity of his career. Literally reborn as an American novelist in the early fifties, with a command of an adopted language that includes words found only in an unabridged *O.E.D.*, Nabokov produced in *Lolita* (1955) and *Pale Fire* (1962) two works superior to what earlier Russian writing I have read in translation, the second of which, more than the first, belongs with the new American fiction.

In retrospect, 1959 clearly emerges as the turning point; for just as the older novelists find it a barrier, nearly all of the best fiction written since then is by previously un- or little-known writers. Moreover, despite the wide range of personal styles and subjects, nearly all the most interesting and original of recent works fit into two distinct patterns, one concerned with depicting the absurdity of life in an appropriate form and the other with the madnesses of the individual. This is not to suggest that the patterns were pre-established by critical fiat — they were not — but that the novelists today seem to find certain areas of concern more congenial than others. Each pattern includes works which are, in crucial dimensions, unprecedented and successfully realized. In general, their newness stems less from formal revolutions — these are not entirely absent, though — than from their metaphysical theme, absurdity, and the ways this theme is realized; and, in the other strain, their rendering of a certain range of universal experience, mental derangement.

The first group, which includes the novels of John Barth, Joseph Heller, Thomas Pynchon and Mordecai Richler, resembles the absurd theatre of contemporary Europe in that the author creates a series of absurd (i.e., nonsensical, ridiculous) events — repetition of similar action forms the novel's structure — to depict the ultimate absurdity (i.e., meaninglessness) of history and existence. Thus, these works embody absurdity both in the small events and the entire vision, the subject matter and the form. In world literature, their ancestors include James Joyce's Nighttown sequence and, especially, French 'Pataphysics which, in Martin Esslin's summary, "like its sister philosophy, existentialism, . . . sees the universe as absurd; unlike existentialism, though, it does not take that knowledge as tragic but, on the contrary, as a matter for laughter." Its spiritual father, Alfred Jarry (1873–1907), once, in a preposterous imitation of mathematics, "proved" that "God is the tangential point between zero and infinity." In American literature, progenitors include Nathanael West's *The Dream Life of Balso Snell* (1931) and, in key spots, the works of William Faulkner, S.J. Perelman, and Henry Miller. In contemporary world literature, its analogue is Samuel Beckett's masterpiece, *Comment c'est* (1961), in which the absurd situation of a lone man crawling through mud becomes a paradigm of existence (How It Is).

The second trend includes Vladimir Nabokov (in his American genesis), Bruce Jay Friedman, Walker Percy, Irvin Faust, Michael Rumaker, and William Burroughs, all of whom create realized *internal* portraits of mental distress, running from mild neurosis to hallucinatory insanity, with a sophistication, depth, accuracy, intimacy and/or terror that is, in crucial degrees, unprecedented. Its ancestors include that long line of European works that descend from Dostoevsky's *Notes from Underground* (1864), and probably the best of the few American portraits, the Jason Compson section of *The Sound and the Fury* (1929). These Americans, it should be pointed out, diverge from the Jamesian tradition exemplified today by Nathalie Sarraute, which is concerned with the subtleties of more normal consciousness.

The absurdity of society, the madness of the self — these are the overarching themes of an American fiction considerably different from both postwar American writing and trends in contemporary European fiction.

II

John Barth is unquestionably the most brilliant and promising novelist to appear in America in the past ten years. No other writer as young as Barth (b. 1930) is so thoroughly equipped with the verbal resources and energy, imaginative range, literary sophistication, intellect, courageous originality, independence and, most important, the literary genius to transform these virtues and talents into fiction that continually reflects his capacities. Moreover, Barth has distinctly and considerably matured in the course of his three-novel career— *The Floating Opera* (1956), *The End of the Road* (1958), and *The Sot-Weed Factor* (1960); and since the third of these novels is one of the greatest works of fiction of our time, the potential limits of Barth's achievements are beyond pre-definition, if not compre-hension.

Set in late seventeenth- and early eighteenth-century England and Maryland, filled with characters who speak accurately rendered eighteenth-century dialect with appropriate contemporary references, *The Sot-Weed Factor* (an archaic term for a Tobacco merchant) for 806 pages tells of the adventures of one Ebenezer Cooke who at the age of thirty makes a two-fold vow— to preserve his treasured virginity and to devote himself to poetry. Having convinced a rather dumfounded and generous Lord Baltimore to be his nominal patron, Cooke confers upon himself the rather dubious title of "Poet and Laureate" of Maryland and sets out to write an epic in praise of the New World, his Marylandiad. A summary of all the twists and turns of the maze-like plot, all the little digressions, disguises and coincidences, and the natures of all the characters is, for the moment, unfeasible; suffice it to record that Stanley Edgar Hyman attests that "The plot contrivance is the most fantastic of any book I know."

On its most basic level, *The Sot-Weed Factor* is a mockery of written history; for Barth systematically distorts— mostly debunks— the accepted versions of the past. In this narrative, Sir Isaac Newton and Henry More, the Cambridge neo–Platonist, emerge as lubricious pederasts who provide refuge for orphaned boys. The intellectual coffee-house conversation which Addison described, actually, says Barth's novel, sooner turned to sex. The third Lord Baltimore, known to history as an undistinguished Catholic ruler, runs a network of spies and saboteurs in his war against the Prot-estants, and he informs Ebenezer that in the New World poets are as rare as virgins; and the most successful and self-confident woman Ebenezer en-counters in Maryland is Mary Mungummory (note her initials) who claims to have been "swived" 28,000 times. Boatloads of whores regularly arrive in America, and at one point American pirates intercept a ship carrying Moorish virgins to Mecca and take their pleasure until "The deck looked like a butcher's block." Barth's most extensive debunking comes with the piece-by-piece discovery of the *Secret Historie* of John Smith and *The Privie Journall of Sir Henry Burlingame*, both written in magnificently faked seventeenth-century prose. These "authentic" documents, to deny the ac-cepted version, reveal that John Smith was a lecher who first obtained Powhatan's friendship by giving him pornographic pictures, later won his confidence by satisfying the chief's otherwise insatiable wife, and, finally, thanks to a secret "Eggplant" potion manages to deflower the much-tried, but previously impenetrable virgin Pocahontas. The Indians, likewise untrue to historical form, confiscate Smith's immense collection of erotica. Whereas Ebenezer Cook (without the "e") is known to history as the pseudonymous author of *The Sot-Weed Factor* (1708), a bitterly satirical attack on life in Maryland, Barth's Cooke writes a mildly unfavorable, Hudibrastic ditty that Londoners interpret as a sign of Maryland's high cultural achievement — it even persuades some of them to settle in the New World. ('Pataphysical proverb: "Only the unusual exists and . . . everything is unpredictable, especially the predictable.") Among other historical figures, William Penn, John Coode, Sir Edmund Andros all make their appearance, albeit in somewhat unfamiliar dress.

Though one character rejects sentimental interpretations of history, saying, "More history's made in the bed-chamber than the throne room," Barth is sophisticated enough to suggest that not much history is made in bed either. To Barth, history is thoroughly disordered; and the search for first causes or definitive interpretations uncovers only confusion. A chapter heading near the book's end expresses the reader's befuddlement as well as Ebenezer's:

> The Poet Wonders Whether the Source of Human History Is a Progress, a Drama, a Retrogression, a Cycle, an Undulation, a Vortex, a Right- or Left-Hand Spiral, a Mere Continuum, or What Have You. Certain Evidence is Brought Forward, but of an Ambiguous and Inconclusive Nature.

In addition to burlesquing written history, *The Sot-Weed Factor* thoroughly ridicules literary conventions and, thus, undercuts art's ways of understanding life. The satirical blade is aimed obliquely at all fat popular historical novels (this being too fat, too difficult, and totally faked as history) and particularly at the eighteenth-century novel whose chapter headings and pet plot devices are exaggerated *ad absurdum:* the search for the father, reversal of roles, the accidental recognition scene, transformation through disguises (Burlingame, Cooke's Sancho, assumes a plethora of identities), moments of near incest, and, especially, preposterous coincidences all appear with excessive abundance. Thus, Barth successfully transforms a serious two-fold quest — Cooke's for his muse and Burlingame's for the identity of his parents — into a long series of incidents so incredible that high comedy becomes the book's overall tone. The traditional picaresque structure is further subverted by making the book's main character a congenital unsuccess, a *shlemiel*, whose innocence, in another inversion, turns out to be the single quality that saves him in the rough, cynical, greedy society of America. Indeed, one of the book's main themes is that in a world which throws up hazards and sharpsters at every turn — the novel is almost a catalogue of man's sins—innocence is stronger protection than the mild worldliness of, say, the diseased prostitute, Joan Toast.

Finally, Barth's debunking is universally extended—it starts with the novel's main character, includes the most minute facets of society, ends in the book's final passages with Barth himself, spares no one, and offers no reforms. In mocking the conventions of the eighteenth-century novel, by overusing them to absurd lengths, in suggesting that the history we know is as unlikely as his rewriting of it ("This Clio was already a scarred and crafty trollop when the author found her."), in mocking both Ebenezer's quest and the society that is inhospitable to poetry—in doing these things with such a thoroughness and breadth of reference, Barth ultimately says, not only that the single events of life are preposterous (i.e., absurd), but also that life as a whole, which resists any ordering interpretations, is likewise totally absurd.

As well as being thematically neat—indeed, it seems to be a programmed illustration of a pre-determined theme—*The Sot-Weed Factor* displays on nearly every page Barth's verbal brilliance. It is, at once, one of the most eloquently written books of our time and one of the funniest. Few writers can turn as many striking phrases as Barth or coin as many quotable aphorisms, such as the double-entendre of: "Who gives a man horns must beware of goring." And nobody else would have written this or many other scenes:

> *We were fetch'd into the small circle and station'd before the altar of* Venus *(to look whereon brought the blush to my cheeks), whereupon the Salvages lay'd hands upon my Captain, and with one jerk brought his breeches low. From where I stood, wch chanc'd to be behind him, the sight was unprepossessing enough, but the Salvages before all suddenlie put there by clamour. The emperour shaded his eyes from the morning Sunne, the better to behold him, and Pocahontas, maugre her bonds (wch nettered her as fast as those, that* Vulcan *fashion'd for his faithless spouse), this Pocahontas, I say, came neare to breaking her necke with looking, and the unchast smyle, that erst had play'd about her mowth, now vanish'd altogether.*
>
> *My Captain then turning half around to see, Whether I was at hand? I at last beheld the cause of all this wonder, and as well the effect of all his magick of the night past— the wch to relate, must fetch me beyond all bownds of taste & decencie, but to withhold, must betray the Truth and leave what follow'd veil'd in mystery. To have done then, my Captains yard stood full erect, and what erst had been more cause for pity than for astonishment, was now in verie sooth a frightfull engine: such was the virtue of his devilish brewe, that when now his codd stood readie for the carnall tilt, he rear'd his bulk not an inch below eleven, and well-nigh three in diameter—a weapon of the Gods! Add to w^{ch}, it was all a fyrie hue, gave off a scent of clove & vanilla, and appear'd as stout as that stone whereon its victim lay. A mightie sownd went up from the populace; the Lieutenants, that had doubtlesse been the Princesses former suitors, dropt to there knees as in prayer; the Emporour started up in his high seate, dismay'd by the fate about to befall his daughter; and as for that same Pocahontas, she did swoone dead away.*

More than just mere joking, this is truly superior comedy, stemming from Barth's ability to mesh frustrated expectation, witty language, vivid description, timing, parody; so that, one kind of joke enhances another (just as Harpo complements Groucho) and all the comic effects fall together into a neat whole. As sophisticated comedy, it is funnier if one reads the archaic language with some ease, is familiar with the conventions of pornography, colonial history, the literary references and the geography of Eastern Shore Maryland; but even without this erudition, the reader finds this novel often hysterically funny. Though capable of a wide variety of comic tricks and of turning nearly everything he touches to laughter, Barth never makes what is, to my taste, a cheap joke, and rarely does he concoct an unsuccessful or a corny one.

As well as being one of the funniest, most erotic and pervasively scatological novels since Henry Miller's best gems, *The Sot-Weed Factor* is also one of the intellectuallly richest. Not only is Barth acutely aware of how ideas can function in and be illustrated by fiction, he is also, without doubt, the most erudite novelist of excellence we have ever had in America; perhaps only Vladimir Nabokov and Thomas Mann could rival him among modern writers. In his work, especially in *The Sot-Weed Factor*, there is conspicuous evidence that he is extensively knowledgeable in music (in fact, he studied composition at Julliard), English literature, pornography, ethics and the history of philosophy (he was once a Ph.D. candidate in "aesthetics-of-literature" at Johns Hopkins), American colonial history, English cultural history (his characters of both centuries familiarly refer to the music, books and popular ideas of their respective times), the development of the English language and etymology (he literally seems to have checked the accuracy of every archaic word and the origin of every modern one in the *O.E.D.*), existentialist philosophy, and a variety of critical theories of the American mythos, ranging from Philip Young's reinterpretation of Pocahontas and R.W.B. Lewis' *American Adam* to Leslie A. Fiedler's insight into our writers' preoccupation with the inter-racial homosexual romance and Ralph Ellison's image of the trickster as archetypal American (tricksters and Adamic innocents prosper in the novel; others don't). Thus, *The Sot-Weed Factor* inspired Fiedler to report that it embodies "all the obsessive themes common to our classic novel: the comradeship of males, white and colored, always teetering perilously close to, but never quite falling over into, blatant homosexuality; sentimentalized brother-sister incest or quasi-incest; the anti-heroic dreams of evasion and innocence; the fear of the failed erection"; and, thus, as Fiedler added, it is "closer to the 'Great American Novel' than any other book of the last decade." Stanley Edgar Hyman, surely among our most erudite critics, wrote, "The novel has so many literary sources that it would be easier to list the books that it does *not* copy or burlesque." The book, I predict, will become a gold mine for symbol-, source- and influence-hunting academic critics, all of whom will be implicitly mocked with each discovery they make. Yet, as remarkable as Barth's knowledge is, more extraordinary is his ability to use it in fiction — to use it at the same time he parodies and debunks it. All his academic interests are at the service of a true fictional energy; and in this respect, although the book is far from what is called a dry, academic novel, it is still the kind of book only an academic could write.

In comparison to the lushness of *The Sot-Weed Factor*, the earlier novels are distinctly minor works in which Barth seems to be lightly, if not blithely, testing his talents and his ability to win publishers. *The Floating Opera* is a rather conventional absurd novel, outfitted with an unconventional twist that makes it a parody of Camus' *The Myth of Sisyphus*. Its narrator is a typical twentieth-century middle-class man — Todd Andrews, a fairly eminent lawyer in the small Maryland town of Cambridge, born in 1900 (and, thus, a child of the century), a bachelor, an adulterer, a man of little religion and no family. Writing in 1954, he remembers the day, seventeen years before, when he planned to commit suicide. Discovering his own inability to explain life — that the reasons people have for attributing value to things are ultimately arbitrary, and that nothing around him is truly important — he considers taking his own life; but being fairly logical, Todd then discovers there is no justification to death either. "Hamlet's question is, absolutely, meaningless." A very neat novel — the intellectual joke is clearly and efficiently made — *The Floating Opera* is stylistically undistinguished and, once the joke is fathomed, not very interesting.

Although it contains some scenes more brilliant than those in the earlier book, *The End of the Road* is the weakest of the three novels because of its inability to coalesce around anything, even the theme Barth has publicly attributed to it. Its narrative center is the psychic health of Jacob Horner, an indolent graduate student and sometime teacher of "prescriptive grammar" at Wicomico State Teachers College. Suffering from emotional paralysis, which seems to stem from existentialist *angst*, he is remobilized through therapy with a Negro witch-doctor. Finding himself in need of an abortionist for a friend's wife, whom Horner probably impregnated, Horner selects the witch-doctor, who bungles the abortion, killing the woman and leaving Horner suffering from paralysis again. The novel ends with him hailing a taxi to drive him to the "terminal," ambiguously either to his death or to the train headed for the witch-doctor's Remobilization Farm. Unnecessarily uneven in tone, uninteresting in language, never quite focusing on the announced theme — Horner's evasion from responsibility — and lacking any other unifying thread, the novel has one brilliant chapter. The therapy scene is brilliant absurd comedy — two desperate people talking at cross-purposes; and it stood as an excellent short story in *Esquire*.

Coming after the earlier novel, *The Sot-Weed Factor* leaves the critic with the same impression that Joyce's *Ulysses* must have implanted after its first appearance — that nothing, but nothing, is beyond the competence of its author. He has the literary intelligence, the fictional adroitness, the self-awareness, the mature control, the ideas — indeed, all the basic virtues (except, perhaps, psychological insight) to produce fiction more extraordinary and more original than any other writing today. Unlike too many American novelists, he seems to plan his fiction well in advance, announcing with the publication of *The Floating Opera* that it was the first in a series of novels concerned with various aspects of nihilism: "Each will concern some sort of bachelor, more or less irresponsible, who either rejects absolute values or encounters their rejection." So far, he has shifted emphasis from the first pattern to the second, defining in progressively larger chunks a world without order or value.

The author of three novels before he turned thirty, Barth has since 1960 slowed down his pace. Only two of his short stories have appeared, rather undistinguished pieces in *Esquire* (February, 1963) and *Southwest Review* (Summer, 1963); and he has also published an obtuse essay on his native Eastern Shore Maryland, the locale of his three books, in *Kenyon Review* (Winter, 1960) and an afterword that is immensely illuminating (on his own works too) to the Signet edition of Smollett's *Roderick Random*.

Still, his forthcoming novel promises to be more extraordinary, if not larger, than *The Sot-Weed Factor*. In a letter to me, dated August 7, 1964, Barth described *Giles Goat-Boy* as follows:

> [It] will be a two-volume work, each volume consisting of three reels, each reel consisting of seven chapters. It isn't an easy book to synopsize sensibly. George Giles, the narrator of the story, is a young fellow whose complex fate it is to have been raised as a goat on the stockfarms of New Tammany College, one of the richest, strongest, and largest colleges in the whole University. As a kid, George learns from his keeper (a pacifist polymath named Dr. Max Spielman) that the modern University is divided into two armed campuses, presently pitted against each other in a kind of Quiet Riot, but perennially on the verge of EATing one another alive. (EAT stands for Electroencephalic Amplification and Transmission, the ultimate weaponry of WESCAC — the West-Campus Automatic Computer — and equally of its counterpart EASCAC: Dr. Spielman helped invent it during Campus Riot Two.) Many are convinced that only a new Grand Tutor can lead studentdom away from the wholesale flunkage of modern terms and set it on the way to Commencement Gate; and a great many signs indicate — to George, at least — that he himself may be destined for that hero-work: that indeed he may be no mere Goat-Boy but the true GILES — the *G*rand-tutorial *I*deal, *L*aboratory *E*ugenical *S*pecimen — prepared some years earlier by WESCAC in a supposedly abortive experiment. In the first volume George leaves the goat-barns, makes his way to the Great Mall of NTC, and after sundry encounters and vicissitudes contrives to pass the Trial-by-Turnstile, slip through Scrapegoat Grate, and matriculate as a Special Student, not without having met a rival claimant to Grand-Tutorhood. In volume two he must

address himself to his Assignment, which he conceives to be (perhaps mistakenly) passing the finals himself, declaring his Grand-Tutorhood, descending into WESCAC's *Belly* — the basement chamber where its EATing-tapes are stored — and changing its AIM, or Automatic Implementation Mechanism, to more passéd purposes: something only a Grand Tutor might presumably accomplish without being EATen alive. He may fail.

The twenty pages of discarded fragments Barth enclosed hinted that the novel would be even more imaginative (is that possible?), more difficult and just as comic as *The Sot-Weed Factor* and that the book would describe a world just as nihilistic and absurd.

Barth's plan, I conjecture, is to follow his demonstration of the absurdity of history with a novel about the absurdity of technological "developments," both novels taking faint swipes at religion and academia. To pursue the logic of his plan, he could then progress to philosophy or to various modes of art, or even to language itself, again to expose his theme, always illustrated with encyclopedic learning, immense imaginative energy, and unquenchable wit, that human culture is ultimately as absurd as life itself. The world yields to our efforts no ordering scheme; there is no central truth, only nonsense, with each twist of complexity multiplying itself to infinite degrees.

Like *The Sot-Weed Factor*, Joseph Heller's *Catch-22* is a rather unrealistic narrative of supposedly historical happenings which becomes the author's stylized vision of life as absurd; but where Barth sees absurdity in history's disordered confusion and man's inability to understand it, Heller in his portrait of American soldiers in World War II describes a world which is absurd because there is no relation between intention and result. This is the law of Catch-22, the book's central symbol, introduced in the following dialogue between Yossarian, Heller's main character, and Doctor Daneeka:

> "Is Orr crazy?"
> "He sure is."
> "Can you ground him?"
> "I sure can. But first he has to ask me to. That's part of the rule."
> "Then why doesn't he ask you to?"
> "Because he's crazy.... He has to be crazy to keep flying combat missions after all the close calls he's had. But first he has to ask me."
> "And then you can ground him?"
> "No, then I can't ground him."
> "You mean there's a catch?"
> "Sure there's a catch. Catch-22. Anybody who wants to get out of combat duty isn't really crazy."

Thus, in a world ruled by the laws of Catch-22, it follows that Major Major Major Major should impress people by "how unimpressive he was," that

"Colonel Cathcart was so awful a marketing executive that his services were much sought after by firms eager to establish losses for tax purposes," that the same Cathcart who ruthlessly sends his pilots on an excessive number of missions will become a hero in the eyes of the *Saturday Evening Post*, that Yossarian should be told he is jeopardizing his traditional freedoms by exercising them, and that syllogistic logic is destroyed by contradictions: If war is crazy, the book continually says, and if soldiers go to war, then soldiers are crazy; but all soldiers who, like Yossarian, want to run away from war are abnormal — therefore, crazy. Of course, Heller's principle of opposites does, in fact, govern much of modern behavior. The army hospitals are rated, I am told, by how few deaths take place within each of them; thus, authorities quickly transport all near-death patients elsewhere, thereby increasing the likelihood of death. Or, in a more heroic example, President Kennedy in the Cuba *affaire* of October, 1962, had to use the threat of violence to reduce tensions. In an interview, Heller speaks of a more mundane example: "There is a law of life: People in need of help have the least chance of getting it."

Heller's potential point, as I get it, is that a society that has so distorted the natural correspondences between intention and result, between need and fulfillment, is thoroughly absurd; and in this respect, *Catch-22* is not at base a war novel. "Certainly," Heller has written, it "is not about the causes or results of World War II or the manner in which it was fought. *Catch-22* is about the contemporary, regimented business society." The book also has a secondary, unabsurd theme: nothing, but nothing, is worth a human death. But this is undercut by the absurd paradox, suggested by Heller's Major Danby, that the Second World War had to be fought, that there was in Nazism a real enemy, that people had to *die* to *preserve* human life.

The novel itself exhibits a rich talent for comic invention, exemplified by Heller's ability to run the whole gamut of comic devices from pun to slapstick to irony. Many of the characters, most of them defined by single passions, are memorably resonant; and though slightly preposterous, most are imaginatively convincing. Heller's failings stem more from a want of craft. No other recent novel I know has such a needlessly wild discrepancy in the style of representation, running from naturalism through surrealism, from the grotesque to parody and comic satire to symbolic fantasy. Moreover, the book's structure shifts from a series of vignettes that jell into common themes (the influence here, Heller says, was Celine's *Journey to the End of Night*) to, in the last seventy or so pages, something of a conventional narrative. Coupled to this is a shift in authorial stance from Olympian detachment to social-protest engagement. For these and other reasons, Heller's literary future remains unpredictable. In the spring of 1964, some three years after the completion of *Catch-22*, Heller told a *Book Week* reporter that he had not yet started writing his second novel. Yet it is hard to believe that Heller could not do as well again.

Closer to *The Sot-Weed Factor* in style, if not, indeed, influenced by it, Thomas Pynchon's *V.* is a lushly brilliant novel, exhibiting on every page its author's huge and versatile talent and erudition. At first, the novel seems to evade coherence with every ridiculous turn of its incredible plot; but precisely in this incoherence and preposterousness is the key to the book's theme. Very much like Barth, Pynchon relentlessly illustrates — through two separate and faintly inter-connecting plots, one American and the other international in scope, through a variety of absurd quests and counter-quests, a gallery of inane characters, and a plethora of pseudo-factual details that give the book a pretense of historical narrative — his personal vision of human life as thoroughly and irrefutably nonsensical.

Two-thirds of the way through the book, one of Pynchon's internal narrators, who has his own story to tell — Fausto Maijstral — writes clumsily and suggestively: "No apologia is any more than a romance — half a fiction — in which all the successive identities taken on and rejected by the writer as a function of linear time are treated as separate characters." A few lines later he adds, "It isn't so much to pay for eyes clear enough to see past the fiction of continuity, the fiction of cause and effect, the fiction of humanized history, endowed with 'reason.' " Maijstral, then, is one of Pynchon's identities, creating an incoherent story within an incoherent story; and his tale, like Pynchon's, is a calculated denial of the principle of continuity in fiction and, thus, its usefulness as a way of understanding human history.

Like Barth, Pynchon endows his theme with a wealth of original inventions, burlesques of religious practices and literary styles, and absurd events. Of the two key images, a yo-yo and the letter V., the first, which previously and tellingly appears in Barth's second novel, is used to describe the book's characters, particularly Profane, as they bounce from one place to another, spinning free on the string of life, coming to rest only through the exhaustion of energies. The letter V. is Pynchon's most imaginative projection, the central symbol of the book, first introduced as the object of Stencil's search (indicatively, he was born in 1900, another child of the century); and like much else in the novel, V. is capable of meaning many things: a wide variety of similar, perhaps successor, characters, ranging from Victoria, an English girl seduced in Cairo in the late nineteenth century, to the grotesque Veronica Manganese with a jewel in her navel; as well as, in Stanley Edgar Hyman's summary, "Some great female principle [the searchers are all male], . . . she is the goddess Venus and the planet Venus, the Virgin, the town of Valetta in Malta, the imaginary land of Vheissu with its iridescent spider monkeys and Volcanoes. She is Vesuvius, Venezuela, the Violet of the vulgar mnemonic; ultimately, she is the V of the spread thighs and the mons veneris." Pynchon's special achievement is devising a symbol for metaphysical reality defined not by ambiguity as, say, Moby Dick is, but by nonsensical multiplicity.

Behind *V.* is a superior intelligence, perhaps not quite equal to Barth's, but still capable of making familiar references to a wide variety of historical, scientific and social phenomena and of using phrases from Latin, Yiddish, Spanish, German and French with facility and appropriateness, steeped in modern world history, widely and eccentrically familiar with contemporary literature and thought and, most unusually, knowledgeable in science. Not only did Pynchon study engineering at Cornell, before enlisting in the Navy and transferring to literature upon his return, but more than any other American novelist today he uses scientific ideas to understand reality. Surely, his knowledge of Quantum theory must have influenced his desire to reject causality in literature, and his short story in *Kenyon Review* (spring, 1960) entitled "Entropy" expresses a two-fold image of that scientific concept — one side from thermodynamics and the other from information theory. In the first sense, the story depicts the possibility that if the earth's temperature stays constant at 37° F. then human life will become, on its surface, randomly disordered and, at its base, stasis. Second, entropy is, in information theory, a measure of the disorder present within language, and in the story the term refers to the failure of Saul and his wife to communicate with each other. The story, then, describes a scene in which entropy, in both senses, has reached its maximum levels. (If absence of motion is the apocalypse of "Entropy," a vision of universal violence concludes a story Pynchon published as an undergraduate in *Epoch* [Spring, 1959], "Morality and Mercy in Vienna," which seems an early draft of the style of *V.*)

The failures of *V.* are perhaps unavoidable, given the nature of Pynchon's attempt; portraying incoherence, he succumbs to incoherence himself. The book is wildly overdone and, to my taste, better on the page than as a whole. At times Pynchon seems to have little control over his imagination's excesses, piling unclear images and references upon obscure bases, until some paragraphs are needlessly impenetrable. Not only does he create some of the most unimaginably complicated visual descriptions I have ever read; he also spins off an unusually high number of what strike me as unsuccessful jokes.

On the one hand, I suspect that Pynchon's characters would be more engaging if he paid more attention to human essences than to surfaces; Pynchon probably understands people less well than any other writer discussed here. On the other hand, *V.* is in many ways a story about its author's not-understanding things — as Benny Profane, Pynchon's main character, comments upon his own experiences, "I'd say I haven't learned a goddam thing [about life]." Still, Pynchon has faced the problem of depicting human absurdity and his own incomprehension of life quite successfully, perhaps not wrenching it as neatly into form as Ionesco does in *The Chairs*; but Pynchon's strategies, like Barth's, are towards statement by overstatement, rather than understatement; by reference to a wealth of images, rather than a single pregnant scene. In many ways, this is an extremely impressive book, making Pynchon, who was born in 1937, easily the most accomplished and original very young American writer today, whose *V.* seems, as "Morality and Mercy in Vienna" did in 1959, an imposing sign of wonderful books to come.

Like the other novels here, James Purdy's *Malcolm* (1959) describes the voyage of an innocent young man into the absurdity of society; but in contrast to Pynchon and Barth, Purdy employs a wispy, low-keyed style, keen psychological and emotional sensitivity, a knack for creating the telling moment and the resonant line — in general, a greater artistic control — to produce a more pruned absurd novel. Malcolm, a fifteen-year-old boy stranded alone on a park bench, is befriended by a Professor Cox, an astrologer, who in turn instructs Malcolm to visit all his friends. They include Estel Blanc, a Negro undertaker; Kermit Raphaelson, a midget artist, and his wife Laureen; Girard Girard, a tycoon; and Melba, a teen-age popular singer, whom Malcolm finally marries. Each wants something of him; and though Malcolm responds to their needs — having no essence and being passive towards others, he is capable of a wide variety of responses — he still never thoroughly adjusts to any of his masters. This is why the novel is, as Jonathan Cott suggests, an allegory of growing up into an absurd world, one which offers a young man neither satisfaction nor frustration of his needs and ambitions, has nothing worth his clinging to, and also evades his understanding; and in allowing Malcolm to die in his teens of an excess of alcohol and sex, Purdy seemingly says that these retreats from life are inevitably the only outlets for a young man. *Malcolm* is by far Purdy's best work; his other novel, *The Nephew* (1960), is just another savage portrait of the emptiness of mid-western life, albeit with a few nice moments; and of his stories, which are, in general, extremely uneven, the best, such as "Goodnight, Sweetheart" and "Don't Call Me by My Right Name," depict in muted tones persons in extreme distress and are realized by Purdy's uncanny ability to strike a perfect moment in which human tensions are implicitly and resonantly announced. Though some of his work is marvelous — a few of his scenes are truly great — his work, I find, lacks the immense verbal resources, the grandness of vision, the sheer imaginative energy that I admire in Barth, Heller, and Pynchon.

Of the young Canadian writers, one whose work seems promising is Mordecai Richler. On the one hand his *The Apprenticeship of Duddy Kravitz* (1959) strikes me as highly derivative, its hero a compound of Augie March and Sammy Glick; its prose undistinguished and its minor characters undefined. In contrast, his more recent and most interesting fifth novel, *Stick Out Your Neck* (1963), shows that Richler has abandoned his preoccupation with heroism for a fiction that focuses upon the situation — the absurdities of Canada's love-hate dependence upon American culture. An Eskimo, Atuk, takes Toronto's literary society by storm, wins the high-minded national heroine, a swim champion, for his mistress, becomes the founder of a prosperous Eskimo-trinket business and, subsequently, an inhumane capitalist, is accused of the murder (by cannibalism) of an American colonel, and finally becomes the martyred hero of Canadian nationalism. Against Atuk's career, Richler creates a gallery of Canadian hypocrites — a rabbi who champions national culture also invites "Jerry Lewis to give readings from the Book of Esther at the up-and-coming Israeli bond drive"; an entrepreneur encourages at-cost prostitution for male teenagers in hopes they will "acquire a taste that in later, higher-income years, they would find hard to give up," and so forth. The polemical point, made quite strongly, is that Canadian society has fallen into the particularly ridiculous situation of denouncing with one hand what it imitates with the other, a situation that creates an emptiness of value which makes the society absurd.

In his first forays into fiction, Kenneth Koch, whose mock-epic poem *Ko* (1959) is a comic masterpiece, has written some realized, though minor absurd fiction. His novella, "The Postcard Collection," first published in the first issue of *Art and Literature* (March, 1964), is a tight, ingenious parable of Koch's major idea about the nature of artistic understanding: true art, truly experienced, produces ambiguous responses that signify the observer's ultimate non-comprehension; thus, any clear meaning one discovers in an artwork is forcibly imposed on it and is, therefore, a violation of art's inherent ambiguity. Creating a perfect vehicle for embodying the theme of the absurdity of trying to understand art definitively, Koch has his first-person narrator examine a collection of postcards, written some time ago, filled with hand-scrawled French (art is a foreign language), only to find himself unable to decipher their messages; thus, the narrator uses the fragments he can comprehend as touchstones for writing his version of the message; and throughout the story, Koch continually draws the necessary analogy between the postcards and art itself. Although the esthetic thesis, for a variety of reasons, strikes me as untrue — indeed, Koch's neatness of composition verges on an implicit denial of his polemical point — the story is, on its own terms, a successful absurd parable. What I have seen of Koch's projected novel, *The Red Robins* — those sections published in the first issue of *Location* (Spring, 1963) — suggested the book would be an attempt to dispense completely with plot, character and definite setting and create a fictional world of pure spatiality, complete possibility and underlying absurdity. Such a novel could quite easily disintegrate into its own method or, more likely, attain the richness, comedy and scope of the best absurd novels; even in fragments it is another sign of the ambition for artistic originality that informs all of Koch's work.

Though, of course, attuned to the same impulses in contemporary culture to which the absurd novel responds, several recent works in this strain seem considerably less successful, if not embarrassingly imitative.

The polemical point of Ken Kesey's *One Flew Over the Cuckoo's Nest* (1962) — it is absurd that the guards of a mental institution should be more insane than the inmates — is enhanced by some marvelous comedy but considerably blunted by a relative absence of true and deep madness anywhere in the book. His second novel, *Sometimes a Great Notion* (1964), hardly rises above being an energetic, obfuscating exercise in rapidly shifting the point-of-view. Jack Ludwig's *Confusions* (1963), whose narrator tries to define his own identity through a mass of superficial, conflicting signs, never lived up to the promise of the brilliant short story, "Confusions: Thoreau in California" (1960). The best stories in Donald Barthelme's collection, *Come Back, Dr. Caligari* (1964), such as "To London and Rome," employ absurd surfaces to depict the absurdities of affluence; but Barthelme so far has created just a series of eye-catching tricks, useful only once, rather than an interesting or personal style. Both Lawrence Ferlinghetti's *Her* (1960) and Harry Mathews' *The Conversions* (1962) are often originally comic, but lacking in consistency, resonant symbols, stylistic variation and other undergirding necessities. *Cat's Cradle* (1963) by Kurt Vonnegut, Jr., fails to transcend its surface confusions and fix absurdity in a viable form. Finally, William Peter Blatty's *John Goldfarb, Please Come Home* (1963) is probably the first of many watered-down, denatured novels which absurd fiction will spawn. As the new absurd novels attract more of a following — nearly all have appeared in paperback — more imitations, we should expect, will flood the market until its conventions, like the patterns of late nineteenth-century writing, will become fossilized.

Still, at the moment the American absurd novel thrives, both in distinguishing itself from the small-scale European absurd novel and in attracting publishers, readers and critics alike. More than anyone else in America, these novelists announce, collectively, that the novel is neither stale nor dead, nor has the audience for high-quality fiction disappeared into the void in front of the TV screen. In his introduction to the Signet edition of *Roderick Random*, John Barth wrote a "post-naturalistic, post-existential, post-psychological, post-antinovel novel in which the astonishing ('out-wandering'), the heroical — in sum, the adventurous — will come again and welcomely into its own." Though one questions whether these major characters are heroes — they seem too slight for the role and are used more to reveal the character of the world — the kind of novel Barth describes is blossoming in force.

III

As the absurd novelists sometimes defend personal eccentricity, if not madness, as the most viable strategy for encountering absurd life, so the other stream of new novelists explores these madnesses *from the inside*; that is, they depict the workings of the mad mind itself, rather than carefully noting external symptoms. This internal-external dichotomy illuminates the crucial difference between the progenitors of inside portrayals of madness, such as Nikolai Gogol's "The Diary of a Madman" (1835) and the first part of Dostoevsky's *Notes from Underground*, and the rather objective observation of a madman's odd behavior, such as Herman Melville's "Bartleby" (1856), Hendrik Ibsen's *Rosmersholm* (1886), and Sherwood Anderson's *Winesburg, Ohio* (1919). A third tradition was initiated by Kafka, whose greatest works symbolically objectify the patterns of a neurotic mind. Neither an external record nor an inside portrait, Kafka's fiction is like dream-work itself, a conscious ordering of psychic symbolism.

Although a few novels of the early fifties had realized portraits of mental derangement, such as Salinger's *Catcher in the Rye* (1951), Shirley Jackson's *Hangsaman* (1951), and William Styron's *Lie Down in Darkness* (1951), only in recent years have so many of the very best novels dealt with madness. The most original, especially in form, is Vladimir Nabokov's *Pale Fire* (1962). Its protagonist is the most recent incarnation of the figure that haunts so much of Nabokov's fiction — from the early Russian novels through *Lolita* (1955) to the present — the writer as fool; and not only is Charles Kinbote psychologically the most interesting of these creations, he makes *Pale Fire* Nabokov's best work as well as one of the most hysterically funny novels in contemporary literature. Incidentally, this novel belongs to American literature, rather than Russian, because its frame of reference, its language, its realm of action and its expressed values are primarily American.

Developing an idea faintly presented in *The Gift* (1937), that the act of literary criticism could be the novel's subject and determine its form, Nabokov gives *Pale Fire* an unprecedented structure of three unbalanced parts: a 999-line poem entitled "Pale Fire" by the American poet John Shade (who considers himself second only to Robert Frost), a foreword to it and a critical commentary. These are the work of Shade's admirer, Kinbote, who for a semester was guest professor of Zemblan, his native tongue, at Wordsmith College, where Shade himself taught. The poem itself is a prolix, occasionally tender piece about Shade's development, written in a fairly orthodox form, which at various times echoes (and implicitly parodies) Alexander Pope, T.S. Eliot, Robert Frost, and Wordsworth's lines about the growth of the poet's mind.

Whereas the best comedy in Nabokov's early books stemmed from his cutting descriptions of external phenomena, here the satirical blade is swallowed, so to speak, by an ironic narrator who unintentionally wields it against himself. The third section, Kinbote's line-by-line commentary, is the novel's comic center, for his remarks are a masterful example of what in graduate school is glumly called "over-reading," in the outside world "egomania," and in literature, brilliant comic irony. Most of the humor stems from the ironic relation between what Kinbote sees and what the reader perceives is actually happening. A passage from the foreword — Kinbote describing his early days at Wordsmith — is a sample of Nabokov's technique:

> On one of my first mornings there, . . . I noticed that Mr. and Mrs. Shade . . . were having trouble with their old Packard in the slippery driveway where it emitted whines of agony but could not extricate one tortured rear wheel out of a concave inferno of ice. . . . Thinking to offer my neighbors a ride to campus in my powerful machine, I hurried out toward them, . . . and I was about to cross the lane when I lost my footing and sat down on the surprisingly hard snow. My fall acted as a chemical reagent on the Shades' sedan, which forthwith budged and almost ran over me as it swung onto the lane. . . .

Kinbote's characteristic fault is missing the point, and being doubly gifted he can persuade himself that his failures are really virtues; and Nabokov, being even more gifted, can create a commentary in which Kinbote's blabberings consistently reveal more than they explicitly tell.

Kinbote the egomaniac insists upon understanding Shade's poem "Pale Fire" as a symbolic recreation of all the Zemblan history that Kinbote unloaded on Shade's disinterested ears. Therefore, in his interpretation, Shade's trivia actually tell of Kinbote's life, perhaps fantasied, as King Charles Xavier II, the deposed monarch of Zembla, and Kinbote pushes his self-importance through what, at first, seems unpromising stuff. Doomed to be a fool and not to recognize it, Kinbote can report that the first time he read Shade's "Pale Fire" he could see no reference to Zembla. Likewise, he fails to recognize that when someone addresses him as "The Great Beaver" the epithet is derogatory, that his capacity to rationalize all mistakes and criticisms is immense, that he regularly commits all sorts of misspellings and greater intellectual errors (which can be interpreted as an undercurrent of ironic commentary), that he is morally arrogant and disingenuous, that he has a natural inclination for overblown and inappropriate similes and needlessly multi-syllabic adjectives and adverbs, and that in his superficially correct index to Shade's poem several names, usually those of young attractive males, do not exist in the text. Quite acccurately, Nabokov shows that his malady produces a variety of secondary ills, including an unselfconscious, thorough insensitivity to the written word — Kinbote's artistic judgments are ludicrous and his quotations from Shakespeare, retranslated from the Zemblan, make one wince — and a general inability to recognize reality.

What is remarkable about *Pale Fire*, then, is Nabokov's ability to realize a three-fold effect — to sustain the sheer comedy of Kinbote's stupidity, to render from the inside consistently and subtly the meanderings of a deeply mad, but superficially functioning, intellectual mind, and to keep us aware of the inescapable terror of Kinbote's isolation and constant failure. Though

Pale Fire is Nabokov's best work, it fails to measure up to Barth's big novel in one crucial respect — an inability to transcend the sense that it is at base faintly trivial. Whereas Barth or, say, Eugene Ionesco in *The Lesson* can lift a similar feeling about the joke of knowledge and life into a basically serious vision of the absurdity of existence, nearly every line of action in *Pale Fire* culminates in just a guffaw; so that, the humor reflects merely on itself, letting Nabokov's work fall short of what we recognize as truly major fiction.

The other novels of madness tend to be less perfect in achievement and less original in form, for their authors, seemingly less in total control of their materials, weave realized portraits of neurotics into rather disjointed contexts. Walker Percy's *The Moviegoer* (1961) depicts in a young, well-connected New Orleans stockbroker, Binx Bolling, an anomic man who finds more "reality" in a movie house than in the life around him. From the movies, he learns how to understand life — he uses film examples to understand experience around him, and the incidents in life continually remind him of more interesting events in the movies. "I keep a Gregory Peckish sort of distance" is his description of his own behavior. In the climax of the book, a moment of desperation, he addresses his confession to a movie star: "I'll have to tell you the truth, Rory, painful though it is...." But precisely because the movies do not explain life, Bolling accepts platitudes as sincere compliments, fails to recognize the ineffectuality of his own social behavior, records "happiest moments" which a detached reader can see are insignificant, and continually rationalizes a life in which nothing happens. Indeed, his apathy is a more realized and profound version of the "paralysis" Barth continually attributes to his characters.

In the novel as a whole, Percy has a religious point to make. The movies have become Bolling's church, the source of otherworldly truth (and thus to them he must confess); and in giving the book the following epigraph from Kierkegaard, Percy perhaps gives too much of his theme away: "The specific character of despair is precisely this: it is unaware of being despair." But the Christian framework seems, in my opinion, rather forced and abstract in contrast to the true feeling and terror of Bolling's neurosis. Other aspects of the novel are rather fuzzy — Bolling's intelligence seems to fluctuate wildly, as does his attitude towards sex and business; but *The Moviegoer* is never more resonant and true than when Bolling is mad about the movies.

With Bruce Jay Friedman's *Stern* (1962), the problem of imperfection is somewhat different. After a brilliant opening section, the remaining two-thirds of the novel falls apart terribly; but in that opening vignette, Friedman creates a deftly concise portrait of a man who sees an enemy behind every strange bush — in Stern's life, there is an anti-Semite behind every gentile face. His feverish mind transforms every event that has an ambiguous significance to give it an ominous meaning. Stern, a new resident of the suburbs, hears that a male gentile neighbor has seen under his wife's

dress and perhaps called her a kike. In his mind, this becomes a rape. . . .
Elsewhere, "As [Stern] drove by, the man was looming up in front of him,
standing, hands in pockets, on the lawn and wearing a veteran's
organization jacket. It meant he had come through the worst part of the
Normandy campaign, knew how to hold his breath in foxholes for hours at
a time and then sneak out to slit a throat in silence." But, on second thought,
the fact that the gentile wears that jacket means absolutely none of these
things; and Friedman shows how Stern's neurotic mind exaggerates the
potency of the enemy to rationalize his own cowardice. What makes the first
part of *Stern* a comic and psychological masterpiece is Friedman's ability to
capture Stern's neurotic mechanisms without ever letting the characterization become a mechanically unlifelike "case study" or allowing us to believe
that Stern's fears might be real. However, once the portrait of Stern's anti-
Semite neurosis is complete, the book disintegrates. For some un-
fathomable reason, Friedman reveals that many of the fears that at first
seemed products of Stern's imagination are quite real; so that the sustained
brilliance of the first part is nearly massacred by the rest of the book.

Friedman's collection of stories, *Far from the City of Class* (1963), is extremely uneven, full of effects too arch to be true, phrases whose flash
obliterates their clarity ("pistol-like bosoms"), themes written in letters so
large they blot out any need for narrative, and trick endings that give no
discernible shape to the tale. Here, too, the best moments are Friedman's
portraits of neurotic behavior or reactions, like "The Good Time," which
tells of a young man's traumatic discovery of all the complicated underwear
under his mother's dress. Out of the situation and characters of that story,
Friedman fashioned his second novel, *A Mother's Kisses* (1964), a Kafkaesque
exercise in psychic symbolism about a young boy's emancipation from his
domineering mother. In this work, too, Friedman has written some truly
extraordinary scenes; but he is unable to sustain his occasional brilliance.

Though his work so far is confined entirely to stories, Irvin Faust,
working with the same materials as Friedman and Percy, appears to be a
considerably more promising writer, showing in *Roar, Lion, Roar* (1965) that
he is capable of depicting convincingly a wide range of madnesses in stories
as stylistically rich as they are well-realized. In the best of the seven I have
read, "Jake Bluffstein and Adolph Hitler," originally in *Carleton Miscellany*
(Spring, 1962), Faust describes, from the vantage point of an intimate third-
person narrator, a mad aging Jew who fondly remembers the days before
and during the Second World War when Jews found good reasons to hate
the gentiles, who tries to stir anti-gentile sentiment by scribbling late at
night the word "JUDE" on the window of his neighborhood butcher and
who believes that all Jews who do not hate gentiles are, like his rabbi,
basically Nazis. In a dream, he addresses the synagogue's members and
imagines himself becoming the Jews' modern messiah: "He saw a great sea

of faces, miles and miles of faces. 'SIEG,' he roared and the uniformed men marching toward him out of the faces, raised their arms for all the millions behind them and roared back, 'HEIL.' " In the story's next and last line — "He was free at last" — Faust suggests that this dream was a catharsis for Jake and that he would resume normality; but in none of these stories has Faust depicted normal men.

What makes Faust such an extraordinary psychological writer is the variety of madnesses he can describe. In the stories I read, he portrays a Puerto Rican boy whose existence becomes so attached to the fate of the Columbia football team that when they lose to Princeton he commits suicide; a rather stupid, dreamy fellow who sets out, accompanied by his Sancho, to be the Albert Schweitzer of Central Park; a lonely stockroom boy so pathologically attached to his portable radio that a girl who makes a pass at him must first destroy the radio before she can attain her end. Faust's wide range of psychological understanding results from his professional work. A guidance director at a Long Island high school by trade and author of a book of case studies in social psychology, *Entering Angel's World* (Teacher's College, Columbia University, 1963), Faust advocates that the counselor must assume, "wherever possible, the character and personality" of those with whom he deals; thus, his fictional interests and professional talents complement each other. But on top of his capacity for empathy, as well as a varied social knowledge, Faust has mastered the ability to evoke in print the frenzied mind dashing between memory and present, fragment and thought, to report its wanderings in an appropriately intense, immediate and elliptical style, and to write with a masterful control over image and metaphor in a variety of idioms.

Though far less original and ambitious than Nabokov and Percy and less psychologically insightful than Friedman and Faust at their best, Michael Rumaker has created some acute portraits of mad young men. Although he functions as a third person narrator, Rumaker gets inside his characters by sensitively reporting their feelings in an empathetic, matter-of-fact tone. "Jim had this tennis ball he found at the hospital," Rumaker writes in the opening of *The Butterfly* (1962). "He walked around bouncing it off the sidewalks and off walls. He bounced it in the library and bugged everybody. He was wearing an imaginary baseball cap until he could get a real one." Two pages later, "Jim cocked his baseball cap back on his head and thought...." Among other psychological experiences, the book contains a remarkably accurate record of a self-castration dream. Yet, as a novel *The Butterfly* seems cut in two, offering no transition between the opening three-quarters and the final fourth, in which Jim, unlike the other mad characters in recent fiction, attains a kind of normalcy. In his novel, as well as his stories, Rumaker exhibits a strong control of description, language and emotion — in short, of fictional craft — that immediately distinguishes him from the "beats" with whom he usually publishes.

Staking out its own area of pathological behavior, Burt Blechman's savage *How Much?* (1961), which is more insightful than his later *The War at Camp Omongo* (1963), focuses upon the compulsive desire to buy things "cheaply," particularly as it turns into a mania that destroys moral and emotional balance. A first story by Mrs. H.W. Blattner, "Sound of a Drunken Drummer," which first appeared in the *Hudson Review* (Fall, 1962), is a brilliant portrait of the disjointed consciousness of a suicidal alcoholic prostitute, somewhat reminiscent of Malcolm Lowry's classic treatment of the same condition in a man, *Under the Volcano* (1947), and yet extremely brilliant and promising in its own right. Indicatively perhaps, the best part of William Styron's disappointing second novel, *Set This House on Fire* (1960), is an incisive sketch of drunken impotence and disorientation originally published in *Paris Review #22* as "The McCabes."

IV

In the past decade, drugs have replaced alcohol and sex at the frontiers of avant-garde experience; and while one sub-strain of the new literature of the self focuses upon madness, the other turns to the new forms of experience provided by drugs. Without doubt, the most extraordinary work in this literature is William Burroughs' *Naked Lunch* (1959), a report of the hallucinatory madness he experienced during a withdrawal from narcotics addiction. The narrator is identified as William Lee; but since Burroughs used that name as a nom de plume for his earlier *Junkie* (1953), one assumes Lee is Burroughs himself. In structure, *Naked Lunch* is a collection of scenes, gathered from notes supposedly jotted down while undergoing withdrawal and not remembered afterwards; and in it Burroughs creates, like Genet, a dream universe, full of characters who have some semblance to real people but who are transformed into nightmare grotesques.

The book's characters fall into two groups, the horrendously evil and the anonymous dregs: Salvador Hassan O'Leary, the mythical international mogul, the Man behind the Man, who "held 23 passports and had been deported 49 times." Doctor Benway, Burroughs' most demonic creation, is the scientific man using his knowledge for super-evil, in charge of "interrogation, brainwashing and control" in Burroughs' totalitarian world and who in the middle of a riot samples the blood of the dead. With shrewd images, Burroughs evokes the nameless bottoms of the drug world, such as the lonely old opium addicts: "A few old relics from hop-smoking times, spectral janitors, grey as ashes, phantom partners sweeping out dusty halls with a slow old man's hand, coughing and spitting in the junk-sick dawn, retired asthmatic fences in theatrical hotels. . . ." The sterility of the external world complements the paralysis of the self; during addiction, Burroughs remembers: "I could look at the end of my shoe for eight hours."

Some of Burroughs' fantasy images are extraordinary creations, unlike, one guesses, anything that could be consciously devised. The scene of the book is an alien city:

> All streets of the City slope down between deepening canyons to a vast, kidney-shaped plaza full of darkness. Walls of street and plaza are per- forated by dwelling cubicles and cafés, some a few feet deep, others extending out of sight in a network of rooms and corridors.

In the end, *Naked Lunch* becomes a vision of the world in total decay, thoroughly without redemption, any outpost of retreat or a possibility for change. Among all the modern books that envision a contemporary world of complete horror, none evokes it more thoroughly, or with such uncom- promising images of decay and violence, as Burroughs' book. In this respect, *Naked Lunch* makes other "end-of-the-world" books, such as Ken- neth Patchen's *The Journal of Albion Moonlight* or Nelson Algren's *A Walk on the Wild Side* (1956), seem pretty feeble. Ferdinand-Louis Céline, perhaps Burroughs' closest competitor in this respect, once boasted that yes he had imitators but no one else could keep up such intense, imaginative negation for a couple of hundred pages; well, Burroughs does. However, whereas Céline intended, perhaps pretended, to describe reality, Burroughs' world is entirely a madman's creation.

What makes *Naked Lunch* such an arresting and disturbing book, the best of all the narcotics fiction to emerge in recent years, is that Burroughs transcends a concern with narcotics as such to render the hallucinatory ex- perience in a realized and appropriate literary style. Like other American fiction concerned with the frontiers of human behavior, *Naked Lunch* opens the reader's mind to the possibilities of perception and literary creation; and in its unfettered exploration of demonic consciousness, it resembles such great American books as *Moby Dick* and *Absalom, Absalom*.

In structure, *Naked Lunch* is a string of scenes from which emerge a coherent sensibility and a set of themes; in this respect it resembles the books of Henry Miller. But because Burroughs relies more upon images than upon plot for unity, his book achieves an overall spatial form that justifies his boast that, "You can cut into *Naked Lunch* at any intersection point." This too is appropriate, for the heroin experience itself is the achievement of timelessness.

Although *Naked Lunch* will, I think, become a modern classic, Bur- roughs himself is fated, I am afraid, to remain a minor writer. His later creative works seem distinctly less impressive. *The Exterminator* (1960), *The Soft Machine* (1961; revised, 1963), *The Ticket That Exploded* (1962), and *The Nova Express* (1964) are relentless pursuits of Burroughs' faith in the theory that certain composing methods viable in painting and music can be ap- plied to literature. Some of these books are produced with the cut-up method: Burroughs writes on several pages, cuts them up, scrambles the scraps and sets down the result in a fixed final form. Others were written with what he calls the "fold-in" method: "I take a page of text, my own or someone else's, and fold it lengthwise down the middle and place it on another page of text, my own or someone else's, lining up the lines. The composite text is then read across, half one text and half the other." Since his books regrettably do not contain prefaces explaining the method used to compose them, it is impossible to tell whether one method provides better results than another. Nonetheless, except for an occasional original image, surely an achievement that has little to do with the method, there is not much here to engage one's interest. Only when Burroughs harnesses his rich imagination and observational honesty to a confining form does he produce excellent writing, as in the letters of 1953 to Allen Ginsberg (whose own letters, in contrast, seem mannered) published as *In Search of Yage* (1963).

In contrast to Burroughs who records the fantasies of withdrawal, most of the other writers on withdrawal, from Alexander King in *Mine Enemy Grows Older* (1959) to more serious novelists, accent the addict's sheer pain and compulsive movements. In two stunning passages that redeem Clarence L. Cooper's confused, otherwise undistinguished novel, *The Scene* (1960), Rudi Black is described as "twisting his body in a half-figure eight," suffering from uncontrollable spasms, constant tickling sensations, shivering, sweating, vomiting, spitting and dreaming of friends who might give him dope. "He tightened his belt until the thin leather bit into his stomach like wire, establishing a new pain, one he could concentrate on to forget the others."

In a chronicle of the day-by-day details of the addict's experience, *Cain's Book* (1960), Alexander Trocchi, a Scotsman who spent many years in America, describes the sheer boredom and emotional impotence of addiction and the addict's lack of concern for past or future, or for other people, in a novel that taunts and eventually succumbs to the intentional fallacy of being a dull portrait of dullness.

The experience of using hallucinogens, non-addicting fantasy-producing drugs, while it greatly interests the educated young in America, has not to my knowledge been the subject of any American prose writing as interesting, original and unselfconscious as, say, Aldous Huxley's *The Doors of Perception* or the French poet Henri Michaux's "Experiments." Some of our poets, such as Michael McClure, have written about their use of hallucinogens, particularly peyote, usually to propagate pet theses about esthetics or existence. Paul Bowles in *A Hundred Camels in the Courtyard* (1963) has spun off rather pat didactic tales advocating kif smoking as superior to alcohol. Hallucinogen experience will, I suspect, interest many young writers in the next few years; and in all likelihood, out of this mass derangement of consciousness some interesting writing will emerge.

V

Scattered other young writers have produced some innovative and interesting fictional work which, in the end, stands outside the two main trends. If Barth and Nabokov exhibit a versatile inventiveness, Hubert Selby, Jr.'s originality is extremely narrow, confined to one aspect of his writing, his style. He has concocted a gritty, grinding, impatient, hard-edged, undertone-less idiom, with the quality of a lawnmower, to tell pro-saic, violent naturalistic stories, as in the following passage from "Another Day Another Dollar" in *New Directions #17*:

> They formed a circle and kicked. He tried to roll over on his stomach and cover his face with his arms, but as he got to his side he was kicked in the groin and stomped on the ear and he screamed, cried, started pleading then just cried as a foot cracked his mouth. Ya fuckin cottonpickin punk and a hard kick in the ribs turned him slightly and he tried to raise himself on one knee and someone took a short step forward and kicked him in the solarplexus and he fell on his side, his knees up, arms folded across his ab-domen, gasping for air and the blood in his mouth gurgled as he tried to scream, . . .

Though his fiction so far offers little interest besides its language, that alone makes it worth reading.

In *American Contemporary* (1963), an uneven collection of portraits of modern pathos and rootlessness, Curtis Zahn creates a variety of styles to carry his basically satirical themes. "Recognition," my own favorite, is the most successful rendering I know in first-person narration of a stupid, inar-ticulate person's inability to cope with experience:

> When we first move here I was born in Saint Louie and Harry Ohio but met in Kansas, Mo, because I was going with this fry cook but Harry had a Chevy convertible. He got married to me in Riverside, Cal, because there is this cousin that has an Olds. But we didn't have much else in com-mon with Riverside except shooting, which is the main route down to Palm Springs where Tony Curtis goes.

In the other sketches, particularly those of California life, Zahn is too apt to let his bitterness obliterate his literary sense.

VI

Although the two strains of new American fiction, concerned with op-posite poles of human experience, are on the surface quite different, they complement each other's view of the world. In an absurd world, man con-tracts the *anomie* that incites and abets mental disability; and widespread madness is one of the factors contributing to an absurd world. Indeed, in two of these novels, madness and absurdity overlap—*Catch-22* and *The Moviegoer*, each of them coming to the center from different sides. In all, then, these novelists present such a narrow vision of contemporary possibility that one suspects either their vision is severely limited or they have succeeded in penetrating to the two-fold heart of the contemporary experience. I believe that the novelist has always been more successful at grasping social essences than facts and, thus, that these writers too reflect, as well as indicate, our predicament. They present images of society which neither sociology nor newsreels can evoke or confirm and offer glimpses into madness which psychological writing does not provide.

Stylistically, too, they have much in common. Unlike the playwrights, they all seem to remain unaffected by the major trends in post–World War II European literature; neither the reactionary realism of the New University Wits, nor the objectivist novels of Alain Robbe-Grillet, the concern with semi-consciousness of Nathalie Sarraute, nor the existentialist realism of Alberto Moravia has fathered propitious parallels in recent American literature. Only one major recent European work I know, Gunter Grass's *The Tin Drum* (1959), greatly resembles the new American writing. If these novels belong anywhere, it is in the great American tradition of non-realistic romance: the novel of man and civilization (such as *Huckleberry Finn*) now receives an absurd twist and the gothic imagination has moved into the haunted house of the mind.

In nearly all these novels, the isolation of the main figure is extreme. Except for Ebenezer Cooke, the protagonist has no discernible father; except for Stern and Jake Bluffstein, he has no wife; and in general, he does not reveal his intimate self to others. Conversely, society is depicted as offering little salvation. No character explicitly considers religion or politics, though Binx Bolling and Bluffstein fantasize substitutes for each. Just as these authors make their characters and situations paradigms for the larger world, they eschew creating explicit contrasts. Sane men are never compared to madmen, rational societies to absurd ones; for what these authors describe will, they believe, inevitably exist. Although none of these writers creates life-giving heroes, worthy of imitation, nor posits a Way Out of the contemporary predicament, the sensitive protagonist in all these books but *Malcolm* refuses to die before his due, for these novels join Samuel Beckett's in speaking a single metaphysical message for our time: Although man has little reason to go on living, in a world so meaningless and hazardous, he still asserts, by the force of his essential will, the right to exist. Finally, by traditional criteria, these writers literally have "nothing-to-say," except to say, 'pataphysically, that there is nothing to say.

The writers themselves are as culturally isolated as their characters are socially; none is largely a product of that main line of American culture that runs from the universities of Boston through those in New York to Philadelphia. John Barth was born in Eastern Maryland, took his degrees at Johns Hopkins, and has taught at Penn State for a dozen years. Joseph Heller worked in advertising in New York while writing *Catch-22*. Nabokov wrote *Pale Fire* in Switzerland; Pynchon is a recluse in Mexico; Faust works in a Long Island high school; Purdy lives aloof in Brooklyn; Percy in New Orleans; etc. Yet these writers have received conventional, if not extensive, educations. All, to my knowledge, have B.A.'s, and many have advanced degrees: Barth and Heller, M.A.'s; Percy, M.D.; Faust, Fiedler and Koch, Ph.D.'s; Nabokov taught continental literature for several years at Cornell, where Pynchon was his student. Most have taken courses in creative writing, if often to rebel against their teachers' pet formulas. Not only are they educated, but they use their learning so easily and extensively that their novels have, to various extents, a pedantic quality; indeed, they succeed best with educated readers.

Their education largely explains why these writers, except for Friedman and Faust, appear to start writing with a theme clearly in mind, rather than a situation, a conflict, or a single character, and then devise ways to best dramatize their point; yet it is not their themes, which are easily summarized, but the method by which these ideas are realized that makes these books interesting and artistically important. Surely, it is rather easy to plan an absurd novel, but it is enormously difficult (if not inconceivable) to give the scheme the embellishment of *The Sot-Weed Factor*. Moreover, all these books are realized primarily as novels — they contain effects only fiction can achieve; but for *Catch-22*, I cannot imagine any of them being adapted into another artistic medium without having its essence distorted or destroyed.

Finally, all of them have experienced an excess of unfavorable and/or uncomprehending reviews: the basic irony of *Pale Fire* was all but completely missed, Heller's novel was nearly universally panned, Percy's and Friedman's were hardly reviewed at all. Yet, in the 1960s, thanks largely to the perseverance of conscientious critics, the mistaken judgments of hasty reviewers — the maltreatment that plagued nearly all original American writers throughout their careers — are with each year being rectified with increasing speed. By 1964, all the novels discussed here at length are widely admired, nearly all have appeared in paperback; and all together, they make American fiction one of the most interesting arts in America and the world today.

The American Absurd Novel (1965)

What we call "absurd literature" embodies a very specific literary convention: a series of absurd — that is, nonsensical or ridiculous — events that suggest the ultimate absurdity, or meaninglessness, of human existence. At the end of Ionesco's *The Chairs*, a particularly neat model of the convention, a hired lecturer addresses a nonexistent audience in an indecipherable tongue. This is the absurd surface. Since the lecturer's message is supposed to represent the final wisdom of a ninety-five-year-old couple, the meaningless message becomes an effective symbol for metaphysical void.

Used precisely, the term "absurd literature" does not apply to all literary works that deal with human absurdity. In the plays and fiction of Sartre and Camus, for contrary examples, the surface is too realistic, the sense of human causality too linear; and the characters, along with the writer and reader, deduce absurdity from the course of credible events. Truly absurd literature does not discover meaninglessness; from its opening moments it accepts the condition and presents it as a theme. Absurd literature has an anti-realistic, preposterous surface; it embodies a stylized vision of human reality, rather than an accurate representation of it. In addition, it treats questions of ultimate significance, such as the quality of contemporary life, belief in final truths, or the underlying pattern of human history. It embodies absurdity in both the small events and the entire vision, in both the subject matter and the form.

The most familiar absurd literature are certain works of post-war European theater, particularly the plays of Samuel Beckett and Eugene Ionesco. In recent fiction, the comprehensively absurd masterpieces are Beckett's later novels; and selected Raymond Queneau, but only in America in the nineteen-sixties do we find a large body of absurd fiction — the novels and stories of Harry Mathews, Donald Barthelme, Kenneth Koch, and particularly three longer novels worth discussing in closer detail: *Catch-22*, by Joseph Heller, Thomas Pynchon's *V.*, and *The Sot-Weed Factor*, by John Barth.

A writer dealing with metaphysical issues must create a microcosm of experience that has enough symbolic resonance to stand for larger human issues. The European absurd writers tend to create a single pregnant image: in Ionesco's play, the hired lecturer addressing the nonexistent audience; in Beckett's last novel, *Comment c'est*, Pim dragging his bag of possessions through the mud of existence; in *Waiting for Godot*, two men awaiting a mysterious Godot who obviously is not coming. The American absurdist, in contrast, resorts to strategies of elaboration and overstatement, rather than a single suggestive scene; and although these American novelists treat larger areas of human experience, they are still exploiting these subjects as symbolic microcosms for even larger issues.

Heller's *Catch-22*, which has the narrowest focus of the three novels, depicts the activities of some American soldiers in the Second World War; Pynchon's novel has two faintly interconnecting plots, one portraying a group of American layabouts, the other a search for a woman whose name starts with the letter V., a search conducted against a background of European history in the twentieth century; and Barth's *The Sot-Weed Factor*, set in the late seventeenth and early eighteenth centuries, tells of the adventures of Ebenezer Cooke, in England and Colonial America, with flashbacks to John Smith's experiences with Pocahontas in the early seventeenth century. And to suit the breadth of their interests, all these novels are huge: both Heller's and Pynchon's run to 500 pages, and *The Sot-Weed Factor* over 800, at 500 words to a page.

On life's surface, each of these novelists finds more disorder than continuity, more incongruity than meaning. Heller, for one, portrays a world in which there is no relation between intention and result. This discrepancy he defines as the law of *Catch-22*, the book's central symbol, introduced in the following dialogue between Yossarian, Heller's main character, and Doctor Daneeka:

> "Is Orr crazy?"
> "He sure is."
> "Can you ground him?"
> "I sure can but first he has to ask me to. That's part of the rule."
> "Then why doesn't he ask you to?"
> "Because he's crazy... He has to be crazy to keep flying combat missions after all the close calls he's had. But first he has to ask me."
> "And then you can ground him?"
> "No then I can't ground him."
> "You mean there's a catch?"
> "Sure there's a catch. Catch-22. Anybody who wants to get out of combat duty isn't really crazy."

In a world ruled by Catch-22, a character with the preposterous name of Major Major Major Major should impress people, as Heller writes, "by how unimpressive he was"; and another character named Colonel Cathcart "was so awful a marketing executive that his services were much sought after by firms eager to establish losses for tax purposes." In *Catch-22*, Yossarian should be told he is jeopardizing his political freedoms by exercizing them; and the book as a whole attempts to demonstrate that since the world's standards of value and behavior are so various and inconsistent, syllogistic reasoning can preach only contradictions.

Like Heller, Pynchon is obsessed with the discontinuity of human experience. Two-thirds of the way through this novel, one of his internal narrators, Fausto Maijstral, introduces his own narrative with these suggestive words: "No apologia is any more than a romance — half a fiction — in which all the successive identities taken on and rejected by the writer as a function of linear time are treated as separate characters." A few lines later, Maijstral adds: "It isn't so much to pay for eyes clear enough to see past the fiction of continuity, the fiction of cause and effect, the fiction of humanized history, endowed with reason." Maijstral, then, is one of Pynchon's identities, creating an incoherent story within an already confused narrative; and Maijstral's story, like Pynchon's, is a calculated denial of continuity as a principle in fiction and its usefulness as a tool in understanding human history. Pynchon's method has affinities with the Quantum Theory which holds that experience that is discontinuous defies precise definition — its direction is indeterminate; and phenomena that have a semblance of meaning turn out, on closer inspection, to suggest a multiplicity of answers.

The letter V, Pynchon's most imaginative projection, is the central symbol of the book and one of the prime indicators of its meaning. "V" is first introduced as the object that a character named Stencil is trying to find — indicatively, as Stencil was born in 1900, he is "a child of the century," and, like much else in the novel, the letter V is capable of meaning many things: such as a large number of similar, perhaps successor characters, ranging from Victoria, an English girl seduced in Cairo in the late nineteenth century, to the grotesque Veronica Manganese with a jewel in her navel, as well as, to quote the summary of the American critic Stanley Edgar Hyman, "Some great female principle... She is the goddess Venus and the planet Venus, the Virgin, the town of Valetta in Malta, the imaginary land of Vheissu with its iridescent spider monkeys and volcanoes. She is Vesuvius, Venezuela, the Violet, of the vulgar mnemonic; ultimately she is the V of the spread thighs and the *mons veneris*." Pynchon's special achievement, then, is devising a symbol for metaphysical reality that suggests not ambiguity as, say, Moby-Dick does, but unbounded multiplicity.

Unlike Pynchon, who accepts basic historical facts as true, John Barth doubts our standard versions of the past; and in *The Sot-Weed Factor* he systematically distorts, mostly debunks, traditional accounts of history to create versions that are just as probable as those in the textbooks. In Barth's narrative Sir Isaac Newton and Henry More, the Cambridge neo-Platonist, emerge as lubricious pederasts who provide refuge for orphaned boys. And whereas Addison described the late seventeenth-century coffee-house conversation as being intellectual, in *The Sot-Weed Factor* the chatterers sooner turn to sex. The third Lord Baltimore, known to history as an undistinguished Catholic ruler, runs, in Barth's book, a network of spies and saboteurs in his war against the Protestants. The book's principal character, Ebenezer Cooke, gives himself the dubious title of "Poet and Laureate" of Maryland, and goes off to the New World to write his *Marylandiad*. In the course of his travels he discovers some supposedly authentic documents, *The Privie Journall of Sir Henry Burlingame*, and *The Secret Historie* of John Smith, both written in magnificently faked seventeenth-century English prose.

These documents provide Barth with his most extensive opportunity for historical debunking, for they reveal a hidden story behind the Pocahontas myth. In the legend, we remember, the English explorer, John Smith, about to be executed by the Indian chief Powhatan, was saved by the intervention of the chief's daughter, Pocahontas. The version recounted in the novel's "documents" reveals that John Smith was a lecher who first obtained Powhatan's friendship by giving him pornographic pictures and later won his confidence by satisfying the chief's otherwise insatiable wife. Later, thanks to a secret "egg-plant" potion, Smith manages to deflower the much-tried, but previously impenetrable, virgin Pocahontas. The Indians, likewise untrue to historical form, confiscate Smith's immense collection of erotic literature.

Although one character in the novel rejects sentimental interpretations of history, saying "More history's made in the bed-chamber than the throne room," Barth's story suggests that not much history is made in bed either. In this novel, history is thoroughly disordered; and the search for the first causes or definitive interpretations uncovers only contradictions; more persistent search, only multiple confusions. A chapter heading near the book's end expresses Ebenezer's befuddlement as well as Barth's and the reader's:

> The Poet Wonders Whether the Source of Human History is a Progress, a Drama, a Retrogression, a Cycle, an Undulation, a Vortex, a Right- or Left-Handed Spiral, a Mere Continuum, or What Have You. Certain Evidence is Brought Forward, but of an Ambiguous and Inconclusive Nature.

In addition to burlesquing written history, *The Sot-Weed Factor* thoroughly ridicules fictional conventions, and in this way undercuts literature's pretensions to comprehending life. The satirical blade is aimed obliquely at all fat popular historical novels (this one being too fat, too difficult, and largely faked as history) and particularly at the eighteenth-century novel whose penchant for digressive chapter headings is exaggerated as absurdly as its favorite plot devices are repeated. The search for the father, the reversal of roles, the accidental recognition scene, transformation through disguises, moments of near incest, and especially preposterous coincidences all occur again and again in Barth's novel.

The Sot-Weed Factor successfully transforms two serious quests — that of

Cooke for his muse and that of his companion Burlingame for the identity of his parents — into a long series of incidents so incredible that their serious purposes are twisted into high comedy. And then, before the novel is over, the book's spine is twisted back again to align with Barth's essentially serious concern with human history. In mocking the conventions of the eighteenth-century novel by overusing them to absurd lengths, in suggesting that the history we know is as unlikely as his rewriting of it, in doing both these things with such imaginative wit and breadth of reference, Barth ultimately says that not only are the single events of life preposterous — that is, absurd — but also that life as a whole, which resists any ordering interpretation, is similarly, at base, absurd. Amid all these facts the novel tells only one truth: that there is no truth. This conclusion, I think, strikes appropriate undertones for our time; for the world yields to our efforts no ordering scheme, only nonsense with each twist of complexity multiplying itself to infinite degrees.

Although these novels are all new in their fusion of absurd base with absurd surface, they descend from several distinct literary traditions. First, they belong with those prose works that reveal the influence of François Rabelais and Laurence Sterne; and, like their predecessors, these new American novelists are, at once, both prodigiously erudite and endlessly imaginative. Neither the form nor the action of their novels bows to accepted conventions of literary realism or propriety; and while they deal with the facts of existence these authors reserve the right to transform those actualities — indeed, to transform all experience — through their rich imaginations. Secondly, these novels belong to the American tradition of anti-realistic romance, particularly those novels concerned with individual man and oppressive civilization, a line that includes *Huckleberry Finn, Billy Budd*, the novels of Saul Bellow and Ralph Ellison. And like their predecessors, these new American novelists all tell us, again and again, that human society is so cruel that individual man, no matter how strong his will, can find no salvation within it.

All these novels seem more extensively considered than most fiction. That is, their authors appear to start writing with a theme in the very front of their minds, rather than a situation, a conflict, a single character or a specific technical device; and then they devise ways to illustrate their theme. Yet it is not their themes, which are easily identified and summarized, but the methods by which these themes are realized that makes these books interesting and artistically important. Surely it would be fairly easy to outline an absurd novel, but to take the absurd formula and give it the embellishment of these novels would be extremely difficult.

The artistic problems in creating an absurd novel are, then, twofold. First the situation described must be an effective enough symbol to suggest metaphysical absurdity. A contrasting failure in this respect is Bernard Malamud's first and best novel, *The Natural* (1952), which has a comic absurd surface. For example, when the manager of the baseball team instructs his batter in baseball slang, "to knock the cover off the ball," the batter pulls the impossible trick of batting the baseball so hard its leather cover falls off. But Malamud's baseball team fails, I think, to become a metaphysical symbol, and his novel never achieves the serious resonance which it constantly suggests. The other hazard of an absurd novel is over-embellishment, particularly as the strategy of surface discontinuity pushes the novel over the line of effectiveness into outright, thorough incoherence. Perhaps the most notorious example of this is William Gaddis's 956-page novel, *The Recognitions* (1956).

To my mind, the novels by Pynchon, Heller, and Barth achieve metaphysical pertinence and avoid the perils of excessive incoherence; and all three are realized primarily as novels — they all contain structures and effects that only fiction can achieve; and, except for *Catch-22*, I cannot imagine any of them being adapted into another artistic medium, such as the cinema, without having its essence distorted or destroyed. These American absurd novels show us that, even in these post–Joycean, post–Gidean, post–Faulknerian times, the novel as an art form is far from dead. Indeed, in an age in which everything artistically appears to have been done, these writers reaffirm the possibility of creating novels that are, in the contemporary sense, crucially new, and, in the traditional sense, realized achievements.

"New American Fiction"
Reconsidered (1967)

Some three years ago, somewhat annoyed at how little of the post–Bellow-Malamud-Baldwin fiction was receiving serious critical scrutiny, I drafted a long essay on "New American Fiction," which became a chapter of a book I edited on *The New American Arts* (1965). In that essay, I attempted to identify, first, the dominant new styles in the best American fiction and, second, both the major works and the emerging talents. At that time, I particularly admired four novels — John Barth's *The Sot-Weed Factor*, Vladimir Nabokov's *Pale Fire*, Joseph Heller's *Catch-22* and William Burroughs's *Naked Lunch*. Whereas I had doubts about the future work of both Burroughs and Heller, I placed a heavy bet upon Barth's next work and lighter wagers upon, to list all the writers I favored then, Thomas Pynchon, Irvin Faust, Bruce Jay Friedman, Walker Percy, Curtis Zahn, Hubert Selby, Jr., Kenneth Koch and James Purdy.

Looking back over both the essay and the novels I discussed there, I find little reason to revise its broad outlines. I have not since reversed my decision on any of the several score novels I disliked then (though regretting the catalogue-quality of my negative judgments), nor have I come across any truly first-rate fiction by native contemporaries previously unknown to me. (E.L. Doctorow's *Welcome to Hard Times* [1960] and Paule Marshall's *Soul Clap Hands and Sing* [1962] are both quite fine, however.) Today, I would still identify the two encompassing themes of the best American fiction as the absurdity of society and the madness of the self; and the best novels I have read since then have only confirmed these hypotheses. Unlike before, however, I now value more highly the stories of Irvin Faust, collected as *Roar Lion Roar* (1965), which I reread with increasing pleasure; and John Barth's *The Sot-Weed Factor* now strikes me as an even more awesome imaginative work. Also, now I find myself more disturbed by the incoherence in Pynchon's *V.* (1963) and the inability of both Friedman and Percy to sustain, respectively in *Stern* (1962) and *The Moviegoer* (1961), the excellence that marks the first-halves of those novels.

Likewise, in the past few years, not one of the older generation of established novelists has risked a jump into frontier territory. Indeed, some of them manage to sustain a current reputation upon works produced long ago—Ralph Ellison, William Styron, J.D. Salinger and William Gaddis. Saul Bellow's *Herzog* (1964) strikes me as excessively pretentious in tone, clumsily written, needlessly compromised in crucial dimensions; Norman Mailer's *An American Dream* (1965) suffers from unconvincing prose and artless excesses, which did nothing to overcome my impression that his better essays of recent years have more style and substance. James Baldwin's short stories, *Going to Meet the Man* (1965), have more art and less ambition than *Another Country* (1962); still, they mine old veins, as do the stories Jerome Charyn collected in *The Man Who Grew Younger* (1967). Alan Harrington's long-awaited second novel, *The Secret Swinger* (1966), was little more than a malevolent *roman à clef*; Francis Pollini's *Glover* (1965) lacked the immediacy and hard integrity of *Night* (1960); Truman Capote's *In Cold Blood* (1966) displayed less journalistic art than Tom Wolfe and little fictional interest. Nabokov has published numerous translations, of both Pushkin's poetry and his own earlier Russian works, introducing them all as equally sacred texts. Leslie Fiedler's three novellas, *The Last Jew in America* (1966), was indubitably his worst fiction to date; Howard Nemerov's *Journal of the Fictive Life* (1965), while more self-honest and artistically ambitious, still suffered from that slickness that plagued his previous fiction. Bernard Malamud's *The Fixer* (1966), so hailed by older critics, I found enormously disappointing— much too close to the style of Isaac Bashevis Singer, as well as too distant from that less parochial milieu of *The Natural* (1952), which I still consider his richest novel. Writers of this generation seem to provide too easily what their publics admired before, rather than achieving a relationship of tension and surprise.

However, most of my favored novelists, it must be acknowledged, have similarly betrayed my hopes. Walker Percy's *The Last Gentleman* (1966) comes as a dreadful mistake, suffering from a protagonist who is both stereotyped and needlessly vague; and for a novel that makes so much of his interaction with society, *The Last Gentleman* has such a deficient sense of milieu that its best dimension, the truth of its portrait of dislocation, is not successfully integrated into the fictional line. William Burroughs has not yet, to quote myself, either transcended or verified "the theory that certain composing methods viable in painting [i.e., abstract expressionism and collage] and music [i.e., aleatoric procedures] can be applied to literature." Indicatively, the revised version of *The Soft Machine* (1966) was hardly an improvement over the original Olympia Press edition (1961). Bruce Jay Friedman's second book of stories, *Black Angels* (1966) suffers from that hokey cuteness that mars the last half of *Stern* (1962); and not since that first novel has he attained that hard perception that, for many readers, had seemed so true. Neither Hubert Selby, Jr. nor Curtis Zahn appears to have published anything new; and Joseph Heller's "Something Happened," (*Esquire*,

1966), while excellent as short fiction, leaves doubts, as an excerpt about its novelistic potential. Of the first novels by new writers, Jeremy Larner's *Drive, He Said* (1964), LeRoi Jones's *The System of Dante's Hell* (1965), and Richard Fariña's *I've Been Down So Long It Looks Like Up to Me* (1966) all suffer from excessive bad writing and conspicuous signs of classroom lessons learned too well, while just the latter attribute mars first novels as various as Robert Coover's *The Origin of the Brunists* (1966), Cynthia Ozick's *Trust* (1966), Joseph McElroy's *The Smuggler's Bible* (1966) and Jay Neugeboren's *Big Man* (1966). W.H. Gass's debut, *Omensetter's Luck* (1966), has so much impressive prose that I am honestly pained by my inability to deduce its contents; and finally whereas James Merrill's second novel, *The (Diblos) Notebook* (1965) is clearly an original work, its possible significances escape me.

II

Of the many new novels I have read in the past three years, only one struck me as fusing the three essential virtues of originality, significance and realization at the highest levels of consistency—Irvin Faust's *The Steagle* (1966), which may indeed be the most perceptive and sustained portrait of a psychotic breakdown in all novelistic literature. Faust's major figure, Harold Aaron Weissburg, is an associate professor of English at a New York college—a man ambitious enough to live above his means, yet not particularly devoted to his work; and the novel relates the two and one half weeks preceding his fall. In structure, *The Steagle* resembles Faust's truly great short story, "Jake Bluffstein and Adolf Hitler," for the theme of mental derangement, evident from the opening scene, is expanded to the protagonist's ultimate breakdown. However, in *The Steagle* the theme is endowed with more detail and incident as Weissburg's disintegration is more gradual and sensitive than Bluffstein's. Faust is particularly shrewd at portraying Weissburg as a psychotic who, unlike a neurotic (such as Walker Percy's Willston Barrett or Sartre's Roquentin), is barely aware of his impending explosion; and as a psychotic, he externalizes his fantasies, really believing that he is a movie star named "Bob Hardy" (of the same family as Andy) or a gruff Italian capable of making a stripper fall in love with him.

In conveying Weissburg's increasing madness, Faust handles several technical problems with especial brilliance. As in "Jake Bluffstein," he is particularly clever at so successfully distorting the lines between fantasy and reality that the reader is never fully sure whether a certain action takes place in dream or in life; for deeply imbedded in his fiction is that psychological truth that the wish can be as significant as the act. Second, Faust is a master of that modern technique of rendering an hysterical consciousness with unerring similitude. As he returns home on the train, Weissburg reads the *New York Times*:

> Back to Arthur Krock. Friendly thickness. The sober seriousness of the
> situation. The responsible analysis of the implication of the sober
> seriousness of the — *Balls, Hesh*. No, listen. Herr Hitler is indicating a will-
> ingness to — *Balls*. No, experts. *Balls, Krock is a crock.* No, negotiate. Cy
> Sulzberger, look, he interviews Nasser. Cy and Nasser? *Schmuck?* No, nor-
> malcy, Rita, blond bullycock, guilt. The squish unsquished, and the
> voice — low, controlled, bored — said, "Isn't that the city?"

As in this passage, Faust's prose is neither clichéd nor fancy; but as an elliptical notation, it attains a distinct kind of frenetic elegance.

His fiction is loaded with simple descriptive lines that reveal so much
about a person's mental state. As Jake Bluffstein prepares to convey his mes-
sianic message to those around him, Faust writes, "He felt like Columbus."
Of Weissburg, he says, "He was feeling calm and yet terrifically excited."
Even in this age of jargons, neither analytical terminology nor leaden symbols mar Faust's descriptive perceptions. Fourth, he effectively evokes
Weissburg's successively more perilous steps, from his impulsive affair with
a fellow professor through addressing his class in the "obb" language of New
York children, through his dream of himself as a rising movie star, to the
final moments when he tells a nurse he picks up that he is "Cave Carson,"
the son of Floyd Collins:

> "Uh. . ." Tired, oh so tired.
> "Sobbay Bobbang Bobbang Swobbeetobby."
> He sagged against the rail. As the pain started up behind the left sinus
> and the heartburn pushed into his throat he looked at her and said, 'All
> right, Louie, drop da gun.'

With a stark conciseness and a clear finality that resembles the final words
in Faulkner's *The Sound and the Fury*, this is among the great endings in contemporary literature.

The book's major failures stem from the curious falseness and
parochialism of certain crucial details. It is difficult to believe that
Weissburg is a college teacher, despite all the references to Elizabethan
authors; the conversation in the dining hall scene, early in the book, has a
tone closer to high school (a milieu Faust knows well) than college; and
Weissburg's own pedantic love of obscure facts suggests more the
autodidact than the scholar with a Ph.D. In addition, the effectiveness of
certain details depends upon a familiarity with New York's Jewish
culture — not just Yiddishisms (for example, that "Hesh" is a nickname for
Harold) but the sort of things that typical Jewish city kids think and do.
Similarly, many other details will date too quickly for Faust to earn posteri-
ty's beneficence. Not only does the import of both the book's title and its
epigraph escape me completely, but also in using as a background the Cuba
Missile Crisis of October, 1962, Faust inadequately integrates public
disturbance into private troubles. Finally, on first reading, I found that

following the narrative line and identifying the speakers of certain quotations both became progressively more difficult as Weissburg's derangement becomes more acute; but on second reading some of these problems were alleviated.

Nonetheless, what is remarkable is Faust's consistency—his unwillingness to compromise his fictional method—and his perseverance with an enormously hazardous subject. He chooses a theme—the progressive derangement of one man—that is basically the material of short fiction and achieves the awesome feat of sustaining it through a novel where nothing, to my mind, is conspicuously superfluous. Though one might say that Faust has rutted himself as a specialist in mental distress, he has hardly exhausted, in my estimate, the fictional possibilities of this preoccupation. Moreover, *The Steagle* establishes Faust as clearly among the most accomplished craftsmen of fiction today.

III

By now everyone who has read John Barth's *Giles Goat-Boy* (1966) appears to agree that it is hardly as great as *The Sot-Weed Factor*; indeed, those early outrageously laudatory reviews were probably intended to repair the reviewers' neglect of his earlier novels. It is, nonetheless, a first-rate book, surely among the dozen or so best novels of the sixties. On its most basic level, that of style, the new work is not as brilliant as its predecessor, suffering from less of the conspicuously eye-catching writing and the natural comic energy that lifted the earlier masterpiece. The opening section of the publisher's editors' reports suggested huge promise, as in the following passage, where one editor chides the negative judgment of another:

> His own daughter, I happen to know, "ran off" from college with a bearded young poetry-student who subsequently abandoned her, pregnant, in order to devote himself to sheep-farming and the composition of long pastoral romances in free verse, mainly dealing with his great love for her. Her father never forgave her, neither has he, it seems, forgiven bearded heterosexuality or things bucolic, and it is the mark of his indiscrimination that he makes a goat-boy suffer for a sheep-boy's sins.

In prose that manages complicated constructions with unerring grace and high wit, as well as combining elegance with the ironic mockery of elegance, Barth defines himself among the great contemporary stylists. However, closer reading reveals that all the editors make judgments in more or less identical language (far superior to that of most publishers' editors I know); and the double framing device—a story within a story within a story—that introduces the novel becomes too complicated and tedious for itself (as well as assuming no discernible meaning). Moreover, while the narrator, the goat-boy, may be an extraordinary imaginative creation, he is by design too innocent to give the novel the consistently comic intelligence its plot needs. Then, to make matters worse, the novel suffers from an excess of jokes that do not flow from their situations and humor that is just plain dreadful. Wholly unsuitable to a comic form is its ending, where the protagonist, instead of succeeding, becomes a tragically martyred hero. Finally, unlike *The Sot-Weed Factor*, whose immense length was necessary for Barth's thematic purposes, this is at 710 large pages far too long for its stuff.

Most of the book's deficiencies stem from Barth's inability to match realization with intention. As before, his subject is historical, and he proposes to comment upon the broadest and most important questions of meaning and direction. Moreover, "The use of historical or legendary material, especially in a farcical spirit," he once wrote, "has a number of technical virtues, among which are esthetic distance and the opportunity for counter-realism." However, the "history" in *The Sot-Weed Factor* is quite different in kind from that of *Giles Goat-Boy*; and in that difference lie crucial problems. The earlier novel is essentially a rewriting of actual history, for nearly all its characters, even its protagonist, have the names of actual historical figures. In Barth's fiction, however, their adventures are considerably different from those their historians document, as Barth attempts to deny that human history has the neat development that the textbooks give it. This large purpose, evident throughout, gives *The Sot-Weed Factor* a clarity that overcomes its confusing surface, as Barth clearly implies that this microcosm has a large historical reference. *Giles*, in contrast, is an historical parable, about the present and the near future — an *Animal Farm* at several times the length. Most of its major places and persons have a one-to-one relationship with contemporary realities — The Grand Tutor as Christ, the University as the Universe, West Campus as the western nations, East Campus as the Communist bloc, student-unionism as Communism, Second Campus Riot as World War II, the Quiet Riot as the Cold War, Revised New Syllabus as the Bible, and so on; but unlike Orwell, Barth draws his analogies from different historical periods, thereby projecting past myths into the immediate present. I suppose that his intention here is a form of intellectual reductionism — the Cold War is nothing more than a silly quarrel between two campuses, Christ's father was the computer WESCAC, etc. all of which contribute to his encompassing vision of worldly absurdities; and the book's sub-title, "Revised New Syllabus," suggests that Barth may have in mind a satirical history of Christianity. Artistically, the symbolic references do not rise smoothly out of the fiction; and though these equations may be devilish jokes, their significance misses me — as insights into current phenomena, they are practically meaningless.

Indeed, it is my distinct impression that as the novel progressed, Barth himself may have become more interested in plot than parable, for precisely on the former level is this fiction most successful. Some of the scenes are comic masterpieces, particularly Giles' descent into the machine (to discover if he really is, as he suspects, the Grand Tutor) and the description of WESCAC's endlessly huge Furnace Room; for Barth successfully imagines horrendous encounters between modern man and distinctly modern depths — a format that successfully exploits his penchant for the comedy of excessive complication. Particularly impressive, to my mind, was Barth's capturing of the goat-boy's point of view — his wide-eyed discovery of things previously unknown to him, such as the experience of riding in a car or discovering the details of a human female body; and Barth's fidelity to the goat-boy's peculiar perspective is among the reasons why Giles is such a successful character. Some of the minor figures, particularly Stoker and Max Spielman, reveal Barth's established talent for efficient caricature. As always, I enjoyed immensely the Barthian parodies — of psychological prose, philosophical jargon, alma maters (even a musical joke!), the capital-initialing acronyms of computers and their processes — which are invariably little gems; some of these were incorporated into the short story "Test-Borings" that Barth contributed to Philip Rahv's otherwise mediocre anthology, *Modern Occasions* (1966). Finally, Barth is the master of a language that fuses contemporary idiom with seventeenth century rhythms:

> Mighty WESCAC was not able to *enjoy*, for example, as I enjoyed frisking through the furze; nor could it contemplate or dream. It could excogitate, extrapolate, generalize, and infer, after its fashion; it could compose an arithmetical music, and a sort of accidental literature (not often interesting); it could assess half a hundred variables and make the most sophisticated prognostications. But it could not act on hunch or brilliant impulse; it had no intuitions or exaltations; it could request, but not yearn; indicate, but not insinuate or exhort; command but not care. It had no sense of style or grasp of the ineffable: its correlations were exact, but its metaphors wretched; it could play chess, but not poker. The fantastically complex algebra of Max's Cyclology it could manage in minutes, but it never made a joke in its life.

Furthermore, Barth handles this style with extraordinary fluency that completely overcomes the affectations that might otherwise fell it; yet sometimes, in *Giles*, he becomes the victim of his talent, committing the Updikean sin of writing where white space might be better.

All these bits of brilliance, however, do not compensate for the overall deficiencies, which are severe indeed. As a step in a career, *Giles Goat-Boy* is no cause for alarm, for Barth still remains among the most extravagantly talented novelists of our day. In the end, I suppose that like Melville, Faulkner and Fitzgerald before him, Barth will be haunted by the awareness that he has published his masterpiece at the age of thirty; and a recognition of the subsequent decline of his predecessors is an awful burden for any writer, particularly an American, to have to bear.

Thomas Pynchon's new novel, *The Crying of Lot 49* (1966), stands to *V.*

(1963) as *Giles Goat-Boy* does to *The Sot-Weed Factor* — a fine novel, but a lesser achievement than its predecessor; and like Barth's new book, Pynchon's offers neither a fictional advance nor increasing talent. *Lot 49* is considerably shorter than *V.* as well as proportionately slighter; it lacks completely, therefore, that rich embellishment of every chapter that so distinguished *V.* Indeed, the new work seems an early draft of something more important, just as some of Pynchon's earlier stories ("Morality and Mercy in Vienna" [1959] and "Under the Rose" [1961]) were embellished to become chapters in *V.* Pynchon's method has always been the marshalling of many facts and scenes (or examples) on behalf of his (seemingly predetermined) symbols and themes. However, in the new work, while the method remains, the symbols receive so much less fictional support that, at one point, Pynchon is forced to tell us (p. 178) that Inverarity's legacy, which is San Narcisco (itself already symbolic of California?), "was America." The other dominant symbol is WASTE (also w.a.s.t.e.) which turns out to be a secret underground society committed to wreaking havoc in America; its members are ideological descendants of another mysterious group, likewise invented by Pynchon, called the Tristeros, who immigrated here in the nineteenth century. On top of all this, Pynchon introduces another favorite symbol — entropy, which he tells us (p. 106), relates [as it did in an earlier story of that title (1960)] to both thermodynamics and information flow. That is, the energy of the world is disintegrating into random movement at the same time that communication between people becomes progressively more impossible.

Within these outlines (and the absurdist vision they imply) Pynchon exercises his art; and the results, even excusing difficulties intrinsic to his method, are still highly uneven. The prose at once appears more mature and yet lacks the high brilliance that so often informed the language of *V.* The dominance of a single character, Oedipa Maas (her nickname of "Oed" suggesting Albertine dimensions), whose investigations into her inheritance become the novel's plot, handicaps Pynchon's earlier fictional strategy of presenting a variety of highly factual but faintly preposterous illustrations of his theme. However, what remains impressive is Pynchon's technique of characterization — the oblique evocation of highly charged aspects that place a person without fully describing him, as in Oedipa's first encounter with her new lawyer:

> That night the lawyer Metzger showed up [at her home]. He turned out to be so good-looking that Oedipa thought at first They, somebody up there, were putting her on... His enormous eyes, lambent, extravagantly lashed, smiled out at her wickedly; she looked around him for reflectors, microphones, camera cabling, but there was only himself and a debonair bottle of French Beaujolais, which he claimed to've smuggled last year into California, this rollicking lawbreaker, past the frontier guards.

Though passages like this express a highly individualized perspective, the short novel suffers from an excess of lengthy digressions, including the plot summary of a pseudo-Elizabethan play (that fails, to my mind, to create a symbolic dimension), as well as too many long paragraphs I found inscrutable. More excusable, again given the method, are all the shaggy dog dimensions; but these might be more tolerable if *Lot 49* were a longer work. At the root of all these critical caveats is the criticism that the novel suffers from a whopping lack of consistent scale.

The only novelist I read whose second work strikes me as significantly better than his first is Harry Mathews; for his new work *Tlooth* (1966), with its stronger narrative line, is considerably more controlled and accessible than his much-admired *The Conversions* (1962) which, after several attempted readings, continues to evade me. The opening sentence of *Tlooth* successfully sets the book's tone: "Mannish Madame Nevtaya slowly cried Fur bowls! and the Fidest batter alert to the sense behind the sound of her words, jogged toward first base." While the language continues to be as sober, if not as circumspect, as the narrator's vision is innocent, the events described are consistently preposterous: the narrator, who is the catcher, tosses out a dynamite-equipped ball which soon disappears down a drain; toward the novel's end, Mathews reveals, much to my surprise, that the narrator is female. The novel's ingenious plot is that of travelogue-adventure in which all places are very much the same, even if they are called Afghanistan, Russia, India, Morocco; and in this respect, *Tlooth* very much descends from Apollinaire's *Zone* (1913) with its unbounded sense of literary space and the (higher-) non-sense fiction of Lewis Carroll and, especially, the Frenchman Raymond Roussel. The novel's meaning lies in its method (and even in its title); for *Tlooth* is a realized example of absurd fiction, where the pointlessness of surface event fuses with the theme of underlying absurdity. Unlike previous American forays into the form — Barth's, Pynchon's, Heller's — *Tlooth* has a neatness and brevity that is positively European (perhaps reflecting Mathews's own expatriate status); but it is precisely this difference in degree of elaboration that, to my mind, separates the major American works in this form from the minor.

IV

In rereading my essay of three years ago, what bothers me most today is my generally optimistic conclusion about the future of American fiction; at the time I failed to realize how much junk is produced (even though I had read a good deal of it) — even worse, how much junk comes from writers possessed of some serious following, if not favorable critical standing. Perhaps the deception can be traced to my sense that other literatures are currently less interesting — that English writing is only beginning to reawaken to modernism, that French fiction has not transcended fads that do not equal their publicity. Even more important, I did not then realize that in the reading of fiction I would find so little excellence. That is, after one has read the classic moderns, as well as Jorge Luis Borges and Samuel Beckett (whom I consider the two living masters) and begun to treasure their works, nearly all recent fiction seems distinctly derivative and prosaic. In another sense, now that I have become more familiar with the other arts, I recognize that the fictional scene today simply lacks the polemical drive, as well as the experimental ambition, that so richly informs recent American painting and music. To be frank, no new novels seem as monumentally significant to the art of fiction as, say, Milton Babbitt's *Relata I* (1966), John Cage's *Variations V* (1965) or Robert Rauschenberg's *Oracle* (1965) are to their respective arts.

In contrast, the problem with fiction is not that it suffers an exhaustion of formal possibilities — Barth, Borges and Beckett would seem to repudiate that academic piety — but that too many first-rate novelistic intelligences too easily settle for pouring old wine into even older bottles. Where today is that kind of special passion that must have animated James Joyce in *Finnegans Wake* (1939), Gertrude Stein in *The Making of Americans* (1926) and William Faulkner in *Absalom, Absalom* (1936)? I have found an inkling of this sort of possibility in American short fiction, particularly the works of Faust, Donald Barthelme, Kenneth Koch, Tillie Olsen, which I have discussed in the introduction to my anthology of *Twelve from the Sixties* (1967); but nothing that is currently happening in the novel strikes me as a significant breakthrough. More than once I have looked at Milton Babbitt's programme notes to the Columbia recording of Arnold Schoenberg's Violin Concerto and thought that a novel attaining such intricate levels of relatedness would revolutionize the art of fiction. Moreover, such books as R. Buckminster Fuller's *Nine Chains to the Moon* (1963) and Milic Capek's *The Philosophical Impact of Contemporary Physics* (1963) strike me as filled with suggestive formal ideas applicable to fiction.

The other half of the novel's problem is that many of its traditional functions have been usurped by other genres or media. Where novelistic fiction once offered the most penetrating analysis of new styles and manners, the journalistic art, or pseudo-art, of a Tom Wolfe itemizes the Hugh Hefners and Robert Sculls with an efficiency and economy equal to Sinclair Lewis's portrait of George F. Babbitt; multi-disciplined intellectuals such as Herman Kahn and Marshall McLuhan illuminate more insightfully the hidden realities of life in the 1960s; today's most persuasive visionary utopias appear not in novels but in books of thought — Norman O. Brown's *Life Against Death* (1959) and R. Buckminster Fuller's *Education Automation* (1962). The problem here is not, as Phillip Roth contends, that the unprecedented ridiculousness of our world evades the imagination, but that the imagination of novelists has not coped with these actualities as well as non-novelists.

This lack of pioneering artistic ambition probably accounts for the per-functoriness of nearly all fiction criticism in America, where the same nice words more often than not describe semblances of what we have read before. Prosaicness feeds upon prosaicness, as everyone writes around the circle. One explanation of this situation is that since American literary in-tellectuals have not fully assimilated the impact of modernism, too many critics are content to use archaic values to praise comparably archaic works. Thus, established novelists are not goaded, as major contemporary artists are, to move on to different, if not greater, things. Quite indicative of this deficiency is, I think, the generally insufficient recognition of Beckett and Borges, for I can make a huge list of acknowledged critics, supposedly of "current" fiction, who have not to my knowledge confronted these master figures with any thoroughness; and if they have not dealt with these touchstones, how can such "critics" respond to a fiction that might move beyond these points?

In each of the arts today, two avant-gardes exist — those that would preserve and develop the essence of an art and those that would combine with (or draw their creative ideas from) other arts. In music, this is the difference between, respectively, Milton Babbitt and John Cage; in paint-ing, between Frank Stella and Robert Rauschenberg; in dance, between Merce Cunningham and Ann Halprin; in poetry, between John Berryman and "concrete" poets. The combinational impulse has barely informed fictional arts, except by acknowledging cinematic montage, although cer-tain writers (Barthelme and Doctorow) would seem to emulate conceptions first developed in other arts — treating, for instance, a single event from several points of view has analogies with cubism in painting, while distort-ing a pulp-fiction formula resembles "pop art." Future formal invention in fiction, let me suggest, will stem more from this cross-fertilization impulse than from a novelistic purism. I could well imagine a novel where typography of various sizes would be crucially important or where the pages would contain just a set of related drawings. Why, after all, shouldn't novelists follow Alfred Jarry's example in *The Exploits and Opinions of Doctor Faustroll, 'Pataphysician* (1911) and introduce a succession of algebraic equa-tions; for there really exists no limits upon the kinds of fictions that can be put between two covers. All this only echoes what I said earlier — that novelists have not contemplated deeply enough the formal possibilities of the fictional format. The point is that fiction today necessarily assumes a competitive position, where, if it is to earn its audience, it must be as in-teresting as the latest endeavors in the other arts.

*   *   *

Addendum, 1967

How John Barth's *Giles Goat-Boy* became such a best-seller is one of the more puzzling questions of the recent season. Hardly the sort of book that would earn such popularity all by itself, it contains little of the stuff of which money-making fiction is customarily made, being horrendously difficult, terribly pedantic, skimpily pornographic, and thoroughly blasphemous; and no one but a fairly well-educated reader would find its 710 pages an unalloyed pleasure. It is, I think, reasonable to assume that, since no serious novel is a natural best-seller, something extrinsic makes it so, whether that be a huge advertising and promotion campaign, a relevance to current events, previous public interest in the author or his subject, or a widely acknowledged reputation for literary excellence. Prominent and favorable reviewing is more a contributing cause than a sufficient one, for many books receive, as Barth's did, lead reviews in the *New York Times Book Review* and *Time* only later to die on the remainder tables.

It is no secret that late in 1964 an earlier draft of *Giles* was circulated among New York publishers, and since more than a dozen rejected it, one heard premonitions of Barth's literary death. In 1965, however, his literary currency began to firm, as he was included among the "black humorists" and later, in my own essay, among the "absurd novelists"; *Book Week* invited him to be the only novelist contributing a personal manifesto to its retrospective issue on post–WW II American fiction. In 1966, the *Times Book Review* published a puffy front-page article devoted entirely to his work, Brandeis gave him an award for distinguished achievement, as did the National Institute of Arts and Letters. Then came the deluge of featured reviews. Furthermore, it could scarcely be said that Barth helped make himself famous (as Norman Mailer, say, did), as he has refused to do journalism, television interviews or other publicity-generating gimmickry.

His recent success must therefore be attributed to the efforts made by others on his behalf, and that observation suggests, in turn, a pet hypothesis of mine. Such unlikely best-sellers become popular thanks to the backing of certain identifiable opinion-making forces in our culture. For instance, much of Saul Bellow's recent eminence can be attributed, historically, to the persistent efforts of Jewish critics in hailing him as the most promising living novelist, while James Gould Cozzens's high reputation of some years ago originated with an older generation of mostly gentile literary men, many of whom are now especially enthusiastic about John Updike. Norman Mailer's recent eminence can be traced to the media-socialites who run between *Esquire* and *Paris Review*, between the television cameras and the latest New York mammoth cocktail party, although one suspects that Mailer would like to think that both his literary-political origins and his most loyal audience lay elsewhere.

None of these established forces, however, were responsible for Barth's success, which represents instead the ascendency of what I shall call, in lieu of a better name, the Underground. Different from previous literary powers, it consists of newer, mostly younger people — the assistant editors, just-graduated professionals who move in literate circles, the new blood in advertising and the media, aspiring critics (me!), graduate students, fresh-faced bookstore managers and salesmen. The Underground is not as well organized as other establishments, and even less aware of its own existence. By definition, it consists at base of those people within the organized system who feel a large cultural distance between themselves and the aboveground world. People in the Underground frequently quarrel with their bosses, and they tend to pass from job to job, still approaching each new one with disillusioned hope. They recognize each other through the expression of similar cultural enthusiasms. Barth's awareness of worldly absurdity, along with his devotion to personal craftsmanship, perhaps corresponds to their own attitudes toward society and personal work.

These are probably the same people who contribute to establishing the reputations of Marshall McLuhan and Buckminster Fuller when the more entrenched powers either neglected or dismissed them. Other Underground favorites include, let me conjecture, the sculptor Claes Oldenburg, the composer John Cage, the film-maker Kenneth Anger and magazines like *Ramparts* and *The Realist*. Its enthusiasm does not extend to James Baldwin or Robert Rauschenberg, whose staunchest admirers belong to an older cultural generation (regardless of their chronological age), or to Andy Warhol, the Beatles, and Timothy Leary, whose followers form other groups that have yet to develop their novelist-heroes. This Underground may well be the most incipiently powerful cultural force at the present time, and its rise may, among other things, spell the dissolution of certain ethnic, racial and geographic factors that unified earlier groups. Not only do we now recognize that such criteria falsify both the ineluctable pluralism of cultural America and the more fickle processes of human taste but, as this analysis suggests, the grain of cultural conflict nowadays is more accurately defined in other terms.

* * *

Addendum, 1971

Irvin Faust's next project was an historical novel based upon Marinus Willett (1740–1830), a chronic loser who was mayor of New York City for a year at the beginning of the nineteenth century — he sided with Aaron Burr, opposed the development of the steamboat and the building of the Erie Canal, lost by a landslide in a gubernatorial election, etc.; but this work, which seems, curiously, more typically Barthian, has so far remained unfinished. In 1970 appeared *The File on Stanley Patton Buchta*, whose protagonist is a fairly sensitive Long Island WASP who, after serving in Vietnam, decides to become a policeman. Being college-educated and more sophisticated than his colleagues, Buchta is enlisted to become an undercover agent assigned to spy upon both a militant right-wing group and their leftish antagonists.

This more "newsy" subject seems to popularize Faust's earlier virtues — the intimate relationship to New York City, the appreciation of ethnic diversity, and occasional passages of startlingly acute psychological understanding; but just as the plot is often needlessly confused and less credible, so is the style considerably thinner than before. Its successor, *Willy Remembers*, which appeared the following year, has another Middle-American for its narrator, Willy T. Klienhans, now well into his dotage, whose opening sentences indicate that his recollection is, to say the least, hopelessly scrambled: "Major Bill McKinley was the greatest president I ever lived through. No telling how far he could have gone if Oswald hadn't shot him." This novel is richer in literary excellences than *Stanley Patton Buchta*, and it resembles *The Steagle* in its portrayal of insensitive psychosis. However, though Klienhans, in Faust's hands, becomes more imposing than the silly old fool he seems to be at the novel's beginning, he is scarcely as compelling, or socially resonant, as Weissburg or Bluffstein, or even Buchta; and the portraiture is extended far too long, suggesting perhaps that the material of *Willy Remembers* would have worked better as a short story or a novella. For the while, then, *The Steagle* establishes Faust among the most accomplished psychological novelists today.

Short Story Anthologies and a History (1966)

Most of us would agree that it is more than a bit presumptuous for any anthologist to entitle his book "The Best. . . ." without explicitly stating his criteria for selection. "Taste," as an implicit explanation, simply will not suffice; for, in fiction as in food, what is apple pie to one man might be unpalatable to another. Since neither Martha Foley nor her sometime co-editor David Burnett, of the annual *The Best American Short Stories*, have not bothered in the past six years to offer any outline of their preferences (their chatty introduction disappearing from *1965*), this task of definition must be assumed by another.

The editors' strongest bias is for urban realism—straightforward, unadorned portraits of upper-middling people who live in cities, particularly New York; and the most frequent plot is an encounter between two people in which the protagonist, invariably more sensitive, is considerably moved by the experience. Often, in *Best*, an innocent figure has a shocking encounter with the world's ugly realities. The prose of a *Best* story tends to be as plain and efficient as a reporter's, rather than as embellished and evocative as a poet's; and its authors exhibit little taste for ironic techniques, elliptical narratives, or complicated structures. The settings are generally contemporary and familiar; the characters tend to be mildly educated, fairly agreeable, inclined to predictable responses; and the events are of the most common sort. These *Best* stories have no homosexuals, no scenes of violence, no seducers, no drugs, no mad people or nihilists, although so much of city life, unlike that in rural areas, is defined by marginal people and experiences. To their credit, the editors eschew that mistaken notion that seems to plague so many recent collections—for examples, *Stories from the London Magazine* (1964) and the new pulp reprint periodical *Short Story International*—that short fictions are, at their best, surrogates for reportage from foreign lands. Nonetheless, the best *Best* stories are often slightly—and only slightly—sentimental.

In both *1964* and *1965*, five of the selected stories appeared previously in the *Saturday Evening Post*, which, though considerably finer than the interred *Post* of a decade ago is still hardly a highbrow magazine. Curiously, an unusually high percentage of the authors are women — eight out of twenty in *1964*, seven out of twenty-two in *1965*, eight out of twenty-three in *1963*, seven out of twenty-two in *1962* — many, if not most, of whom live in New York. Some of them seem to have been regular pupils of Martha Foley's creative writing classes at Columbia (see the correspondence columns of the summer 1964 issue of *Mutiny*). Although the editors explicitly stated in *1964* that they do not include extracts from novels, three of the selections in *1964* and three in *1965* are actually sections of longer work.

While one may consider this consistency of taste as a mark of the editors' integrity, their bias does not prepare them to cope with those stories that descend from the great tradition of modern short fiction. From Chekhov's "A Boring Story" through Hemingway's "A Clean Well-Lighted Place," Kafka's "The Penal Colony" and William Faulkner's "The Bear" to the contemporary masterpieces of Samuel Beckett and Jorge Luis Borges, the modern short story, in Europe and America, has eschewed all that Foley and Burnett seem to admire in short fiction. The great modernists are interested in extreme situations (or extreme dimensions in ordinary situations) and unusual people; they reject factual realism for representational styles that evoke the feel of things, reject straightforward authoritative narrative for discontinuous plot, ironic narrators, and shifting points of view. Most of all, they transcend conventional syntactical procedures to exploit the possibilities of language — to create a distinctive, highly individualized prose. In short, they strive to make both the form and the content of the story as original, interesting, appropriate and perceptive as it can possibly be.

In contrast *Best* contains stories of 1964–65 chosen primarily with taste honed before the advent of modern literature (1920) and barely affected by subsequent developments. "To be technically out of date is a genuine defect," the American novelist John Barth once wrote; "Beethoven's Sixth Symphony or the Chartres Cathedral, if executed today, would be embarrassing." The stories here do not imitate models quite as ancient, but many of them are, as "contemporary" structures, just as embarrassingly archaic. As a selection of the "best" recent short fiction, this series is wholly inadequate, hardly aware of the finest writing being done in America today. Moreover, whereas past collections of *Best* often contained at least one brilliant story, such as Tillie Olsen's "Tell Me a Riddle" (1961) or H.W. Blattner's "Sound of a Drunken Drummer" (1963), both the *1964* and *1965* editions contain nothing genuinely worth remembering.

Its traditional competitor, *Prize Stories: The O. Henry Awards*, has always been the lesser anthology; and once a critic as well-intentioned as Richard Poirier took over the editorship in 1961 (more recently joined by William Abrahams), a change for the better was expected. The annual has, in general, improved, but it is still not an adequate guide to current achievement. If *Best* suffers from its self-defeating, retrograde bias, *O. Henry's* failing is little distinct taste at all. Indeed, the choice is so eclectic that the book suggests two editors so often at odds with each other that they have to make numerous compromises. The series' main problem springs, perhaps, from the wrong-headedness of its encumbering title; for O. Henry is the father not of the great American short story — Hawthorne, Poe, Melville and James are more deserving of the title — but of its bastard heirs, nowadays called "Detective" and "Pulp-Slick."

Too many of these recent selections, instead of achieving rare effects, are either irrevocably common or, in fewer cases, unsuccessfully experimental. One story from *1965* (Mary McCarthy's) has paragraphs so overly loaded with specific facts that one suspects it might actually be a parody of Dreiser; a second (Eva Manoff's) has an ending that would make even a soporific reader moan in agony; and a third (Warren Miller's) is so arch and heavy-handed in conception that one is surprised that its author did not discard its outline. In the *1966* selection, three authors (Tom Cole, Christopher Davis and first-prize winner John Updike) exploit that tired Jamesian plot of the American's confused encounter with the mysterious ways of Europeans (too much foreign reportage again); and in each story, the style is as undistinguished as the action. Another (Sallie Bingham's) has a plot so pat — a woman disappointed in marriage finds divorce even more disillusioning — that its awful ending makes it an inadvertent contribution to the camp canon. In *1965*'s collection, Poirier wrote, quite rightly, that in a truly good story, "The reader is made to care about extended significances." However, these *O. Henry* collections contain too many stories in which significances hardly extend beyond the page; indeed, some carry no discernible significance within themselves.

In general, what is most lacking in both these anthologies are stories exhibiting large doses of extraordinary style; not only are nearly all of them uninteresting and unmemorable (the exceptions being Donald Barthelme's "Margins" and Flannery O'Connor's "Revelations" in 1965 *O. Henry*), but a day or two later they are barely distinguishable from each other. Not one story in either of these anthologies merits the same enthusiasm I have for several other brilliant, modernist stories first published in the same period as those collected in the earlier pair of books (Winter, 1963, to Summer, 1964): Irvin Faust's "Philco Baby" in *Paris Review* and his "The Dalai Lama of Harlem" in *Sewanee Review*, John Yount's "The Scattering" in *Contact*, Kenneth Koch's "The Postcard Collection" in *Art and Literature*, and Donald Barthelme's "To London and Rome" in *Genesis West*. Indicatively, just as both pairs of editors generally neglect those magazines in which the best contemporary avant-garde fiction appears — *Contact* and *Genesis West* (both recently and regrettably deceased) and *Paris Review, Transatlantic Review, Evergreen Review, Art and Literature* — so neither anthology has ever included such more original, if not flagrantly radical, promising American short story writers as Curtis Zahn, Hubert Selby, William Burroughs, James Schuyler,

Michael Rumaker, Irvin Faust, Paule Marshall, John Hawkes, Kenneth Koch, Lynn Lonider, and Susan Sontag.

William Peden's critical history, *The American Short Story* (1964) grows out of presuppositions about the nature of modern short fiction similar to those of Foley-Burnett, and thus inadvertently reveals how a preference for realism so sorely blinds the critic's understanding of modern writing. Having little sense of the purposes of art, Peden discusses short stories as though they were newspaper feature articles, giving us their plots, locales and summary descriptions of the major characters; he avoids questions of style, form or overarching themes. Thus, Peden feels most comfortable with plot-and-locale writers, such as Peter Taylor and John Cheever, and somewhat baffled by more modernist authors. His comments on individual writers can be positively ludicrous; under the rubric of "stories of manners," he lists collections by writers as drastically diverse in style as Tillie Olsen, Harvey Swados, Grace Paley and George P. Elliott. As a bibliography of short stories since 1940, this book is passable. As literary history, it is hampered by irrelevant categories, rather indiscriminately applied; as criticism of literature, it is worthless. We still do not have either a good book on the American short story or perspicacious anthologies of recent achievements.

Notes on the American
Short Story Today (1967)

All media are active metaphors in their power to translate
experience into new forms. — Marshall McLuhan.

The Americans have handled the short story form so
wonderfully that one can say that it is a national art
form. — Frank O'Connor.

The medium is a metaphor in its ability to offer an image of experience
which, though not an exact replica, in some way recreates experience; and
in contrast to the novel, whose length makes it capable of presenting a broad
picture of reality, the short story devotes its attention to a small area of
human existence. If, however, this microcosm is sufficiently resonant, the
short story will become a complex symbol for larger worlds. On its surface
it may portray a single situation, but in its depths it can comment upon
universal issues. For this reason, as a medium the short story is more
metaphoric than the novel, which in turn is more metaphoric than reportage. In the great modern short stories, the techniques of representation
stem not from realism, which emulates reportage, but from symbolism,
which descends from poetry.

The nature of realism as a literary mode is discussed in the following
passage from Erich Auerbach's *Mimesis*, perhaps as profound a study of the
various forms of reality in literature as has ever been written. Here Auerbach describes the style of representation in Homer's *Odyssey*:

> All this is scrupulously externalized and narrated in leisurely fashion. The
> two women express their feelings in copious direct discourse. Feelings
> though they are, with only a slight admixture of the most general con-
> siderations upon human destiny, the syntactical connection between part
> and part is perfectly clear, no contour is blurred. . . . Clearly outlined,
> brightly and uniformly illuminated, men and things stand out in a realm
> where everything is visible; and not less clear — wholly expressed, orderly
> even in their ardor — are the feelings and thoughts of the persons involved.

What distinguishes nearly all the best works of modern literature is the rejection of this kind of realism as a literary mode; and since short works of fiction are — by their nature — uncomfortable with lengthy, detailed portraits, the contemporary short story, in all Western literatures, accentuates this non-realistic tendency. But in America, as nowhere else, short-story writers from the times of Washington Irving, Hawthorne, Poe, and Melville to the present have always discarded realism for elliptical and symbolic representational styles. To this day, the best American short stories have presented experiences which are not typical but so extreme that they strain the reader's "willing suspension of disbelief," and actions that are not explained by the author but are presented without comment for the reader's interpretation. The author depicts in depth rather than in breadth, and the world described is not varied and definable but narrow, disordered and ambiguous. What American short-story writers have always offered is a vision of life that must transcend reportage with metaphor if it is to succeed as literature.

Of course, many novelists today are still in the realist tradition, but even the best of them write works that are less interesting, less provocative — indeed, of lesser stature. Yet some of the realistic fiction writers, like Mary McCarthy in America and like Dan Jacobson in England, support their work with essays in which they try to discount the particular achievements of great nonrealistic modern writers. These critics assert, in short, that we measure a novelist by how many full-bodied characters he can create, by how wise and authoritative his narrative voice is, and by how accurately he evokes the reality of what he describes. In fact, we can use these criteria to judge Tolstoy, Dickens and George Elliot; but, when we apply them to Faulkner, Proust, Gide, and Joyce, they become irrelevant and reactionary since they do not subsume the modern writers' special intentions and achievements. Just as the political reactionary wants to abolish the income tax and return to the free-economy days of yore, so the reactionary novelist-critic wants to discredit the innovations in the form, perception, and content of modern writing. Although this double-barreled defensive maneuver has some conversational notoriety, it has but little influence upon the most important fiction written today.

A rejection of realism and its concomitant values is a prerequisite for realizing a second ambition of contemporary fiction writers — to stake out for fiction its own unique territory. If a color film can transport us to life in an exotic land more intimately and completely than prose, the novel would be foolish to compete; if a poem can present a concise image, fiction writers should not try to equal poetic economy with the less precise tools of prose. If sociologists and sociological journalists can define shifting patterns of social feeling, and if the essayist can change social behavior and literary taste, the novelist may as well pass up both these tasks. Indeed, when a novel provides the most accurate portrait of bad working conditions in the Chicago meat-packing houses — as Upton Sinclair's *The Jungle* did — then the novel's impact represents not the achievement of fiction, but the failure of sociology to do better. Modern novelists have realized that the essence of fiction is prose style — no other medium can imitate it; and without a special, heightened language, no work of fiction is truly interesting as literature. At the center of the fiction writer's purposes, then, is the creation of a unique style which enables him to penetrate the experience fiction best describes — not the quantifiable, verifiable elements of society and man (really the realm of reportage) but the hidden qualitative phenomena that only a man of vision, the novelist, can perceive.

The revolution against literary realism responds to a shift in the structure of the short story. The traditional mode was linear development: things happened realistically, in credible and usually chronological succession, until the story created a pattern of expectation that was concluded by the story's logical end (or sometimes undercut by an equally credible, but less predictable, reversal). Whereas the old short story (whose doddering contemporary heirs are the mystery and the pulp-slick) emphasized the ending (which packed as much surprise and moral punch as possible), the modern short story emphasizes the middle. Unlike their predecessors, contemporary writers of short stories devote their energies largely to the techniques of telling — the use of figurative language, metaphor, the evocation of sharply symbolic (rather than comprehensive) details, well-turned phrases, strategic placement of the climax, manipulation of the point of view, and similar devices — in order to create a fiction not of surface and simplicity but of depth and complexity. In modern short works of fiction, plot, tone and (often) theme are established fairly quickly, and the story becomes an elaboration of the opening elements: it is intensified rather than developed. Moreover, in modern short works of fiction, the narrator is rarely a reliable observer — indeed, his unreliability itself often becomes the fiction's central issue. Although Frank O'Connor's assertion that, "in the great modern short stories, there is no character with whom the reader can identify himself" is not true for every first-rate short story (exceptions include works by Samuel Beckett, Faulkner, and Sherwood Anderson), his perception is certainly more often true of short stories than of long works of fiction. In modern short stories, the reader observes the scene instead of participating in it.

Ideally, in modern short stories, each new paragraph should offer a succession of surprises or intensifying symbols; and since the writers concentrate intensely upon shaping every moment of the story, the resulting fiction is closer in form to poetry than it is to traditional fiction. This is also why the best new short stories can be more *rereadable* than the old ones. Whereas foreknowledge that his wife sold her hair to buy the fob and the husband sold his watch to buy the comb may keep us from enjoying O. Henry's "The Gift of the Magi" a second time, the sheer beauty of style, the esthetic economy, the symbolic perfection, the balanced conflict of moral issues, and the depth and scope of human truths in great modern short stories — such as Joyce's "The Dead," Isaac Babel's "The Sin of Jesus," Kafka's "The Penal Colony," and Hemingway's "A Clean, Well-Lighted Place" — make them worth reading again and again.

II

The modern short story of Chekhov, Joyce, and Hemingway departed from the traditional form. In the past few years there have been signs of a new, similarly international development both within and against the modernist canon. These new formal changes are rather quiet and subtle, but they are distinctive enough to suggest another reshaping of the structure of the short story. In Joyce's pervasively influential theory of the short story, we remember, the fiction turned upon an epiphany, a moment of revelation in which, in Harry Levin's words, "amid the most encumbered circumstances it suddenly happens that the veil is lifted, the burthen of mystery laid bare, and the ultimate secret of things made manifest." The epiphany, then, became a technique for jelling the narrative and locking the story's import into place. The classic example is the "Pok" of opening the champagne bottle in Joyce's "Ivy Day in the Committee Room," the gush of air bestowing meaning on the entire story. What made this method revolutionary was the shifting of the focal point of the story from its end — as in, say, Boccaccio, Voltaire, and Balzac — to a spot within the body of the text, usually near (but not at) the end.

In the new short story, on the other hand, the epiphany is abolished, and the writer's theme or perception is diffused throughout the work, which becomes, in effect, a succession of revelatory moments. Donald Barthelme's "To London and Rome" (1963), for instance, is a series of very brief scenes in each of which an excess of money permits the narrator to commit some ridiculous act. One event is not enough to convey the theme, and no one scene is necessarily more important than another; but, through repetition and cumulative impact, the story establishes its point. A similar strategy shapes such a thoroughly ironic work as Jorge Luis Borges' "Pierre Menard, Author of Don Quixote" (1939), essentially a parody of a critical article about a writer whose "admirable ambition was to produce [out of his mind] pages which would coincide — word for word and line for line — with" *Don Quixote*. Here Borges' attitude towards the absurdity of some literary values and styles is diffused through every paragraph of the story. Neither Barthelme nor Borges announces his themes, though in Barthelme the theme is more clearly implied than in Borges. This recent shift in the structure of the modern short story pulls the genre further away from its roots in narrative (which, in our time, is more successfully appropriated by history and reportage) and pushes it closer to the nonlinear spatial forms of modern poetry.

Although the origins of this new short story lie in the past — in Maupassant (particularly "La Horla," *not* "The Necklace"), in Chekhov ("A Boring Story"), in Alfred Jarry ("The Supermale"), in some of the fiction of Franz Kafka and Isaac Babel, and in most of Jean-Paul Sartre's early stories — the change itself is largely the accomplishment of post-war writers: in England, of Samuel Beckett, Dylan Thomas, Ted Hughes, and B.S. Johnson; in Sweden, of Stig Dagerman; in Russia, of Abram Tertz; in France, of Alain Robbe-Grillet and Pierre Gàscar; in Italy, of Tommasso Landolfi and Vera Cacciatore; in Spanish America, of Jorge Luis Borges and Adolfo Bioy Casares; in German literature, of Klaus Roehler, Günter Eich, and Jakov Lind; in Ghana, of Peter Kwame Buahin; and in America, of Donald Barthelme, William Burroughs, Kenneth Koch, Jack Ludwig, James Purdy, Hubert Selby, Jr., Thomas Pynchon, and Curtis Zahn (but not, at least not yet, of Bernard Malamud or Isaac Bashevis Singer).

III

The esthetic development of the modern short story, then, may be divided into three distinct historical stages; and what has happened in American literature, our example for the moment, has parallels in English and continental fiction. In the pre-1920 short stories of, say, Henry James, Ambrose Bierce or Edith Wharton, the pace of the fiction is leisurely; most of the important events and thoughts, as well as themes, are fairly explicitly presented; the characters are more exceptional than average; the story's meaning emerges from its surface action; the presentation of events is strictly chronological; the representational mode is a realism seemingly calculated to produce a shock of familiar recognition; the narrator is (except in James) always omniscient; the tone and plot are fairly optimistic, if not moralistic; and the end of the story coincides with the logical termination of the action.

In the short stories of the 1920s — those of Hemingway, Faulkner, and Katherine Anne Porter — the action is greatly pruned until the story appears rather plotless. Yet every detail serves an artistic function; nothing seems unconsidered or accidental. The short stories in the Twenties exhibit greater emotional complexity and ambiguity, as well as a more discriminating sense of emphasis and an increased brevity of representation (in short, a modified, more selective, realism). Their authors let the crucial thoughts and themes remain implicit and elusive, often presenting them in symbolic form; chronology is distorted, usually through flashbacks; the overall attitude is unsentimental, if not aggressively pessimistic; and the characters emerge as fairly undistinguished, typical people who seem, nonetheless, hardly attached either to each other or to traditional social institutions. Instead of concentrating on plot development, the authors resort to rhetorical strategies of parallelism and repetition; the narrator often speaks in the first person and may be a major participant in the action rather than just an observer of it; and the story's end comes as an anticlimax after the earlier epiphany.

The American short stories of the 1940s — particularly those of Lionel Trilling, Shirley Jackson, Mary McCarthy, Delmore Schwartz, J.D. Salinger, and J.F. Powers — are descended directly from the short stories of the 1920s. But, whereas the writers in the Twenties were obsessed by meaninglessness (epitomized by Hemingway's "A Clean, Well-Lighted Place"), the writers in the Forties represented something of a reaction: not only did they favor a more nearly chronological plot with an ending that clamped the fiction into a thematic vise, but they also displayed an overarching concern with moral ambiguity. The 1950s, in retrospect, seem to have been an eclectic decade, productive of little truly original work in the short story, but of many masterly, almost studied, realizations of essentially earlier styles. The chief common tendency in writers as varied as Bernard Malamud, Saul Bellow, Carson McCullers, Flannery O'Connor, and George P. Elliott is towards the development, usually through plot, of an effective symbolic character or situation; and the major theme of short stories during this decade is moral failure — either the inability of a certain moral code to cope with the realities of existence, or (conversely) the individual's inability to find a viable morality.

In the 1960s, the modernist impetus revives, and some of the works during this decade illustrate the third stage in the esthetic development of the modern short story. In these works, the narrative is more discontinuous and the chronology even more distorted (perhaps as a reflection of the formal revolution implicit in quantum theory and in electronic media). Rather than push his characters through a plot, the author fills in the picture, often changing his (and the reader's) attitude towards the scene. The story sometimes gives the impression that it could go on forever — its ending seems less an integral conclusion than a reflection of the author's artistic decision to stop. Particularly in rendering human consciousness (and in using first-person narrators), the writers are more elliptical; they execute transitions in time, scene and (Tillie Olsen, in particular) point of view more sharply, sometimes even without conspicuous notice. Their characters are more radically marginal, if not irrefutably isolated; and most of their stories have extremely limited, if not nonexistent, moral dimensions. Though hardly sentimental, the stories are less ruthlessly pessimistic than their predecessors; and unlike the narrators in the stories of the Forties, the narrators in those of the Sixties rarely make any discoveries (indeed, their inability to understand is often the reader's discovery). The prose style of the stories, while not traditionally literary, is characterized by the use of heightened language that only print can produce, and many of the writers experiment with more original and economical ways to exploit the medium of the printed book. Finally, the stories suggest that a crucial shift in the use of symbolism has occurred: although certain objects, characters, and events have symbolic dimensions, in most of the stories the central theme is not evoked primarily through symbols. (In rare cases, however, the story as a whole becomes a symbol: for example, the milieu portrayed in Thomas Pynchon's "Entropy" is symbolic of the scientific concept named in the title.) Not one of these writers can claim to represent things accurately (the rejection of literary realism is complete), but they do evoke actions and mental processes directly, even though the significance of these events generally remains implicit. The meanings of the stories are comparatively clear and definite, although the unconventional techniques may put off the unwary or lazy reader. Thus, not only do the writers of these new short stories endeavor to find a special technique that enhances the experience (for example, Irvin Faust's great mad character Jake Bluffstein needs an over-the-shoulder, third-person narrator — just as Beckett's narrator requires a twisting, dulling prose style); but, more radically, they emphasize the technical elements so strongly that the story can even become a nonnarrative succession of fragmented impressions whose connecting strands fall into place when (and not until) the story is finished or reread. In addition, the main interest is often centered less upon the plot or theme than upon the processes of composition, which are sometimes so conspicuously exposed that they cannot help dominating the story. The short stories of the 1960s represent, then, an extension of the modern revolution, on modernism's terms; and in America at least, the most important recent stories take off from, rather than react against, the most fruitful decade for short works of fiction — the 1920s.

IV

In recent American fiction, many of the best works — both long and short — express one of two complementary themes: the absurdity of society and the madness of the self. The European absurd novel (of, say, Sartre and Albert Camus) reveals through description of rather normal activities a disjunction between values and behavior, intention and effect, belief and reality, which proves so broad and irrefutable that it renders the world meaningless. In contrast, the American absurd novel is — like European absurd theatre — an exuberant, nonrealistic portrait of thoroughly ridiculous events which, in toto, suggest that the world is ultimately senseless. In the novel form, the absurd writer can take on history itself (as Thomas Pynchon, John Barth and Joseph Heller do) and show in a sprawling, diffuse narrative that history — both in its single events and on the whole — is absurd. Given the limitations of the short story, the absurdist writer is able to treat only a single experience. In Samuel Beckett's brilliant but undeservedly unknown short stories, the action immediately attains metaphysical overtones; but American short-story writers confine their absurd vision to more modest, mundane activities. To Donald Barthelme, in many of his stories, the capacity to spend large amounts of money renders life absurd. To Kenneth Koch, in "The Postcard Collection" (which perhaps echoes Jorge Luis Borges), the absurd activity is the vain attempt to define in declarative sentences the ambiguous experience of art; to Jack Ludwig, in "Thoreau in California," it is all situations that reveal the nonsensical discrepancy between social demands and images on the one hand and individual desires and identities on the other.

In treating the madness of the self — a theme better suited to the short story's capacities — the writer in recent American fiction describes psychological derangement *from the inside*. That is, he dissects the workings of the mad mind itself, instead of carefully noting external symptoms. This internal portraiture distinguishes the first part of Dostoevsky's *Notes from Underground*, say, from the rather objective representation of a madman's odd behavior in Herman Melville's "Bartleby." Nowadays, the external portraiture seems better suited to the medium that deals best with surface symptoms, the movies; while fiction and poetry (Sylvia Plath, *et al.*) seem better suited to conveying the *feel* of madness. In recent short stories the portraits of mental imbalance range from Michael Rumaker's institutionalized young man, who comes to accept a toy as a human being, to Irvin Faust's Jake Bluffstein, who imagines himself becoming the Messiah of the Jews. Saul Bellow's Herzog, in the story "Sono and Moso" (later revised and included in the novel), suffers from severe, inexplicable depression, whereas H.W. Blattner's "Sound of a Drunken Drummer" echoes Malcolm Lowry's *Under the Volcano* (1947) in depicting the alcoholic's disjointed consciousness.

Of course, not all of the best recent short stories can be said to express one or the other of these two themes. Influenced by the modern tradition of experiment in multiple points of view, many young writers, invariably products of classes in creative writing, have produced accomplished, rather academic, semblances; Tillie Olsen, however, has employed this technique — in "Tell Me a Riddle" — with such emotional depth, structural fluency, deftness and beauty of language that the story as a whole transcends its ancestry. She has successfully adapted what was originally a novelistic technique to the short-story form, defining the scene and its people from several, differing perspectives; and she never ceases to weave beautiful figures as in the description of the dying grandmother: "Light she grew, like a bird, and like a bird, sound bubbled in her throat while the body fluttered in agony." In value, "Tell Me a Riddle" is surely among the great works of American fiction of recent years.

James Purdy's interests and achievements are more difficult to define. On the one hand, his best novel so far, *Malcolm* (1960), is a minor masterpiece in the absurd tradition — taut, resonant, and almost European in its strong control of every element. In his stories, on the other hand, he has perfected the modern technique of keeping everything implicit and of creating a pregnant moment — a situation, a dialogue, or even a line — that suggests many things. In context, the rather simple line that concludes Purdy's "Goodnight, Sweetheart" — " 'God,' Miss Miranda whispered. 'Dear God' " — achieves its power by suggesting a multitude of prayers. Mastery of compression, together with sensitivity, characterizes Purdy's best work, especially his two early stories, "Don't Call Me by My Right Name" and "63: Dream Palace," both of which were written in the Fifties.

Unlike nearly all contemporary writers, Thomas Pynchon builds his fiction upon sophisticated scientific ideas. The structure of his novel *V.* (1963) reflects the concept of reality expressed in quantum theory, and his story "Entropy," mentioned above, subsumes two possible senses of the scientific term used as the title. Simply and roughly, the term "entropy" signifies in thermodynamics "a measure of disorder within a closed system" or in information theory "a measure of disorder within language." In the first sense of "entropy," Pynchon's story depicts the imminence of the heat-death: If the earth's temperature should stay constant at $37°$ F., then human life would become, on its surface, randomly disordered and would come to exhibit, at its base, stasis. In the second sense of "entropy," the story depicts — explicitly — the failure of Saul (ironically, an information theorist) and his wife to communicate with each other, and — implicitly — the failure of everyone to communicate at the Washington party. In the story's scene, then, entropy in both these senses has reached maximal levels.

V

The overarching theme of the best contemporary short stories is less the imminent apocalypse our political history would suggest than the meaninglessness that would seem the inevitable outcome of our intellectual development. Just as absent as an omniscient narrator (even the third-person narrator is close or over the shoulder) is the definite moral stance; and where one can discern a moral statement in these stories, its authority seems pragmatic and tenuous. Mrs. Blattner suggests only one criterion for judging the alcoholism and high-class prostitution of her character — it drove her to her death. With Donald Barthelme's and Kenneth Koch's narrators, moral judgments would seem to emerge from a critique of their styles — they make fools of themselves; therefore, they are not worth emulating. This overarching nihilism debases the satirical impulse, surely implicit in, say, Barthelme and Koch, which as it refuses to offer contrasts turns satire into irony; and irony is too intrinsic in what we have come to call "black humor" — comedy which suggests that there is a gaping pit in life. This world-view, too, probably accounts for the open form of these stories — the only event that seems capable of terminating an action is the death of a major character; otherwise, as noted, the story seems capable of going on forever. Open form, as many critics have noted, is characteristic of an age that feels it does not have a strong hold on experience.

The period from 1960 to 1965 has witnessed, I believe, an ascendancy of the short story. Not only has the experimental impulse revived to produce some successful works, particularly in the broken continuity and the heightened economy of Barthelme and Olsen; but a number of new short-story writers have emerged: most of the writers discussed in this essay, as well as Bruce Jay Friedman, William Burroughs, Uli Beigel, Curtis Zahn, Myron Taube, John Yount, Hubert Selby, Jr., Ivan Gold, Susan Sontag, and Philip Roth. None of them has written many stories (in sharp contrast to such essentially repetitious writers as John O'Hara and John Updike), possibly because they regard the writing of a short story as a difficult art that requires nearly as much planning as a novel and nearly as much precise execution as a poem. This great attention is necessary, especially if the short story as a form is to salvage its own identity. The Sixties, so far, have been a good decade for short works of fiction.

Ralph Ellison (1969)

The more books we read, the sooner we perceive that the true function of a writer is to produce a masterpiece and that no other task
is of any consequence. — Palinurus, *The Unquiet Grave* (1945).

Ralph Ellison handles himself with a dignity, elegance, contained
comfort, and disdain for the trivial that is positively as aristocratic as any
American can be; and he is so variously talented and awesomely well-
conditioned that one might think he devoted his entire day to self-
cultivation. He has high-style hobbies like gourmet cooking, art-collecting,
building hi-fi sets, recorder-playing, taking photographs, designing his
own furniture; his distinguished appearance makes him a propitious subject for elegant photographic portraits; and he belongs to one of New York's
most respectable clubs, The Century, in addition to serving on some of
America's most powerful cultural commissions. Indeed, Ellison's multiple
success demonstrates that a fatherless American Negro really does have the
opportunity to become the author of one of America's greatest novels, *Invisible Man* (1952), as well as an aristocratic presence and an all but universally
respected literary figure.

As a writer, Ellison has a particular passion for demolishing the
stereotype, especially by showing how simplistic images forbid a more complex and perceptive understanding of human life in general and American
Negro experience in particular; and the realities of his own history run
thoroughly counter to a gamut of popular sociological clichés about the im-
prisoning quality of Negro disadvantage. Indeed, he talks about his life with
unusual subtlety and understanding, largely because certain truths were
gained at the expense of personal pain and he wants to insure that nothing
he puts into print will contradict the complexities, and the implications, of
his own experience. Ellison was born March 1, 1914, in Oklahoma City,
Oklahoma, just two years after it gained statehood. His father had been a
professional soldier in the Philippines, in China, and in the Spanish-
American War and, later, a construction foreman; and he was then
operating a small ice and coal business. The family, while not especially rich
in formal learning, was literate and active; and Ellison insists that his father
destined him to become a writer by bestowing on him the Christian name of

Ralph Waldo. "After I began to write and work with words," he once re-marked, "I came to suspect that he was aware of the suggestive powers of names and of the magic involved in naming."

Ellison senior died in an accident when Ralph was three; so to support her two sons, his mother became a domestic and then an apartment-house custodian who made a practice of bringing home the discarded copies of the latest magazines. Young Ralph took on a variety of kid jobs, such as selling newspapers, collecting bottles for bootleggers, shining shoes and clerking in a swanky haberdashery; and some of these tasks he exploited for other advantages. "After all," he once wrote, "the most meaningful tips do not always come in the form of money, nor are they intentionally extended." While quite young, Ellison assimilated the notion that he should excel at everything he tried, perhaps because "my mother had some sense of the value of excellence, and she often said that she didn't care what I became as long as I tried to become one of the best." In fact, he has since done remarkably well at so many things that he all but approximates the Western image of a Renaissance Man; and this ideal, he says in retrospect, first entered his mind, as well as the aspirations of his childhood friends, in the Negro community of Oklahoma City.

He went to the local high school, where he played varsity football, dabbled in writing, and began to concentrate on music. "I remember that in my themes at school I tried to get some of the Shavian quality into my writing; but no one paid any attention to it and I didn't take it seriously." To his good fortune, Ellison won an Oklahoma state scholarship to attend the most famous of Deep South Negro colleges, Tuskegee, founded by Booker T. Washington himself; and unable to afford the fare, he rode freight trains from Oklahoma to Alabama. "I went there as one who wanted to be a composer," Ellison remembers. "They had a good band and an orchestra, and I was a trumpeter. And they also had William L. Dawson, who was a composer and who had become quite famous as a choir director. The Tuskegee Choir opened Radio City Music Hall while I was still in high school, and this really got me excited." Elsewhere, Ellison judged that Dawson "was, and probably still is, the greatest classical musician in that part of the country. I had no need to attend a white university when the master I wished to study with was available at Tuskegee."

To deny another cliché, Ellison today does not regard this segregated education, in the Deep South, as particularly disadvantageous. "You got there to study music, and you studied music; and it wasn't any easier because you were in a Negro college," he explains (pronouncing the next-to-last word as "nig-row"). "The teachers themselves held degrees from Oberlin and the Boston Conservatory and so on; and Hazel Harrison, who headed the piano department, had been one of Busoni's prize pupils and lived in a house with other young composers in Berlin. You know, you don't think about the problems of being a Negro when you're trying to get an

education. When you're in the classroom, you're thinking about the problems before you, not the larger sociological problem, although you are quite
aware that you are Negro."

It was at Tuskegee that Ellison discovered modern writing, not
through his courses, which were mostly in music, but through his own
adventurous reading and the encouragement of Morteza Sprague, then
head of the English department there and the dedicatee of Ellison's second
book, a collection of essays entitled *Shadow and Act* (1964). "When I went to
him about T.S. Eliot and such people — he hadn't given much attention to
them; they weren't taught there — he told me to read the criticism and where
to find it. Once I read *The Waste Land* I became very much involved with
modern letters. I couldn't really analyze it. Emotionally I was intrigued; so
I started reading all the commentaries. My friend Al Murray tells me that
I was actually trying to write poetry in those days — something which I've
blanked out; incidentally, I never wrote a decent poem; but the conscious
concern with writing began there, without my being conscious that this was
what I was doing."

To earn his spending money, particularly to support an *Esquire*-
inspired taste in clothes, Ellison worked part-time in the university library,
and there he came across the major modern books that were not included
in the literature courses. "In Macon County, Alabama," he once wrote, "I
read Marx, Freud, T.S. Eliot, Pound, Gertrude Stein and Hemingway.
Books which seldom, if ever, mentioned Negroes were to release me from
whatever 'segregated' idea I might have had of human possibilities." He
continued elsewhere, "Why should I have wished to attend the white state-
controlled university where the works of the great writers might not have
been so easily available?" Here, as before, Ellison made the best of a
discriminatory situation, which had its own opportunities as well as disadvantages; and his wisdom is that everybody's life is similarly riddled by
superficially restricting and yet opportune experiences.

He came to New York City in the summer of 1936, after his junior year,
intending to get work and then return for the fall semester. With only
seventy-five dollars in his pocket, he stayed at the Harlem YMCA, which
also turned out to be a good place to meet people. However, a steady job
was not his fortune, and New York's excitement was so persuasive that he
never returned to get his degree and has, off and on, lived in Harlem ever
since. He took a job as a counterman at the Harlem Y, and then worked
briefly as a substitute receptionist and file clerk for Dr. Harry Stack
Sullivan, the eminent American psychiatrist. "This was a job of short duration, but one of the most interesting I ever had," he told a Congressional
Committee in the summer of 1966. "After that, oh, I worked in factories and
I sometimes had no work and slept in St. Nicholas Park below City College.
I lived as I could live."

He sought work as a musician, once playing first trumpet for a small orchestra that Alex North, now a famous Hollywood composer, then conducted for his wife, the dancer Anna Sokolow; however, Ellison could not amass enough funds to join the musician's union. He studied composition briefly with the American composer Wallingford Reigger and even took a few classes in sculpture. Late in the thirties he regularly played chess with Jacob Lawrence, who has since become a well-known painter. Thanks in part to his old friendship with the blues singer Jimmy Rushing, who once carried ice for Ellison's father, he also made the acquaintance (and reacquaintance) of many Oklahoma-born jazz musicians, among them the guitarist Charlie Christian (an elementary school classmate of Ellison's younger brother), the bassist Walter Page, the trumpeter Hot Lips Paige, as well as the members of Count Basie's band and even Duke Ellington. Like the novelist John Barth, who also studied music extensively, Ellison as a writer even now has the regular working habits of a composer.

Two days after he got to New York, Ellison ran into the Negro philosopher-critic Alain Locke, whom he had met before at Tuskegee, and another man, who turned out to be the writer Langston Hughes. On the spot, Hughes asked Ellison to deliver a few books, granting the young man permission to read them on the way; and since Ellison made a practice of capitalizing on such unintentional tips, he discovered two of the most influential works he ever read—André Malraux's *Man's Fate* and *Days of Wrath.* "A few months later I met Richard Wright, and he asked me to review a book for a magazine he had come to New York to edit," Ellison reminisced with a slight but perceptible drawl. "And my review was published, and then he asked me to do a short story. Now I had never tried to do a piece of fiction in my life; and I made my first attempt at a short story for a magazine of Wright's called *New Challenge.* The story didn't come out, but it got as far as the galley-proof state. By then, I guess I must have been hooked."

In 1937, after his mother died "at the hands of an ignorant and negligent Negro physician," he joined his younger brother in Dayton, Ohio. The two were so poor that they hunted by day, sometimes consulting Hemingway's stories as a manual of detail, felling birds they later sold to G.M. officials. It was there and then that he vowed to become a writer, arranging his life so that writing, rather than something else, would be his primary interest — "to stake my energy against the possibility of failing." He started a novel, only to discover that he did not know how to finish it; and after recognizing that, as he now puts it, "art is a system of techniques," he embarked upon a systematic study of the novelistic craft — reading a lot of criticism, as well as the prefaces of Henry James and Joseph Conrad, and later querying Wright about fictional devices.

Returning to New York in 1938, he joined the Federal Writers' Project as a researcher at the salary of twenty-two dollars a week. Here he assembled scholarly data for a study of Negroes in New York, as well as collected folklore. "I went from apartment to apartment, talking to anyone who would allow me to." Some of this experience, gained as an outside observer, informed the internal narratives in *Invisible Man*. In 1942 Ellison resigned from the Writers' Project to join Angelo Herndon, then breaking away from the Communists, in editing *The Negro Quarterly*. Although Ellison sympathetically frequented left-wing circles and wrote reportage and criticism for *The New Masses*, which was then one of the few places that would publish tough-minded Negro writers, he never joined the Communist Party or accepted its dictum that social realism was the sole appropriate literary style.

Just before *The Negro Quarterly* dissolved, Ellison joined the merchant marine as a civilian, partly because he had been a member of the National Maritime Union since 1936, when he picketed for them, and largely because "I wanted to contribute to the war, but didn't want to be in a Jim Crow army." He worked as a cook and touched Europe for the first time; but after a particularly wracking voyage, in which his convoy came under attack, he returned home suffering from low blood pressure and went to recuperate with friends in Vermont. It was there, in 1945, in his own early thirties that he started *Invisible Man*, still wondering if, indeed, he would be able actually to finish a novel. At the book's beginnings, he was reading Lord Raglan's study of *The Hero*, thinking about how myth got into fiction, and considering "the nature of politics and Negro leadership, which was based on outside support, rather than the dynamics of the Negro community." He wrote the novel's prologue and opening sections rather quickly, publishing in Cyril Connolly's journal, *Horizon* (1947), the "Battle Royal" sequence as it more or less now stands. "I had an idea where I was going," he explains, "although the actual writing took years. Once I got a pattern going, the pattern parlayed itself; that's what I call 'organic form.' "

In July 1946 he married Fanny McConnell, a petite, slender, freckled, fair-complexioned Negro who resembles Katharine Hepburn and looks after her husband well. Around this time he resumed his pre-War acquaintance with the critic Stanley Edgar Hyman, who has since been one of his closest literary friends. They came together in the early forties over Ellison's admiration for Kenneth Burke, whom they hail in unison as the greatest American critic, and Hyman's enthusiasm for Negro blues, which both of them regard as great folk poetry; and the novelist has since characterized the critic as "an old friend and intellectual sparring partner." Particularly after the War, Ellison frequently stayed at the Hyman house in Bennington, Vermont, where he wrote by day and spent the evening in drink and talk with Hyman and his wife, novelist Shirley Jackson.

Ellison worked seven years on *Invisible Man*, as well as on a shorter work which disposed of a related theme and eventually went unpublished; and the book appeared in 1952 to a fanfare of favorable reviews and eventually the National Book Award. In retrospect, the novel is an ambiguous and somewhat disconcerting achievement that combines much hard visceral detail with a surrealistic sense of perception and event, some of the lushest writing in contemporary English literature with some un-distinguished prose, a sense of authentic immediacy with an almost academic net of myth and ritual; and its plot all but begs to be misread by an undiscerning reader. One reason would be, as the novelist James Baldwin put it, "Mr. Ellison, by the way, is the first Negro novelist I have ever read to utilize in language, and brilliantly, some of the ambiguity and irony of Negro life."

The problem in understanding *Invisible Man* is the nature of the nar-rator, whom some critics erroneously take to be autobiographical and whom most white readers regard as a blameless Negro boy subjected to all the indignities that white society inflicts upon its blacks. He gets a scholar-ship to a Negro college only after passing through a hair-raisingly violent "battle royal," gets expelled from the college for betraying its dirty underside to a white trustee, goes North to discover that his "letters of recommenda-tion" deceitfully advise against him, that jobs are hard to find, and that the ones he gets are more dangerous than congenial. After undergoing an operation that seems like a lobotomy, he gets involved with various radicals, communists as well as black nationalists, all of whom eventually betray him in other ways; and the narrative closes with his escaping into an underground cave where, surrounded by light-bulbs, he contemplates the pattern of his experience.

In one sense, many of the choices the individual narrator makes could be regarded as symbolic of more general political persuasions that certain Negroes have historically espoused and some have followed; and since most of these solutions continue to have their advocates, as well as to fail their hopes for similar reasons, the politics of *Invisible Man*, like those in all great political fictions, seem remarkably current nearly two decades later. In another sense, the gist of the novel could be interpreted as a descent ritual, where the narrator must undergo suffering before he gains the power to speak as an artist. Since the body of narration is actually a flashback, the novel is also, to Albert Murray, "*par excellence* the literary extension of the blues. It was as if Ellison had taken an everyday twelve-bar blues tune (by a man from down South sitting in a manhole up North in New York singing and signifying about how he got there) and scored it for a full orchestra." Moreover, as a novel by a Negro American writing in a Western language, *Invisible Man* draws and comments upon Negro folklore, American literature (with epigraphs from Melville and T.S. Eliot), and Western literature, with specially conspicuous debts to Dostoevsky, Voltaire, and Greek myths. ("I think I still have the copy of *Candide* that I bought at Tuskegee.") Like jazz, *Invisible Man* is a product of American Negro culture, which is indubitably American (and only minimally African) and also Western, which is to say, an extention of Europe.

Most white readers take the story as a catalogue of an innocent Negro's adverse experience; but Ellison, in his usual position of countering a cliché, regards this as "an incorrect and sentimental interpretation, inasmuch as the narrator of the book could have stopped much of his experience, had he been willing to accept the harsh nature of reality. He creates much of his own fate, but I don't look upon him as heroic in that way. I think he made a lot of mistakes; but many white readers, certainly, are so sentimental about the Negro thing that they can't see that. He has a sort of wrong-headed desire to take on identities imposed on him by the outside, always stopping to let someone else tell him what to do and even give him a name; but we know very well that each individual has to discover himself, for himself. Usually, this is done through some sort of pain; but I must say that this is a tough guy, because he goes through many, many experiences which should have driven him to himself and to his reality. He should have understood what Bledsoe had to say; he [Bledsoe] was wise in comparison, though you don't have to approve of him."

Many critics have interpreted the title as suggesting that white America finds the predicament of Negroes invisible. "Well, I wasn't writing about 'the Negro,' " Ellison retorts, a bit amused. "I was writing about a specific character, in specific circumstances, at a specific time. As for the invisibility, well, there's a joke about that, which is tied up with the sociological dictum that Negroes in the United States have a rough time because we have 'high visibility' — high pigmentation, as the formula has it. No one will ever mistake me for white. However, the problem for the narrator of *Invisible Man* is that he creates his own invisibility to a certain extent by not asserting himself. Even though he has the responsibility not to get done in, he does not recognize how evil people can be or how to do the thing that will break the pattern and reveal himself, until far along in the book. He is a type of character that transcends race, although a lot of people don't take him that way." Ironically enough, for a book that is so misunderstood, as well as so texturally rich it could spawn two hundred pages of detailed criticism, *Invisible Man* has done remarkably well, going through several paperback editions; and not only has it been read by nearly every literate young person, but in 1965, a poll of two hundred American critics and writers judged *Invisible Man* the most distinguished novel of the post-War period.

For over a decade now, Ellison has been working on a second novel, as yet untitled; and the sections that he has published in various magazines, as well as read aloud, suggest that it will be just as brilliant and extraordinary as his first book. It will be a political novel, set partly in Washington and partly in Oklahoma. One reason why it was not finished sooner is that the story has become inordinately long — perhaps over one thousand pages — and complicated. Another reason is that Ellison is something of a perfectionist, with a more than usual dose of second-novel jitters. In the spring of 1966, I saw on his desk four thick, bound volumes of typescript, from which he read me miscellaneous passages. "I try to deal with large bodies of experience," he told me then, "which I see as quite complex. There's a tendency to reduce the American experience, which is quite complex, especially when it centers around the Negro American experience. So, I'm constantly writing — I write a lot, but too much I have to put aside. Once it jells, I come back to it; and if I still react positively, if I can still see potentialities of development, then I keep it." One old friend, who has read a good deal of it, says, "Ralph is insanely ambitious. He actually writes quickly, but won't release this book until he is sure that it is the greatest American novel ever written." He has become so embarrassed about his inability to finish the book that he gets visibly upset whenever acquaintances ask about it.

In 1964 he published *Shadow and Act*, which contains miscellaneous essays of twenty years, including all the lengthy interviews that Ellison gave up to that time, his criticisms of jazz, literature, and culture, and his contributions to a famous polemical exchange with the misguided critic Irving Howe, in which Ellison scored all the points and revealed all the truths. These essays are invariably densely argued and difficult to read; but if nothing else, they demonstrate that Ellison is an immensely intelligent author with an unusual care for language and that everything he publishes is thoroughly premeditated.

Ellison himself is just under six feet, broadly built, visibly muscular (particularly his arms), and the color of well-creamed coffee; like nearly all American Negroes, he is not black but, as he would put it, "part-white." He has a broad mouth, moderately full lips, a flattened nose, flaying nostrils, and a precisely trimmed graying mustache that runs quarter-moon shapes down from his nose across to the ends of his upper lips. A broad scar between his right eye and temple, the result of a childhood swing accident, seems less a blemish than a handsome punctuation mark, and his normal expression is pensive, perhaps a bit distant, intimidating, and severe. Reserved by instinct, he is not at all as comic as his books might suggest. He has begun to gray noticeably in the past few years, combing his loosely kinked hair across the back half of his head and leaving the front part bald to the elements.

Containing his nerves well, he used to smoke cigarettes but now puffs a pipe, filling it at home from a large can of Nouve Egberts Amphora. Always erect, he moves with the graceful balance, and incipient energy and perceptible hauteur of a star halfback crossing the campus. He is guarded and yet considerate in manner, except when drink loosens him, as well as unusually formal, even addressing his guests at home "Mr. X" and "Miss Y" long after most Americans would use first names. However, whenever his oldest close friend, a live-wire writer and retired Air Force major named

Albert Murray, pulls into his house, the tempo picks up. (At times, Murray seems to carry Ellison's wilder side, and his own essays seem jazzier renditions of ideas and attitudes they have worked out together.) But for his hair and two rather deeply articulated lines on his face, running from the base corners of his nose to points slightly beyond the corners of his mouth, Ellison would look far younger than he is.

Very concerned about his appearance, a trait he insists is particularly Negro American, he dresses well, in clothes of conservative cut, and sensitively, sometimes condescendingly, notices how others dress; and he also attributes his aristocratic manner to Negro American culture. "You now find," he remarks, "that the great nineteenth-century tradition of elegance and oratory is most alive within the Negro community." When he dons a dark suit and black homburg, encases himself in a dark overcoat, and climbs into his black Chrysler, he looks more like a prosperous banker than a novelist.

From his earliest days at the YMCA, Ellison has always lived north of 110th Street, usually in the nicer areas of Harlem west of Eighth Avenue — in a room at 530 Manhattan Avenue in 1936, on 122nd Street near Manhattan Avenue, on Hamilton Terrace near City College, on St. Nicholas Avenue between 147th and 148th Streets (where most of *Invisible Man* was written), and since 1952, on upper Riverside Drive in the 150s in a spacious eighth-floor apartment with a spectacular view of the Hudson River and the New Jersey Palisades. The Ellisons' apartment is high-ceilinged, large-roomed, comfortable, scrupulously kept, and filled with the best of everything, all so tastefully appointed that it may well adorn certain fashion pages.

There are paintings and sculpture on the walls, soft carpets under the foot, Mies van der Rohe Barcelona chairs, a Marcel Breuer leather-strap chair, a handsome standing sculpture of Ichabod Crane atop his sprinting horse, an improvised cart containing African violets grown under fluorescent light, two television sets (one color, the other black and white), a stand holding four recorders in various sizes, a wall full of hardbound books, several pieces of silver-frame furniture designed in Miesian style by Ellison himself, a plastic humidor filled with cigars, waist-high speakers from a hi-fi set housed in a closet, a Nagra portable tape recorder, an Ampex tape deck, a bright red office-size IBM typewriter, a small replica of Botticelli's *Venus* over the typewriter, a mounted National Book Award, and more than the usual panoply of security devices. The luxurious effect of the three front rooms — the living room, the dining room, a study, all open to each other — is overpowering, as well as somewhat surprising; it is not the sort of elegance that most people, their minds cluttered with stereotypes about Negroes, "ghettos," and writers' homes, expect to find on the edge of Harlem. Bookshelves and records inundate all the hallway walls, sometimes to the point of inconvenience, while a guest room in the back is filled to capacity

with more bookshelves and miscellany as the Ellisons hesitate over throw-
ing things out. (Early in 1968 he retrieved a batch of usable files from an
office high above Rockefeller Center; here some of *Invisible Man* was written.) Their constant companion is a large, frisky black labrador retriever
who answers to "Tucka," which is a nickname for Tucka Tarby of Tivoli.
Although the Ellisons are more than comfortably ensconced in New York,
they fulfilled in 1967 a long-fomenting ambition to have a house in the country. However, the farm they purchased in Plainfield, Massachusetts,
burned down in their presence later that year, tragically destroying several
irreplaceable possessions and a half year's worth of revisions that Ellison
had made on his second novel.

Although he is certainly free to move elsewhere, Ellison has always
lived in Negro communities, in stark contrast to many other dark-skinned
writers and even certain self-appointed spokesmen for "black" America;
and for this reason, he thinks that his soulful books, unlike those of certain
other Negro authors, speak to blacks and browns as well as whites: "I have
to hear the language," he explains. "My medium is language; there is a
Negro idiom. In fact, there are many Negro idioms in the American
language, and I have to hear them sounding in my ear. You know, also,
a place like Harlem or any other Negro community has an expressiveness
about it which is almost Elizabethan. Things are revealed in speech in the
streets; there is a lot of humor. I never know when I'm going to hear
something just in the street that is going to be the making of a piece of fiction
that I'm trying to write."

It seems symbolically appropriate that Ellison should live so close to
Harlem and yet only a few blocks away from the National Institute of Arts
and Letters, to which he was appointed in 1964. Even better, the location
of his house approximates what he identifies as a chief characteristic of
American art — the fusion of vernacular and effete, of local traditions with
Western myth, of the mundane and the universal. Ellison remembers that
he derived this idea from the poems and essays of T.S. Eliot, whom he also
regards as one of the greatest influences upon his own writing. "Eliot is full
of American folklore. He knew quite a lot about it. It would have been inescapable for him, coming from St. Louis, not to recognize the odd juxtapositions you get in this country. High culture and popular culture are
all mixed up; and the poet can mix them any way he wants. It amuses me
that the 'Under the bam/Under the boo,/Under the bamboo tree' line in
'Fragment of an Agon' comes out of a Negro song written by James Weldon
Johnson as part of one of the popular musicals of the 1890s, when a group
of Negroes dominated the American musical stage. Anything and
everything is there to be used. There is this kind of irreverent reverence
which Americans are apt to have for the good products of the past. I think
you get all of this in Eliot"; one could add, in much of American jazz and
Ellison himself. Indicatively, he regards the "Afro-American" identification

as rather irrelevant, if not phoney; for just as T.S. Eliot could never wholly forsake his heritage to become an unalloyed Englishman, so American Negroes culturally cannot honestly be anything but American.

Very much aware of how inappropriate words can corrupt our understanding of important things, Ellison persuasively objects to the use of the word "ghetto" to identify segregated communities. " 'Ghetto' implies a cultural and religious distance. It comes from Europe; it had a content there. However, used in this way, it only helps to obscure the relationships between American whites and American Negroes. They have so much in common — language for one thing, the patterns of myth — universal myth, Christian myths and so on, as they have been given embodiment in terms of Negro patterns. It is not too difficult to find the Hercules myth in John Henry, if you are aware of the connections, if you know where to look. Between Americans white and black there is not a religious wall, nor a cultural wall. Most Negroes are, just to start with religion, Protestant. That's unmistakable; you have communication there. On the other hand, everywhere you look, even in the deepest, most rabid part of the South, the Negroes are not separate but right in the bedrooms, in the kitchens. They are everywhere, even in the clubs and in the cars; they know all the intimate conversations.

"American English would not have the same music in it if it were not for great numbers of Negroes, and great numbers of white Southerners who learned their English partially from Negroes. In Harlem — in fact, in most so-called black ghettoes — you have a lot of people who do not spend most of their time there. They work outside, for instance as domestics in white homes. They're cooking, taking care of children, changing their diapers, teaching them their manners. They are so completely involved on that level of association. The music and the dances that Americans do are greatly determined by Negro style — by Negro American style at that, by American Negro sense of elegance, by the American Negro's sense of what the human experience should be, by what Negroes feel about how an American should move and express himself. So, the word 'ghetto' obscures this. It is much better to say that you have segregation and slums. This is very difficult to get people to see."

Although literature is his trade, Ellison becomes more passionate nowadays, if not adamant, in talking about politics; but rather than offering the usual phrases of terror and protest, he most vehemently objects, as perhaps a writer should, to those homilies that corrupt or contradict his sense of immediate reality, such as an indiscriminate use of the word "ghetto," or those current sociological generalizations about the "disintegrating Negro family." He finds that much that is written about Negroes, as often by supposed friends as by avowed enemies, is fallacious and, if transformed into social policy, pernicious. "Most of those who write about Negro life today," he once wrote with bitterness, "seem to assume that as long as their hearts are in the right place they can be as arbitrary as they wish in their formulations." In particular, he angrily objects to sociologists and social workers who propagate an image of Negro life as riddled by degradation and self-hate, not only because such interpretations are on the whole simply untrue, but also because such influential studies attribute to Negro society certain behavior patterns which are just as characteristic of the white culture as well. "One of the most insidious crimes occurring in this democracy," he writes in *Shadow and Act*, "is that of designating another, politically weaker, less socially acceptable, people as the receptacle for one's own self-disgust, for one's own infantile rebellions, for one's own fears of, and retreats from, reality. It is the crime of reducing the humanity of others to that of a mere convenience, a counter in a banal game which involves no apparent risk to ourselves."

Anger and outrage are clearly in Ellison's repertoire of responses; yet he is perhaps too scrupulous an intellectual, or too aristocratic a brown-skinned gentleman, to traffic in the obvious and familiar epithets of protest spokesmanship. In one of the many memorable passages of *Shadow and Act*, he implicitly offers a partial explanation for his chosen role. "But there is also an American Negro tradition," he writes, "which teaches one to deflect racial provocation and to master and contain pain. It is a tradition which abhors as obscene any trading on one's anguish for gain or sympathy; which springs not from a desire to deny the harshness of existence but from a will to deal with it as men at their best have always done." This is another way of explaining why the most remarkable heroism often remains invisible to the audience of hero-worshippers.

In dealing with those popular sociological clichés, Ellison as usual refers to his own experience as a fatherless child; and although he knew his father well enough to suffer the loss, he realizes that while "a certain companionship was gone, and my mother had to be more severe than she otherwise would have liked," other social disadvantages were more debilitating. "The white family," he adds wryly, "is in just as much chaos." Furthermore, he fears that such theories give people an excuse for nihilistic behavior; and he remembers with horror watching a Negro teen-ager on television after the Newark riot explaining his own destructiveness with a gamut of sociological clichés. The kid patently got his lines from "the new apologists for segregation," as Ellison calls them, who serve to rationalize a new sense of white supremacy by giving white people superficially persuasive reasons not to associate with "culturally deficient" Negroes or grant them equal opportunity. "The decay of the cities," he warns, "will not be stopped by whites moving to the suburbs, and the public peace should be protected, regardless of who is upsetting it."

Because he refuses to join the chants for "black power," Ellison is sometimes dismissed as an "Uncle Tom"; but since his temper is hardly servile or humble and he has the courage of his convictions, often to the point of personal pain, as well as refusing to repress his anger, that derogatory stereotype is no more appropriate than other reductionist clichés. Ellison does not deny that injustice, discrimination, hypocrisy, and poverty all exist; but he insists, partly from personal experience, that these disadvantages are not as totally determining as certain social commentators make them out to be. First, he notes that all men confront disadvantages of some kind and that the measure of a man's character is his will to overcome them. Second is "the broad possibility of personal realization which I see as a saving aspect of American life." Third, he believes that democratic processes and black-white cooperation, rather than violence or racism in any form, are more likely to alleviate those problems and that the liberal approach, in spite of hypocrisies, does bring discernible change. "Barriers are torn down through law and the interaction of people," he declares, adding, "I just don't see how a resort to violence can be successful. It's foolish to believe that it might, because like the character of Ras in my novel, they cannot commit themselves to what they say. They don't have the supplies and the organization for guerrilla warfare." He pauses and chuckles to himself, "I know something about shooting, and those snipers aren't particularly good." Perhaps the final irony of Ellison's relation to the young "militants" is the suspicion that the opening of LeRoi Jones's play, *Dutchman* (1964), closely resembles the scene that closes Chapter 12 of *Invisible Man*.

Indeed, Ellison is disturbed by how eagerly the mass media play up the statements of "black power" advocates who are hardly as representative of Negro American feeling as are ministers or the leaders of the older protest organizations. "People have been making extreme statements in Harlem for decades — some of the guys now on 125th Street and Seventh Avenue were there when I first came to New York; but now television feeds their ideas into many homes. A false sense of reality is disseminated. Most Negroes who see them on television are as scared and awed as white people." Ellison paused to cast for a definitive version of his thought. "We now see revived the old myth of the black bogeyman in a new metamorphosis. He used to scare children in the South; now this myth, propagated by the big media with a few militant-sounding Negroes as their agents, is used to titillate the fears and the masochism of a great audience of whites. This does the causes of equal opportunity, responsibility, and fraternity no good." A tone of tempered frustration, perhaps personal, entered Ellison's voice as he said, "Some old Negro preacher could be the wisest man in the United States, and no one could hear him. The media wouldn't pay attention."

The remark is obliquely applicable to Ellison himself, even though his views do have some circulation and he did testify to Congress in the summer of 1966; for wisdom, along with courage in stating the unobvious truth, is the quality most deeply characteristic of Ellison's mind. Very much unlike his nameless narrator in *Invisible Man*, who is perhaps an obverse of himself, Ellison has a tough and guarded intelligence that refuses to be persuaded by

anything that refutes its senses of value and reality. As a writer professional-
ly concerned with articulating the truth one perceives, he has particular
contempt for hypocrites and hypocrisies, regardless of how intelligent or
superficially high-minded the deception.

Against the herd of current intellectual fashion, he thinks that the
NAACP has achieved "real victories in changing the legal structure regarding race" and praises Lyndon B. Johnson, quite justifiably, as the President
who has done more for the "Negro thing," as he likes to call it, than any of
his predecessors. "He's knocked the pins out of the great structure of racism
in this country," Ellison remarks, "by making changes in the basis of
political power. In sticking his neck out on many appointments, he has
recognized the justice of equal rights and done things that Roosevelt and
Kennedy didn't dare. He knows that it must be seen that Negroes play an
important role in the life of the country—that we must have a full share in
political power and responsibility."

Ellison insists that Negro Americans should keep their eyes fixed on
the classic goals—integration, cultural autonomy, freedom of movement,
equal opportunity, and a share of political power. Now that these goals are
within realization, he fears that various distractions may sabotage the
effort. Similarly, it takes genuine courage for a writer to go against the ma-
jority opinion of his own profession, but this is precisely the personal
strength which Ellison consistently displays, as in publicly defending
American involvement in Vietnam, less out of patriotic enthusiasm than
tragic necessity. "I don't see us withdrawing from the war," he said, for once
looking out the window and then back at me. "We have certain respon-
sibilities to the Vietnamese and the structure of power in the world. It's too
bad, but that's the way it is."

In unison with other cultural elder statesmen, he can become rather
piously alarmed about the young, as much in response to the stereotypes
he sees on the television and reads about in the newspapers as out of his own
sense of values—the media would seem to have the ecumenical power of in-
suring that we all commit the same sins toward each other. Marijuana and
such he regards as *déja vu*. "I knew about drugs from the time I was a kid.
What do these kids think they are doing by using them that way?" He is
shocked by the illiterate style in the Underground-Press newspaper (that
regularly comes, unsolicited, to his home), worried that too many intelligent people are accepting any well-publicized idea that comes along,
alarmed that they are denying any "sense of limits" to proclaim "anything
is possible," dismayed by the new dances which, as he sees them on television, strike him as graceless and uninteresting, and afraid that purveyors
of revolutionary rhetoric will be done in by their pretensions. "Whenever
you speak in the name of a people and you're not truly their representative
and they have no way of bending you to their will," he angrily warns, "then
there is bound to be treachery and betrayal."

Like many writers before him, Ellison is a political novelist who has used his eminence as a stepping stone into politics, not as a self-proclaimed spokesman (a role he obviously detests) but as an influential adviser and respected participant in important commissions — less as a prophet than as a wise man; in life, as well as in literary style, he would seem to emulate the example of André Malraux. He is haunted by the sense that, as he irreverently puts it, "when writers write about politics, usually they are wrong. The novel at its best demands a sort of complexity of vision which politics doesn't like. Politics has as its goal the exercise of power — political power — and it isn't particularly interested in truth in the way that the novel form demands that the novelist must be." In an offhand moment he once conjectured, with an uneasy laugh, that by refusing the invitation to become a Negro spokesman he spurned the opportunity to make a cool million.

Out of his concern with the arts and society, Ellison has in recent years accepted appointments to cultural committees, such as the National Council on the Arts and the Carnegie Commission on Educational Television, as well as served as vice-president of both the American PEN club and the National Institute of Arts and Letters and trustee of both the Citizens' Committee for Public Television and the John F. Kennedy Center in Cambridge. Partly because he is a Negro who does not espouse racial apocalypses, but primarily because he is a great novelist, Ellison is, of course, an ideal choice whenever integrated boards are selected; so since he hesitates to take time from his novel and tries to distribute his energies as propitiously as possible, he likes to pick among the offers and then function as an aggressive, if not dominant, participant in all committees to which he belongs.

For about two thirds of the days of the year, Ellison gets up early, takes breakfast, and goes straight to his desk in the large study adjacent to the living room. He used to walk Tucka every morning; but since his wife Fanny resigned her job as Executive Director of the American Medical Center for Burma, she has assumed that task. Before, he would cook himself a hamburger for lunch, but now she brings it to his desk. He likes to work until four, when he will flip on the large-screen television or return some of the calls his wife has answered earlier in the day. He feels the victim of the world's nuisances and lets the world know his feelings; and should he pick up the phone himself, the caller invariably hears a suspicious-sounding "Who is this, please?" He can sometimes be very curt and forbidding; other times, he talks with ease for over an hour. He takes no total vacations and, on trips away, carries notes pertaining to his novel.

Actually, Ellison is such a slave to his work that interruptions and distractions are as feared as disease. I once inadvertently arrived a little earlier than he expected, and he took an hour to unwind from the invasion of his working time. However, once released from bondage, he feels more uninhibitedly free. Lecture invitations come frequently; but since those fees and the royalties from his two books comprise his entire income, he usually takes only the most lucrative ones and does about a dozen a year. He has taught for brief spells at various universities — Bard, Rutgers, Bennington, and Chicago among them — but has recently given that up, with the prickly advice that serious writers should stay at one school no more than three years. "The first year everybody is very nice to you; the second, they give you a little clerical work to do; but by the third year the demands begin to get all out of hand." As a lecturer, he has the most extraordinary capacity for working out his thoughts without a note, occasionally stumbling but usually hewing to the thread of his argument; and I have seen him talk for hours without a glass of refreshment. In the question periods that follow, he invariably has a complex and extensive answer for every query; if challenged, he is more stubborn than gracious in argument, yet usually persuasive in give and take.

Ellison is very much a literary gent, and those he identifies as his closest friends are likewise middle-aged writers — the theologian-literary critic Nathan A. Scott, Albert Murray, Stanley Edgar Hyman, the novelist Robert Penn Warren (who nominated Ellison to the Century Club). He is less a Negro writer than a writer who is Negro, if there is a difference to be discerned; but it is not quite just to say, as William Faulkner did in one of his rare statements on his peers, "So far he has managed to stay away from being first a Negro; he is still first a writer." While Ellison is, like most serious authors, perhaps more ultimately loyal to the great traditions of literature than the parochial demands of his social group (and so perhaps was the classic blues singer), he identifies his own purposes as originating where these two sets of demands intersect: "As I see it," he said in an address at the Library of Congress, early in 1964, "it is through the process of making artistic forms — plays, poems, novels — out of one's experience that one becomes a writer, and it is through this process, this struggle, that the writer helps give meaning to the experience of the group. And it is the process of mastering the discipline, the techniques, the fortitude, the culture, through which this is made possible that constitutes the writer's real experience as *writer*, as artist."

It is this sense of having contemplated much-cogitated problems more honestly, profoundly, and persuasively than anybody else that gives Ellison his particular importance and power nowadays; for to paraphrase T.S. Eliot's famous remark about Henry James, Ellison has a mind so tough that no consciously perceived deceit could violate it. He knows full well that the most profound influence a writer can have comes not from lending his name and reputation to propaganda but from the ultimate quality of his writings — their final relevance and persuasiveness in contradicting current piety, in explaining how inappropriate ideas are responsible for an ineffective policy, in distinguishing illusion from reality, and in telling the complex truth about subjects nearly smothered by simplistic and/or fallacious cliché, and in demonstrating intellectual opportunity and freedom merely by the influence of his ideas. One reason why Ellison has not been able to complete his second novel is that all these distractions demand so much of his attention, as much to flush the ideological junk out of his own head as to speak about corruption in the social world. "I can be free," he once wrote, "only to the extent that I can detect error and grasp the complex reality of my circumstances and work to dominate it through the techniques which are my means of confronting the world."

It is almost as if it were harder today to be a Negro writer than a white, not because Negroes suffer discrimination on the literary scene (indeed, reverse discrimination is more often the rule), but because they have so many more clichés to discard. Also, white readers (and critics) expect their stereotypes of Negro existence to be confirmed, literary agitprop and "militant" rhetoric are tempting, and supposed friends select themselves as tutors on how Negro authors should write, speak, and maneuver. "It knocks me out," Ellison once wrote, "whenever anyone, black or white, tries to tell me — and the white Southerners have no monopoly here — how to become their conception of a 'good Negro.' " It is easier for Negro novelists to betray their professional tasks and be widely praised for their betrayal. Against this background, Ellison's achievement and integrity are the more remarkable. His insistent point is that the truth is invariably more complex than cliché; and like his own novel, the man himself casts a various and unconventional image, at once relevant and yet puzzling, that evades easy definition.

As he resists compromise with current literary and political fashions, so he will not relinquish his rather aristocratic style of commitment, in one sense remaining above the frays, while on the more profound levels, very much participating down inside of them; and as much by refusing the lie as by telling his truth, Ellison has been consistently and deeply *engagé*, as a man, as a Negro writer, as a representative of Western culture. His reputation often seems on the verge of an eclipse, because of the second novel's delay; but art is more lasting then politics or even literary politics and with each passing year, with each rereading, *Invisible Man* confirms its place among the best American fictions of all times and continues to infiltrate the collective consciousness of new generations of readers. Its mythic resonance, its complex human truth, its political relevance, the wit of its prose, and the energy of its narrative all give the novel an indestructible stature, if not the status of "a classic"; and all these qualities as well attest to Ellison's intelligence as a man and his conscientiousness as an artist. So few second novels in literary history have been so long in labor as Ralph Ellison's forthcoming work, and even fewer have been as eagerly, and yet patiently, awaited.

Leslie A. Fiedler (1972)

There is no doubt that Leslie A. Fiedler aimed from his professional beginnings to be not just a critic but a genuine all-round man-of-letters, publishing not only controversial essays but also poetry and fiction soon after his literary debut; and he has followed all these muses, as well as a powerful one for public speaking, throughout his career. His fiction is, by common consent, less interesting and less original than his criticism (and his poetry even less substantial); and few critics of conscience have ever honored his imaginative work in print. In his opening critical essays, eventually collected as *An End to Innocence*, Fiedler established a knack for controversial argument, full of far-fetched connections and exaggerated remarks, all expressed in equally provocative prose; few since Mencken have provoked so much outrage. Rejecting the simple sentence along with the simplistic idea, Fiedler concocted a robust style composed of long and convoluted clause-compounded sentences riddled by paradoxes, parentheses and charming self-ironies. However, only the tough-minded intelligence behind this forceful style, rather than the characteristic language, informs his fictions, which nonetheless reflect certain ideas in his criticism (which, in turn, sometimes mentions, if not quotes, his fiction!). The key theoretical text is the brilliant title essay opening his second collection, *No! in Thunder*, where Fiedler argues that the great modern writers have responded to ideals, institutions and even people with uncompromised negation — the Melvillian cry of "No! in Thunder" indicating a complete stripping down that reveals inadequacy, deceit, failure and the impossibility of perfection. "The No! in Thunder is never partisan," Fiedler writes, "it infuriates Our Side as well as Theirs, reveals that all Sides are one, insofar as they are all yea-sayers and hence all liars."

The title of his first collection of stories, *Pull Down Vanity*, announces the characteristic strategy of his fiction, for most of the pieces here are shaped around the uncovering of illusory images presented by a person or group; and in this stripping away of human artifice is unveiled another favorite Fiedler theme of universal culpability. Thus, these stories are structured around actions of exposure and embarrassment — a technique admittedly indebted to Nathanael West's *The Day of the Locust* (1939). Thus, should readers come to believe that one of Fiedler's characters might be

103

honest and good, the rug is pulled out before the story is done, leaving that character too sprawled in the fundamental mud. In "Nude Croquet," first published in *Esquire* in 1957, a busty young thing darkens a party's room and then leads a group of middle-aging "intellectuals" in playing croquet in the buff. Not at all uncomfortable, she flaunts her fresh figure, forcing the others to uncover both their masked bodily defects and, then, their spiritual vanities. One has body hair different in color than that on her head, another a withered leg, a third is flat-chested, while on another level one is insanely jealous, another has never completed his projected and much-announced masterpiece, a third has "sold out" to commercial theater. When the group's slightly older idol collapses from over-exertion and dies of a heart attack, the girl screams a long blast as the lights go on. "Molly-o," Fiedler writes, "confronted them in the classic pose of nakedness surprised, as if she knew for the first time what it meant to be really nude." Discovering one's nudity is, symbolically, recognizing comparable inadequacies and culpability.

Fielder's first and best novel takes for its unusual subject the demonic attachment of unrelated twins who, once childhood friends, re-encounter each other over a dozen years. One character speaks of "a comedy of confused identities," and these confusions are not only witty, but also difficult to summarize. The novel's protagonist, Clem Stone, is an unsuccessful writer, while his friend is Mark Stone, an eminent TV intellectual and existentialist rabbi. In the past, Clem was named Mark Stone, and the present Mark's last name was Stein. But as the present Mark changed his surname, his friend Clem, overshadowed by the more successful Mark, became known as Mark the second, or Mark Twain. As the historical author Twain's real identity was Samuel Clemens, Stone takes the first name of Clem. The two Stones have always competed for the same goals, and before the novel is over, Clem seduces Mark's pregnant wife. The novel is similarly erudite in its joking, as in one scene Mark pummels his wife with a rolled-up copy of a magazine entitled *Thou*; and he is described, of course, as unable to stop stuttering "I-I-I-I." Long on such literary gags and arch symbols, *The Second Stone* is also short on credible surface and literary importance.

The protagonist of Fiedler's second novel, *Back to China*, is a college teacher in Montana, whose career in some respects parallels Fiedler's own — a Jew from the East teaching in the West, with a reputation for being the most famous radical on campus, the author of several books, a former wartime Japanese interpreter in the Far East; but whereas Fiedler himself has been a father several times over, Baro Finklestone's main problem is that he and his wife are childless. The reason, as we learn through a series of flashbacks, is that Finklestone's life, as well as the book's plot, turned upon a vasectomy, an irreparable voluntary sterilization, that he underwent in China. His reasons for doing this are never made entirely clear — indeed, the act itself is barely credible — and the novel never quite emerges from a mire of absurdities. Indeed, this slide toward preposterousness, which comes from mixing too much realistic, highly detailed, almost pedantic satire with more wholly symbolic fantasy—a mismating of Sinclair Lewis with Franz Kafka—becomes even more pronounced in the three novellas collected as *The Last Jew in America*; and Fiedler's most recent book of fiction, *Nude Croquet*, adds four slighter stories to those previously collected. A more suggestive step comes in *Being Busted*, an autobiographical memoir devoid of proper names, that successfully elevates to imaginative myth not only Fiedler's 1967 arrest on a marijuana-related charge but also his responses to the life-styles of his children; for Fiedler ranks among the few writers of his post-fifty generation to suffer genuine confrontation and rebirth.

If Fiedler the critic is ambitious and original, as well as appreciative of eccentricity, the novelist is rather conventional in style, structure and subject-matter—his own fiction scarcely acknowledging the innovative literature praised in his criticism; and the impact of his recent rebirth has so far been more intellectual than artistic. A truth of literature's past apparently unremembered in all this effort is that the critics as major as Fiedler have rarely produced consequential fiction, try as much as they otherwise might. With his encompassing theme of deflation, Fiedler's fiction suggests that marriage is insufferable, that adultery is inevitable and just as inevitably disappointing; and his fictions deal as well with ambivalent attitudes toward paternity, to slavish obsessions with seduction's ulterior motives, and the terrors of American professors and intellectuals. This rather limited range is, needless to say perhaps, closer to more prosaic writing than to what Fiedler the critic has defined as the great tradition of American imaginative prose.

Interchangeable Parts (1975)

In his introduction to the anthology *Statements* (1975), subtitled "New Fiction from the Fiction Collective," the novelist Ronald Sukenick claims that the book "presents a selection of previously unpublished fiction in a wide range of styles. These stories are not easy to categorize, a fact which is symptomatic of the new scene in fiction. Not only are the new fiction writers working in a great variety of styles, but these styles bear the mark of individual expression rather than of an avant-garde with its militant ideologies." With this grand assertion in mind, consider this extended passage from the book:

> "Just a fragment!" Harmon sobbed bitterly as he stirred the ashes in the grate and then bent down and transferred a shovelful of the sizzling embers into my lap. I woke up in a panic. Stand up straight or you'll grow up crooked. It is dark. I stare out the window into the darkness. I wanted to be exactly on time. I've come to depend on Arthur more than I care to admit. My solution for the cemetery strike which affected New York City in early June of 1973 is as follows and I offer it to the city as a plan for preventing any such occurrences in future [sic] and as a means whereby cemeteries can be financially self-sufficient and with luck (good or ill) profit-making. They had a good idea when they named this place Plainville. The sun was hanging directly above the island. "Ah, did you once see Shelley plain," one of my mother's beloved lines, delivered on this occasion with some irony as we watched Jasper McLevy, the famed socialist mayor of Bridgeport, climb down from his ancient Model T. Well, yes, but he ended up helping her along in that. They would arrive at dusk so that the large rental truck could pass unnoticed down our main street and through the campus. You won't believe this fucking scene. A baby, rumored to be taking a nap, makes an unanticipated appearance. The young woman sat at the end of the bar near the door. She is not absolutely anything. I will not have her agreeing to be my victim. First, I'll tell the first trip the way he told it to be. It was a Sunday afternoon. He felt two small hits as he listened to the music from the bandshell, as if he had been struck by some pebbles; in fact, if he hadn't glanced at his shoulder and noticed the blood that was seeping through his t-shirt he would have paid no attention to it at all. There seems little point in continuing.

Though the tone and diction in this passage are fairly consistent and "fine," it is actually a pastiche, composed of the opening sentences of fictions respectively by Michael Brownstein, Andrei Codrescu, Ronald Sukenick, Mark Mirsky, B.H. Friedman, Walter Abish, Mark Strand, John Ashbery, Ursule Molinaro, Maureen Howard, Russell Banks, Jerry Bumpus, R.D. Skillings, Jonathan Baumbach, Fielding Dawson, Clarence Major, Raymond Federman, Peter Spielberg, Steve Katz, and Israel Horovitz. ("There seems little point in continuing.") The only statementers not included in this composite are Jerome Charyn, M.D. Elevitch, Ishmael Reed, Frederic Tuten, and Eugene Wildman. Since this tribe speaks in a single voice, Sukenick's claim is so egregiously erroneous that one rightly wonders not only what prompted him to write it, but also how it passed unscathed through his colleagues, his publisher, the house editor, the proof-readers, and lord knows who else? Since most of these identical wordsmiths are full-time university professors, one is reminded, to counter Sukenick again, of an encompassing tag-line to categorize this kind of fiction — academic, yes, uniformly academic.

"The Fiction Collective"
Again (1978)

In a review of the first anthology of the Fiction Collective, *Statements* (1975), I suggested that the contributors tended to sound alike. To confirm my impression, I quoted a paragraph, fairly consistent in language tone and diction, which was in fact composed of the opening sentences of nearly all the stories in the book. In a protesting letter to the editor, Ronald Sukenick, who introduced *Statements*, replied, "Concerning Kostelanetz's nutty claim that all these writers sound alike, all I can say is he must have a tin ear."

Notwithstanding Sukenick's second-hand appraisal of my anatomy, I decided to look at the Fiction Collective's second self-anthology, *Statements 2* (1977); and in its pages I found the following:

> Some four hundred years later, American social workers, with the cooperation of freethinking psychiatrists, launched a campaign to legitimize the utilization of this button for the achievement of better mental health. Be watched him buy tokens. It didn't occur to me to write a novel with A. as a prototype for its hero, Hamilton Stark, until fairly recently, a year ago this spring, as a matter of fact, when I drove the forty miles from my home in Northwood across New Hampshire to his home outside the town of B. He was glad to be back from his trip. But as soon as he said it he realized that being back was just the beginning of another trip. P____ is middle aged, of medium height, neckless, bullet-headed, with features that are unrefined, almost blank. He has been stout, but has been losing weight for no apparent reason. He was in the city, but it was his own block. Packed off to Germany by his father and Admiral Max, who expected him to destroy the republican stinkholes in France and the British Isles, Jude was declared unfit by the regular army on account of his age (fourteen) and pitiful upbringing (tutor Matthew, in his passion to teach Jude the names of Balleneran objects and institutions, hadn't bothered to stuff the infante's head with the practical matters of long division, and the irrational laws of grammar).
>
> I returned from Morocco in September in time for my exhibition of photographs at the Light Gallery on Madison Avenue. Most of the exhibition was devoted to photographs I had taken of the Mosque of Kairouan, and the city of Kairouan which is surrounded on all sides by desert. One day a man swimming off the point returned to shore with much, if not

most, of his left leg missing. He was as surprised as the rest of us to discover what had happened. There was once a recipe, published in the periodical 'Chefs of 3 Continents'—an esoteric gourmet-cooking journal—and this recipe was for a French dish, I forgot the name, which consisted of a fresh, broiled trout served over 'a steaming, swelling bed of firm, ripe, round mushrooms and rice, simply wallowing in its own special deep, succulent, wine sauce.'

The first morning I slipped off the ladder of my loft bed and landed on my ass. I cried. That night, as I slept on the floor in the next room, she died, the pages of the last chapter scattered among the bedcovers and indecipherable notes she had been scribbling at the end. I see blood here I am in myself. But tell me this, my dear: what happened to his ashes? My mother-in-law asked the day after my cremation. And Gwen, I am amused to report, did not know what to say. My God I swear—like the lilies of the field—all of them spread all over the world. What more can we do to ourselves? Is that the question that keeps lights burning in this house through till morning?

The other day as I walked my dog down the beach and watched him sniff the breeze I happened to cut my foot on a rusty piece of iron that was sticking out of the pebbles. I was down on the wharf, I saw this beautiful girl, I sidled over, you know, we got talking and she says You know a cheap place I could stay tonight? "You look like you could use a friend," she said. She sat at the next desk to mine in the Madison Avenue office in which we worked. Everybody knows that men are the true artists. Where are your great women composers, conductors? I know that it was lunch not supper because I remember hours of bad feeling afterwards that corrupted the sweet country air. The beautiful girl stands looking into the store window.

Notwithstanding the rather consistent penchants for unlikely details, sharp transitions and clumsy connectives, *this* passage is drawn from the first and or second sentences in anthologized stories respectively by the following contributors: Peter Spielberg, Thomas Glynn, Russell Banks, Ronald Sukenick, B.H. Friedman, Richard Grayson, Jerome Charyn, Walter Abish, Jonathan Baumbach, Bruce Kleinman, Steven Schrader, Jerry Bumpus, Clarence Major, Marianne Hauser, Elaine Kraf, Leon Rooke, Steve Katz, R.D. Skillings, Mimi Albert, Laura Kramer, Glenda Adams, Ursule Molinaro—in sum, all but two of the twenty-four contributors to *Statements 2*. This *is* the period-style for our time. *Q.E.D.*

Avant-Garde Past (1981)

Now that we have known Samuel Beckett and William S. Burroughs for over two decades apiece, we can associate with each the radical literary development of a single esthetic idea; and the idea identified with each of them has the common quality of previous acceptance in the visual arts. For Beckett, the key idea was lessness or, to be precise, lessness as moreless or, to be more precise, the possibilities of moreness with lessness; for it has been his aim to create not rhetorical splendor (in emulation of his immediate mentor James Joyce) but a language so spare it would render silence resonant.

The quiet of his early plays is universally familiar; his later plays are yet more spare, often consisting of monologues punctuated by silences, so distinctly unique we call them Beckettian. There has been a parallel, if less familiar, evolution in his fiction—away from the repetitious, limited vocabulary (which now curiously seems more Steinian than Joycean) to such non-syntactic flows as these from *Comment c'est* (1961):

> in me that were without when the panting stops scraps of an ancient voice
> in me not mine

To me, one root of Beckett's success is that he is nearly always at once abstract and yet very concrete.

His latest book of prose, *Company* (1980), is likewise filled with images of pointlessness (and thus, by interpretative extension, of meaninglessness), but it is structured not as punctuation-less fragments but as a series of prose vignettes, each a single paragraph in length. Here is a characteristic beginning:

> If the voice is not speaking to him it must be speaking to another. So with what reason remains he reasons. To another of that other. Or of him. Or of another still. To another of that order or of him or of another still. To one of his back in the dark in any case. Of one on his back in the dark whether the same or another. So with what reason remains he reasons and reasons ill [etc.].

Some of the paragraphs have autobiographical overtones that are really beside the point (except to certain scholars), while others intimate a "philosophy" that is no more than an assemblage of modernist platitudes (making most "critical" interpretations of it compendia of clichés). Rather, what distinguishes Beckett — what gives him a secure place in literary history — is his innovative style, which is largely an exploration of the possibilities of linguistic lessness. Nobody wrote like this before him, while everyone who has done so since invariably echoes him.

William Burroughs' debt to visual art was collage — the taking of materials that were not initially created in sequence and do not inherently belong in sequence and then splicing them together not only to make them comment on each other but also to create a quality of awesome leaps in time and space. Onto this style he grafted a vision obsessed by degradation and, at times, by redemption from degradation (an element that I find less attractive than his style). *Naked Lunch* (1958) is the great book that established Burroughs' literary reputation, and it remains a great book, full of both particular passages and a general quality that stick in one's head. However, it seems to me that collage has finally become a terribly hackneyed form, a familiar staple in every art today. Perhaps the surest test of this generalization is that I can think of no distinguished work, *in any art*, that is syntactically based on collage. (Rauschenberg's major assemblages, we remember, preceded 1958, while Karlheinz Stockhausen's awful *Hymnen*, to cite one example among many later collages, was composed well after then.)

Burroughs' new book, *Cities of the Red Night* (1981), is billed by its publisher as a *"magnum opus*, perhaps even more important than *Naked Lunch,"* which it knows as well as everyone else remains Burroughs' milestone. For this new work Burroughs recycles extraordinary characters who appeared in his earlier books, such as Dr. Benway; but he exploits our memory of them, rather than adding to our sense of their specialness. He also exploits a prurient interest in homoerotic-pharmatopia — a subject that has made him a favorite contemporary writer for some who have no other favorites. Remembering a 1966 interview in which Burroughs declared he was "quite deliberately addressing myself to that whole area of what we call dreams," it is easy for us to read *Cities of the Red Night* as a succession of transcribed fantasies. However, whereas *Naked Lunch* was a horrific journey, as difficult in style as in content, this is an accessible travelogue, written mostly in a cornball pulp-novel style that verges on becoming parody, not only of its familiar sources but, alas, of itself.

Nonetheless, glimmers of his earlier genius occasionally appear, usually in his hyperboles and in descriptions of young men:

> Shortly thereafter a boat was lowered and it rowed toward us. Standing in the stern was a slim blond youth, his gold-braided coat glittering in the sun. Beside him was a youth in short gray pants and a shirt with a red scarf around his neck. The boat was rowed by what appeared to be a crew of women, singing as they rowed and turning toward us to leer and wink with their painted faces.

The "women" turn out to be "handsome youths in women's garb"—a dreamy homoerotic revelation that might be more of a surprise to some Burroughs readers than to others. This book is a series of episodes that are arranged neither as linear sequence nor as collage—in essence, a structure similar to a *New Yorker* feature piece or, say, Saul Bellows' *To Jerusalem and Back* (1976)—while the book as a whole suffers from a desultory quality that suggests that it was edited either too much or not enough.

Of all the books that Burroughs has written since *Naked Lunch*, the most extraordinary, to my mind, is *The Third Mind* (1978), which is a collection of dry interviews/explanations and audacious experiments done mostly in collaboration with, or under the influence of, Brion Gysin, the book's ostensible co-author. It includes samples of his cut-up writing (which is not collage, where the parts are chosen to effect each other, but systematic, yet aleatoric mixes of words from different domains). Here Burroughs is broaching a literary territory that has scarcely been explored; but it is others, not he, who presently stand at the frontier. I should add that, though likewise a libertarian, I have trouble with Burroughs' politics, which appears to base our common social philosophy not on sexual freedom or on free drugs—two good places to start—but on the right of everyone to a gun of his choice.

Samuel Beckett and William S. Burroughs are contemporary masters—not guys who have pounded the beat for a lifetime, but the authors of undisputed masterpieces. Lessness and collage were true innovations for literature twenty years ago, but by now they are milestones that, in turn, any avant-garde that is worthy of that name must decisively surpass.

The New Fictions

It is a curious anomaly that we listen to jazz, we look at modern paintings, we live in modern houses of modern designs, we travel in jet planes, yet we continue to read novels written in a tempo and style which is not of our time and not related to any of these influences. The new swift novel could match our modern life in speed, rhythms, condensation, abstraction, miniaturization, x-rays of our secrets, a subjective gauge of external events. — Anaïs Nin, *The Novel of the Future* (1969).

Before there was an art of abstract painting, it was already widely believed that the value of a picture was a matter of color and shapes alone. Music and architecture were constantly held up to painters as examples of a pure art which did not have to imitate objects but derived its effects from elements peculiar to itself. — Meyer Schapiro, "Nature of Abstract Art" (1937).

We are told that our individualist art has touched its limits, and its expression can go no further. That has often been said; but if it cannot go farther, it still may go elsewhere. — André Malraux, *The Imaginary Museum* (1953).

I often have the suspicion that this critical cowardice stems from the disinterest in contemporary literature evidenced by so many academics, but from the fact that writing is becoming something fundamentally different from what it was in the past, so much so that traditional criticism is unable to deal with it.

That we have a multiplicity of trends in every art form today is obvious. It might be that this fact has some deep significance that has, so far, eluded most critics. The old adage that there is no "progress" in art may blind them to the fact that the contemporary arts, if they have not "progressed," may at least be evolving into something very different from what they were in the past. — Richard Morris, "A Dadaist Manifesto" (1982).

Dada and the Future of Fiction
(1968)

Art, if you want a definition of it, is criminal action. It con-
forms to no rules, not even its own. — John Cage, *A Year
from Monday* (1967).

Dada and Surrealism are popularly regarded as nearly synonymous
movements, or as precursor and successor in the step-by-step history of
modern art; but even though their memberships overlapped and both
espoused two major esthetic positions in common — the irrelevance of
nineteenth-century forms of comprehension and the rejection of established
modes of artistic rendering — they differed from each other in one crucial
aspect. Whereas Surrealism was the art of representing subconscious
psychological terrains, the Dadaists dealt primarily with the external
world — the character of the commonly perceived environment, patterns of
intellectual and artistic coherence, standard definitions of meaning and
significance. Therefore, while Surrealistic art represents the experience of
hallucinations, Dada favors the distortion, usually ludicrous, of familiar
contexts, and the rendering of worldly absurdity. Salvador Dali and André
Breton, for instance, purportedly cast their interior fantasies in objective
forms, and, unlike the Dadaists, acknowledged the theories of Sigmund
Freud. Marcel Duchamp, in contrast, drew his model from the mundane
environment (often *finding* his actual material there) and thereby confronted
Art with "non-art," implicitly questioning all absolutist esthetics and
creating impersonal objects that relate not to the psychic life of his audience
but to their perception of the world around them.

The masters of Dada used a variety of esthetic designs on behalf of their
purposes. One consisted of infusing distortion and mundane gesture into
a conventional form — painting a mustache on Mona Lisa, speaking gib-
berish at a poetry reading, fragmenting an image or narrative beyond the
point of comprehension, introducing a urinal into an exhibition of
sculpture, etc. At its best, the dash of nonsense reveals the ridiculous irrelevance of certain social or artistic hierarchies and conventions, as well
as initiating an anti-convention for subsequent modern art (e.g., the artistic

117

validity of all manufactured objects). And this rejection of established forms of order complemented a political bias which was anarchistic. Whereas surrealism is concise and imagistic, like poetry, Dada is more diffuse, like fiction.

A second Dada strategy was the mixing of expressive means in ways previously unknown to the hybrid presentational arts such as opera, the primary mixed-means art of the nineteenth century. Dadaists created performance events in which the sound intentionally did not accompany the movement, or one dimension stood in incongruous juxtaposition to another. By analogy, Dadaists working in a particular artistic medium scrupulously short-circuited the evenly modulated styles and the linear structures of traditional art. "So they came to a new device of literary expression," writes Moholy-Nagy in *Vision in Motion* (1947), "to a crisscrossing, zigzagging thought-pulsation of as many currents and messages as could be transmitted at the same time."

These strategies made all substances available to artists and held that these materials could be combined in any way. (Therefore, all subsequent art that used unusual materials in unprecedented miscegenations has inevitably been hailed as a species of neo-Dada—happenings, combines, Pop art, etc.) Into this absurd context often came an allusion to something traditionally of ultimate significance—the quality of modern life, the meaning of existence, or God himself—so that the work achieved what Jacob Korg appropriately calls "the characteristic Dada blend of hoax and metaphysical statement."

Although prose fiction has always been a major medium by which the intellectual public understands its environment, the original Dadaists, unlike the Surrealists, made no significant contribution to the traditions of imaginative narrative; and, as Martin Esslin judges in *The Theatre of the Absurd* (1961), "The movement never produced a real impact on the stage." Instead, the historical evidence confirms Hans Richter's suggestion, in *Dada: Art and Anti-Art* (1965), echoed by William S. Rubin in his *Dada, Surrealism and Their Heritage* (1968), that the primary revolution occurred in the visual arts. It is true that many of the official Dadaists (as distinguished from spiritual fellow-travelers) committed words to paper, but these writings tended to be poems, manifestos, or chronicles of their own activities, rather than fiction or even theatre [see Robert Motherwell, ed., *The Dada Painters and Poets* (1951)]; and this is perhaps the reason why Dada has subsequently had more apparent influence upon poets than upon fiction writers.

The literary innovations of Dada stemmed from disrupting or, more literally, decomposing conventionally sensible forms. "We began to write series of words having no apparent consecutive sense," remembers Tristan Tzara. "This method presupposed that words could be stripped of their meaning and yet still be effective in a poem by their simple evocative power—a kind of magic as hard to understand as it is to formulate." Around 1917,

Hugo Ball declaimed similarly non-syntactical "poetry" in Zurich, and Kurt Schwitters infused a kind of doubletalk into a satirical love poem entitled *Anna Blume* (1919). The climax to this tendency was Schwitters' *Ursonata* (1924), which Moholy-Nagy describes as "a poem of thirty-five minutes' duration containing four movements, a prelude, and a cadenza in the fourth movement. The words do not exist; rather they might exist in any language. They have no logical, only an emotional context; they affect the ear with their phonetic vibration like music." However, if only because Schwitters uttered these sounds in a situation where poetry was expected, they should be considered not music but literature. "Abstract poetry," he later wrote, "released the word from its associations—this is a great service—and evaluated word against word and, in particular, concept against concept, with some thought paid to sound." Had Schwitters perhaps chosen to announce, in a galvanized gesture, that his words comprised a story, rather than a poem (and since both artists and critics invariably attribute significance to such acts of imposed definition), Schwitters might have made an equally revolutionary contribution to the art of prose fiction, as well as further challenged, as much avant-garde activity does, academic conceptions of the boundaries separating one art from another.

Another extreme literary innovation occurred twelve years later when Marcel Duchamp was asked for his autobiography. "With a typical Dadaist gesture," writes Moholy-Nagy, "he emptied the contents of his desk — notes, drawings and photographs of the last twenty-five years — into a cardboard box. All this was faithfully reproduced and put into a portfolio without chronological or any other order, leaving the 'mess' to be disentangled by the reader." The ultimate theme of Dada esthetics was creative freedom — that literally anything was possible in any art, including the forms of literature; and even though most practitioners could not overcome the constraints that every artist inherits with his training and self-apprenticeship, those who took the leaps of freedom established radical precedents for future work.

The double paradox is that even anti-art inevitably reveals the influence of previous arts, as well as creates esthetic examples that shape future art. Perhaps because the ideas informing Dada were in essence quite simple, although original and unfamiliar to both art history and most artists, its impact upon functioning creative intelligences was liable to be both quicker and more subliminal than the complex thought of, say, Wittgenstein's philosophy or contemporary physics; thus, I suspect that the Dada spirit has probably infiltrated all contemporary minds whose sensibilities were susceptible, slipping, for instance, into the fiction of writers only dimly aware of the original work. What supports this conjectural measure of Dada's impact is my sense that some of the most inventive and profound fictions of recent times are indebted in perceptible respects to its ideas; for as Tzara judged in 1951, he and his colleagues created "a new intellectual climate which still in some measure survives."

II

The novel's forms must evolve in order [for the genre] to
remain alive. — Alain Robbe-Grillet, *Pour un nouveau roman*
(1963).

What makes the Dadaists' neglect of prose fiction so surprising is the
fact that one of their acknowledged precursors, Alfred Jarry, had twenty
years before Dada's heyday written an innovative fiction that realized in
prose many of Dada's esthetic and metaphysical prejudices. *Exploits and
Opinions of Doctor Faustroll, Pataphysician*, sub-titled "A Neo-Scientific Novel"
(although it runs to only eighty pages in Simon Watson Taylor's translation), was drafted in 1898, when Jarry was twenty-five, nine years before
his premature death. Unable to publish his manuscript at the time, he en-
trusted it to friends, who provided it for the first French edition in 1911, just
as the spirits that became Dada were fermenting.

The narrative's opening paragraph, which follows a fictitious document that serves as an introductory framing device, establishes an absurd
tone, beneath a veneer of reasonableness, that the novel sustains:

> Doctor Faustroll was sixty-three years old when he was born in Cir-
> cassia in 1898 (the 20th century was [− 2] years old).
> At this age, which he retained all his life, Doctor Faustroll was a man
> of medium height, or to be absolutely accurate, of $(8 \times 10^{10} + 10^9 + 4 \times 10^8 + 5 \times 10^6)$ atomic diameters: with a golden-yellow skin, his face
> clean-shaven, apart from a sea-green mustachios, as worn by king Saleh;
> the hairs of his head alternately platinum blonde and jet black, an auburn
> ambiguity changing according to the sun's position; his eyes, two capsules
> of ordinary writing ink flecked with golden spermatozoa-like Danzig
> Schnapps.

What plot there is, amidst the numerous digressions, consists of Faustroll's
adventures, in the company of the bailiff Panmuphle and an idiotic creature
named Bosse-de-Nage (literally "bottom-face"); and this narrative starkly
violates several kinds of mundane credibility — chronological,
geographical, psychological, social and biological.

In the course of the fiction, the absurd surface progressively assumes
metaphysical resonance, as at one point Faustroll says in passing, "I am
God," and at another point Jarry introduces "pataphysics," which he then
defines as "the science of that which is superinduced upon metaphysics,
whether within or beyond the latter's limitations, extending as far beyond
metaphysics as the latter extends beyond physics." A few lines later
Faustroll feigns the process of expository elaboration: "Pataphysics is the
science of imaginary solutions, which symbolically attributes the properties
of objects, described by their virtuality, to the lineaments." The climax to

this book, which has a surprisingly linear structure (imposed partly by the adventure story motif), comes in the forty-first and last chapter, which ends a larger section wittily entitled "Ethernity." "Concerning the Surface of God," as the concluding chapter is called, is a fiction in the form of a scientific proof, in which the narrator uses geometrical hypotheses and algebraic equations, the highest rituals of reason, eventually to prove:

> DEFINITION: *God is the shortest distance between zero and infinity.*
> In which direction? one may ask.
> We shall reply that His first name is not Jack, but *Plus-and Minus*. And one should say:
> $\pm$ God *is the shortest distance between 0 and* ∞, *in either direction*.
> Which conforms to the belief in the two principles; but it is more correct to attribute the sign + to that of the subject's faith.
> But God being without dimension is not a line.
> — Let us note, in fact, that, according to the formula
> $$\infty - 0 - a + a + 0 = \infty$$
> the length a is nil, so that a is not a line but a point.
> Therefore, *definitively*:
> GOD IS THE TANGENTIAL POINT BETWEEN ZERO AND INFINITY.
> Pataphysics is *the* science. . .

In *Faustroll* alone, Jarry initiated several revolutionary precedents for modern fiction — among them the familiar devices of "Black Humor" and moderately expressive typography and, more importantly, the related principles that all kinds of printable material could be incorporated into the text of imaginative prose and that literally anything can occur in a fiction; indeed, he suggested stylistic possibilities that went unheeded by the Dadaists themselves. Perhaps because this masterpiece, probably the first thoroughly absurd novel, has gone surprisingly unread — as has Jarry's later fabulous fiction, *The Supermale* (reprinted in *New Directions 18*) — even today, seventy years after *Faustroll* was written, it seems ahead of current advanced fictional practice.

The literary heirs to Dada are hardly plentiful or powerful in the politics of contemporary literature, although they are international in a way that the followers of subsequent Parisian innovations, such as the recent "new novel," are not. Most of the important French fictions in this spirit come from members of the "Collège de Pataphysics," founded in 1949 in Jarry's name and perpetuated by such French authors as Ramond Queneau and Eugene Ionesco. However, in comparison, with their master's work, the fictions of these last two men seem too contrived, too realistic, too linear, too subservient to various conventions. A more imaginative neo-Duchamp conception, though less impressive in realization, is Daniel Spoerri's *An Anecdoted Typography of Chance* (1966), which consists of an elaborate ironic commentary upon all the miscellaneous objects that Spoerri, also a recognized artist, happened to find on his crowded work-write-eat table at a certain time — the process, in which the reader vicariously participates, establishing the form of the whole. Another adventurer in paths reminiscent of Dada is the English novelist B.S. Johnson, whose novels, particularly *Albert Angelo* (1964), mix a variety of prose styles with unusually adventurous typography.

On the other hand, James Joyce's innovations, which are sometimes attributed to Dada, are something else entirely; for whereas Dada aimed for the comprehensive destruction of old forms, merely for the sake of decomposure, Joyce endeavored to create viable new forms, devising an unprecedented narrative structure in *Ulysses* (1922) and then fabricating in *Finnegans Wake* (1939) an original and comprehensible language which consistently conveys a multiplicity of resonances and meanings. Very much as Arnold Schoenberg accepted the disintegration of classical tonality as the first step toward creating a new musical language in the twelve-tone system, so Joyce started from the antithesis of syntactic chaos to synthesize a radically unprecedented technique for putting words together. Similarly, the multiple-narrator structure of Faulkner's *The Sound and the Fury* (1929) stems not from Dada, because its thematic purpose is not the disintegration of narrative but the portrayal of contrasts in perception; however, if perhaps Faulkner has chosen to run the four discrete narrations in parallel columns on the same page, he would have rather closely emulated in print the oral structure and perhaps the perceptual effect of the Dadaist *poème simultané*.

Among the many other authors who echo Dada devices for finally non-Dada purposes are, significantly, the two living masters of imaginative prose, Jorge Luis Borges and Samuel Beckett. The former recalls the Dadaists by casting some fictions as parodies of familiar forms—"Tlon, Uqbar, Orbis Tertius" (1940), is at once an encyclopedia entry and a futuristic fantasy, while "Pierre Menard, Author of the *Quixote*" (1939) looks like a eulogistic, critical article. The narrator of the latter tells of a recently deceased writer, Menard, whose masterwork came from composing out of his own head—not copying or remembering—several chapters of Cervantes' novel. However, Borges here, like Nabokov in *Pale Fire* (1962), is less concerned with debunking literary criticism or ridiculing Menard than with posing complex and ambiguous questions about the process of fictional imagination and the validity of historically relative standards. (Regarding this last point, Robbe-Grillet, whose critical bias is more persuasive than his imaginative practice, has asserted suggestively, "The twentieth-century novelist who reproduces *Don Quixote* word for word writes a totally different work from that of Cervantes.") Beckett perhaps comes closer to the Dada tradition, primarily in his liberties with language and syntax, as in *Comment c'est* (1961); but the tone embedded in his writings is finally too serious, if not ominous, to pass for Dada or even post-Dada.

III

Dada will experience a golden age, but in another form
than the one imagined by the Paris Dadaists. I am firmly
convinced that all art will become dadaistic in the course of
time, because from Dada proceeds the perpetual urge for
its renovation. — Richard Hulsenbeck, "Dada Lives," *transition* (Fall, 1936).

In a Faustrollian fantasy that denies all verification, I once imagined
that certain prematurely deceased Dadaists were reborn as American
writers named John Barth, Joseph Heller, Thomas Pynchon, Harry
Mathews, Donald Barthelme, Claes Oldenburg, William Burroughs and
Tom Veitch (perhaps midwived by Ionesco's acknowledged three greatest
influences — Harpo, Chico and Groucho); for they have realized in ex-
travagant prose fiction certain Dadaist inventions and biases, such as totally exterior representation, the absence of narrative resolution, unmitigated
blasphemous comedy, the decomposition of traditional forms, and the
rendering of worldly absurdity. Unlike the European Dadaists, these
Americans have worked largely apart from each other.

For instance, even though the narrative line of John Barth's *The Sot-
Weed Factor* (1960) is as horizontal as *Faustroll*, the book is a structurally vertical, systematic mockery, mostly in thoroughly detailed parodies, of
several contemporary and ancient philosophical ideas, the eighteenth-
century English novel, seventeenth-century English and American history,
a cartload of literary conventions, and much else besides, all to convey the
Dadaist theme that history itself is as ridiculous as most attempts to understand it definitively. In a more recent story, "Title," Barth creates three
simultaneous but overlapping narrators — one the writer contemplating his
inability to finish a novel, the second the writer considering the decline of
a love affair, the third the writer worried about the decay of the culture; and
in reading this story live, with two of the voices pre-recorded on
stereophonic tape, Barth adapts the Dadaist invention of *poème simultané* to
invigorate the decadent art of a literary recital.

Heller's *Catch-22* (1961), whose subject is the absurdity of modern war,
contains qualities reminiscent of Dada, if not of Jarry, who wrote in *Supermale*, "In fact, Marcueil embodied so absolutely the average man that his
very ordinariness became extraordinary." Conspicuous evidence of Dada
infuses Harry Mathews' less comprehensible but marvelously witty novels,
The Conversions (1962) and *Tlooth* (1966) and the better-known fictions of both
Donald Barthelme and Thomas Pynchon. Claes Oldenburg's *Store Days*
(1967), ostensibly a book about a neo-Dada environmental work of art entitled *The Store* (1962) that Oldenburg had previously constructed, is not a
work of criticism but a critical fiction. Parallelly, Kenneth King's "Super-
Lecture" (1966), reprinted in my *Young American Writers* (1967), is also an

ironic critical fiction cast in the form of a dancer's statement, whose narrator
is partially a fictitious creation, expressing partial sense beneath a veneer
of fantastic nonsense; John Cage's "Talk I" (1965), reprinted in *A Year from
Monday* (1967), recalls Schwitters' *Ursonata* in its intentional incomprehen-
sibility in a situation where sense is expected.

Both William Burroughs and Tom Veitch have successfully exploited
the Dada painters' technique of randomly incorporating whole chunks of
quoted or "found" material into their own narrative texts. The result is a
serendipitous art that even for Burroughs fails more often than not; but
when the technique works, the result can be readily original and yet suggestively coherent. Let me quote in their entirety the stunning second and
third paragraphs of Veitch's fiction, "The Luis Armed Story" (from *Art and
Literature 11*, also reprinted in *Young American Writers*).

> In the dimness of the cafe the manager is arranging the tables and
> chairs, the ashtrays, the siphons of soda water; it is six in the morning.
> I awoke early, shaved, dressed, draped myself with cameras and equip-
> ment, and went on deck to record our entry into the port of Gothenburg.
> In the beginning was the Word, and the Word was with God; and the
> Word was God. The Agon, then. In her tight-fitting Persian dress, with
> turban to match, she looked ravishing.
>
> This is the story of a man, one who was never at a loss. I can feel the
> heatv. . . heatv closing in, feel them out there making their moves, setting
> up their devil droll stool pigeons, crooning over my spoon and dropper I
> throw away at Washington Square Station, vault a turnstile and two
> flights down the iron stairs, catch an uptown A train. . . . For the reader
> familiar with analytical psychology there is no need of any introductory
> remarks to the subject of the following study. An eight-year decline of
> syphilis ended in 1955. "For a pansy." The purpose of this book is to pro-
> vide a concise yet comprehensive guide to the history and understanding
> of philosophy for the general reader.

To achieve this sense of fractured coherence and convey perceptual disorientation, Veitch actually used verbatim the opening sentences — randomly
"found" passages — of several books, including one by Burroughs, that were
lying near his writing desk. In short, several significant Dada strategies —
rendering the fixed unfixed and the comprehensible absurd, appropriating
unretouched materials of the environment, parodying familiar conventions,
creating uncompromisingly thorough blasphemy — continue to inform significant recent fictional work; so that although the original Dadaists themselves did not create any significant prose literature, there was and still is, in
the history of narrative art, a distinctly Dadaist fiction.

IV

The real technical question seems to me to be how to succeed not even Joyce and Kafka, but those who've succeeded

Joyce and Kafka and are now in the evenings of their own
careers. — John Barth, "The Literature of Exhaustion"
(1967).

In a previous long essay, I suggested, "Novelists have not contemplated deeply enough the formal possibilities of the novelistic format."
Since writers are generally more reluctant than other kinds of artists to
break the rules they learned in school, most of the novelists recognized today as important, by newspaper critics and academics alike, appropriate
archaic forms to represent experiences and make comments that invariably
seem similarly outdated; and these are among the primary causes of a sense
many have perceived — the increasing irrelevance of fiction. To my mind,
the necessity for new forms in fiction is as much artistic as philosophical or
even political. The relevance of Dada for the future of fiction lies in its emphasis upon external reality at a time when, since the environment
undergoes greater discernible change than the heads of men (though
change they likewise do), the commonly perceived world is likely to be a
more fertile subject for radical formal invention and, concomitantly, innovative truth than psychological processes.

One thing that is new is the prevalence of newness, the
changing scale and scope of change itself, so that the world
alters as we walk in it, so that the years of a man's life
measure not some small growth or rearrangement or
moderation of what he learned in childhood, but a great
upheaval. — J. Robert Oppenheimer.

Perhaps because the world around us continually evades all neatly encap-
sulating definitions, Dada's esthetic revolutions seem especially persuasive
to writers and readers who seek an appropriate form, if not the semblance
of illusory wisdom, for their not-knowing-profoundly about contemporary
life. Indeed, artfully disordered literature, in posing challenges to comprehension, also serves the beneficial function of honing the reader's mind
for the task of making sense of the chaos in his environment.

A second continually relevant thesis of Dada esthetics holds that any
and all forms and materials are available to literary artists — algebraic equa-
tions, maps and charts, graphic illustrations, pictures, typefaces of various
sizes and styles, unfamiliar or inscrutable languages, etc., etc. The highly
decomposed narrative of Michel Butor's *Mobile* (1962), which I consider one
of the most spectacular forays beyond the frontier, collects and juxtaposes
long lists of words commonly *found* around America, such as billboard
slogans or inscriptions on road signs; and this use of raw verbal data, within
the compositional structure of comprehensive collage, makes *Mobile*, to my
mind, one of the very best microtreatments of the large subject of our country today. Furthermore, since anyone who reads a great number of novels

eventually learns all the old tricks (and perhaps tries a few of them himself),
the problem for creators of imaginative prose is no longer that of infusing
life into familiar conventions but filling up the sheets of paper with persuasive fictions; and to this end, the writer should feel free to employ all the
discipline, cleverness, imagination and intellect he can muster. "A page is
an area," writes B.S. Johnson's narrator in *Albert Angelo*, "on which I may
place any signs I consider to communicate most nearly what I have to
convey."

From the esthetic assumptions of Dada inevitably follows the idea that
a fiction could viably consist primarily of pictures, perhaps abetted by
obliquely relevant texts and or a few attached props like Andy Warhol's
imaginatively conceived but trivially filled *Index (Book)* (1967); and one of
the most extraordinary recent fictional narratives, "Saga" (1968) by the
Frenchman Jean-François Bory (in *Approaches 3*), consists of twenty-eight
pages of photographic illustrations, each of which contains, among other
expressive designs, certain resonant words. (These observations persuade
me to note in passing that certain children's books at times seem formally
more adventurous than adult fare.) In that survey-review mentioned
before, I now find a sophisticated wisdom that I remember asserting out of
innocence: "There really exist no limits upon the kinds of fictions that can
be put between two covers."

On second thought, however, this particular formulation of unfettered
possibility now strikes me as needlessly conservative, if not compromised,
in one crucial respect; for if limits exist not to be respected but exceeded,
why should fictions, even those created out of words, necessarily be printed
on paper of uniform size and bound between covers? And why should a
writer piously accept the convention that all his words be printed in type
of the same size and style and then laid in evenly measured and modulated
grey lines? Why should a work of imagination necessarily have a discernible
beginning and an equally definite end? Why could not a narrative be
framed on a continuous sheet of paper wound, say, between two rollers,
printed not perpendicularly, like the *Torah*, but in lines parallel to the
spindles' shafts? Could not a writer create a room full of words cunningly
chosen, expressively designed, resonantly arranged, and artfully draped,
that would evoke the coherence of both environmental art and literature?
(Maybe such an environmental fiction could be mass-produced or "published" on screens that the purchasing "reader" could then circulate to his
taste around his own home.) In fact, why should the authors of fiction
necessarily deal in linear modes? Just as the French novelist Marc Saporta
created a book, offered in a box, whose unbound pages can be read in any
order, so a fiction appropriate for storage on an advanced computer (which,
given time-sharing, can be electronically linked into an individual reader's
home) should be similarly non-linear. That is, the random-access memory
of an advanced machine would enable the reader to appreciate discrete

segments in any order over his home console; and ideally, every sequence of the fiction's would provide him with more or less the same interest, coherence and pleasure. Indicatively, such discontinuous fictions as *Finnegans Wake* or *Naked Lunch* (1958) or Marvin Cohen's *The Self-Devoted Friend* (1967) would store more suitably on such a machine than nineteenth-century novels or, say, Mary McCarthy's *The Group* (1963).

What will, I think, primarily distinguish fiction of the future from the other arts will be an emphasis upon words, selected and arranged out of a taste for language, a measure of human significance, a sense of potential linguistic articulations, and an awareness of the viable traditions of literature; for the ultimate challenge of the new electronic media to printed literature consists not in appropriating the audience for writing but in forcing everyone who writes to eschew purposes that other media can realize more successfully, and, instead, consider profoundly the most propitious forms for his own devices and the manifold evocative possibilities of words.

Gertrude Stein (1975)

That they have nothing outside of themselves to say should
not be disturbing, even in literary plays, because no
literature, once you are out of school and have heard
everything, is interesting for what it has to say. — Donald
Sutherland, *Gertrude Stein* (1951).

I

What distinguishes Gertrude Stein (b. 1874) from nearly all of her
chronological contemporaries in American literature (e.g., Dreiser,
Stephen Crane, Vachel Lindsay, *et al.*) is that, even a century after her
birth, most of her works remain misunderstood. The principal reason for
such widespread incomprehension is that her experiments in writing were
conducted apart from the major developments in modern literature.
Neither a naturalist nor a surrealist, she had no interest in either the
representation of social reality or the weaving of symbols, no interest at all
in myth, metaphor, allegory, literary allusions, uncommon vocabulary,
synoptic cultural critiques, shifts in point of view or much else that preoccupied writers such as James Joyce, Thomas Mann and Marcel Proust.
Unlike them, she was an empiricist who preferred to write about observable
realities and personally familiar subjects; the titles of her books were
typically declarative and descriptive, rather than symbolic or allusive. Like
other modern writers, she was influenced by developments in the nonliterary arts; yet Stein feasted upon a fertile esthetic idea that the others
neglected — to emphasize properties and possibilities peculiar to one's
chosen medium and it alone. As her art was writing, rather than painting,
Stein's primary interest was language — more specifically, American
English and how else its words might be used. Indicatively, the same
esthetic idea that seems so acceptable in modernist painting and music was
heretical, if not unthinkable, in literature.

From nearly the beginning of her creative career, Stein experimented
with language in several ways. Starting from scratch, she neglected the
arsenal of devices that authors had traditionally used to vary their prose.
Though she was personally literate, her language is kept intentionally
unliterary and unconnotative. Her diction is mundane, though her

sentence structure is not, for it was her particular achievement to build a complex style out of purposely limited vocabulary. An early device, already evident in *Three Lives* (drafted around 1904), is the shifting of syntax, so that parts of a sentence appear in unusual places. Adverbs that customarily come before a verb now follow it, and what might normally be the object of a sentence either becomes its subject or precedes it. These shifts not only repudiate the conventions of syntactical causality, but they also introduce dimensions of subtlety and accuracy. Instead of saying "someone is alive," Stein writes, "Anyone can be a living one." As the critic Norman Weinstein points out, the present participle indicates "the *process* of living." Some parts of speech are omitted, while others are duplicated; and nouns, say, are used in ways that obscure their original function as a particular part of speech.

Especially in *The Making of Americans*, which was also drafted in this period, Stein inserts extra gerunds into otherwise normal clauses. Around this time she also began to remove adjectives, adverbs and internal punctuation, thereby increasing the ambiguity. Because parts of speech are scrambled, it is impossible to diagram even such a superficially simple sentence as this: "Any one being one being in any family living is being one having been saying something." And paraphrase is similarly counterproductive. Such devices not only tend to make her sentences more prolix than normal (in Stein's idiosyncratic heresy), but they are invariably more striking as well. Even rather commonplace perceptions become more witty and, in their ways, more elegant:

> Everybody called Gertrude Stein Gertrude, or at most Mademoiselle Gertrude, everybody called Picasso Pablo and Fernande Fernande and everybody called Guillaume Apollinaire Guillaume and Max Jacob Max but everybody called Marie Laurencin Marie Laurencin.

The subjects of Stein's books tended to be personally familiar — that of *Americans*, say, is the saga of her own family in America; for instead of "making up" plots and characters, she concentrated on inventing linguistic structures. She exemplifies what Hugh Kenner calls the "American preference for denotation over etymology."

In that 925-page milestone, her longest single book, Stein broached what subsequently became her initial notorious device — the use of linguistic repetition. To be precise, she repeats certain key words or phrases within otherwise different clauses and sentences; so that even though the repetitions are never exact, this repeated material comes to dominate the entire paragraph or section. The effect is initially wearisome — the reader's eye wants to leap ahead to something else, because he can quickly discern, by looking at the paragraph, which words will be emphasized. (And experienced readers, like experienced woodsmen, invariably short-cut by instinct.)

However, it would be wise to linger, or even to read the passage aloud, because what makes Stein's repetitions so interesting is the varying relationships that the repeated elements have to their surrounding frames. As phrases are rarely repeated exactly, what initially seems identical is, upon closer inspection, seen to be quite various, for one theme of Stein's repetitions (and near-repetitions) is the endless differences amid recurring sameness. Sometimes the repetition becomes a modifier, introducing degrees of reconsideration apart from punctuation (e.g., "not necessary not really necessary," "the story must be told will be told can be told"). As Kenneth Rexroth observed, "Gertrude Stein showed, among other things, that if you focus your attention on 'Please pass the butter,' and put it through enough permutations and combinations, it begins to take on a kind of glow, the splendor of what is called 'aesthetic object.' "

By dominating the reader's attention, repetitions become a device for focusing and emphasis; a passage is remembered in terms of this repeated material. (One thing that Stein probably learned from painting is the importance of an "after image.") She also believed that repetitions were a tool for penetrating beneath the surface of character:

> I began to get enormously interested in hearing how everybody said the same thing over and over again with infinite variations but over and over again until finally if you listened with great intensity you could hear it rise and fall and tell all that there was inside them.

This kind of comprehension was, in Stein's view, as much implicit as explicit: "Not so much by the actual words they said or the thoughts they had but by movement of their thoughts and words endlessly the same and endlessly different." By emphasizing not what was said but how, Stein paradoxically aimed to communicate, in the course of repetition, meanings that were ultimately beyond the capacities of language. (Documenting this contention remains, in my judgment, beyond the capacities of empirical criticism.)

In reading Stein, one finds that the reapplication of attention, especially after a lapse or rebuff, can produce a range of unusual effects, because the reader's mind is forced out of its customary perceptual procedures. While talking about something else, the composer John Cage once suggested, perspicaciously, "In Zen they say: If something is boring after two minutes, try it for four. If still boring, try it for eight, sixteen, thirty-two and so on. Eventually one discovers that it's not boring but very interesting." Though Stein personally abjured both alcohol and mind-changing drugs, both her work and Cage's rationale prophetically illuminate a certain kind of art that became particularly prevalent around the psychedelic apex of 1967 — works both visual and aural in which certain motifs are repeated to excess.

By itself, *The Making of Americans* seems "contemporary" long after it was written. Originally drafted in the first decade of this century, well before the innovative novels of James Joyce and William Faulkner, it was the first giant step beyond nineteenth-century fiction. Stein's big book also stands as an epitome of the colossal, uneven, excessive, self-contradictory masterpiece that every great American innovative artist seems to produce at least once. Its peers in this respect are Walt Whitman's *Leaves of Grass*, Ezra Pound's *Cantos*, and Charles Ives's Fourth Symphony. Not unlike other American geniuses, she walked a line between brilliance and looneyness, and her work was perceived as original or mad or both.

In addition to defining emphasis, Stein's linguistic repetitions also serve as a structural device, for the repeated word becomes the primary cohering force within a passage. Consequently, expository units, such as the paragraph, are reorganized. Instead of proceeding from a topic sentence through various examples, the paragraph is now filled with clauses that have equal weight within the whole; repetition becomes an effective equalizer.

> Not and now, now and not, not and now, by and by not and now, as not, as soon as not not and now, now as soon now now as soon, now as soon as soon as now. Just as soon just now just now just as soon just as soon as now. Just as soon as now. ["As a Wife Has a Cow: A Love Story" (1926)]

In Stein's view, the repetition of a single word can also evoke connotations, not only by taking on different meanings in varying contexts, but also through the suggestion of secondary qualities. In explaining her most famous repetition of "rose is a rose is a rose is a rose," she once told a university audience: "I'm no fool. I know that in daily life we don't go around saying [that], but I think that in that line the rose is red for the first time in English poetry for a hundred years." Readers struck by the simplicities of much Stein prose tend to forget how intelligent, conscious and literate she actually was, for only an assuredly intelligent author would risk the appearance of stupidity. In his classic *Seven Types of Ambiguity* (1929), William Empson places Stein with Dryden among those authors who "write with the whole weight of the [English] language, to remind one always of the latent assumptions of [English]." Her writing reveals her literacy not through echoes but the scrupulous avoidance of them.

These innovations, simple at base, had radical and complex repercussions. As she neglected subject, setting, anecdote, conflict, analysis and many other conventional elements, *style* became the dominant factor in Stein's writing. It became more important than "theme" or "character"; so that from *Americans* onwards, her books could be characterized as a succession of experiments in particular styles, other dimensions being merely incidental. (Even within *Americans*, her style becomes progressively more experimental.) Secondly, since language is primary, climactic structures become secondary; thus, narrative elements tend to be as flat and uninflected as Stein's language. To put it differently, the kind of structural flattening to which Stein subjected the paragraph was extended to the longer forms of exposition and narrative; so that even in the family history of *Americans*, no event is more important than any other. In this respect in particular, Stein clearly precedes the flat, counter-hierarchical prose of Samuel Beckett and Alain Robbe-Grillet.

This emphasis upon style also diminishes the importance of representational concerns, and that in turn contributes to an entirely different kind of flattening — the elimination of both temporal and spatial perspectives. (Stein herself said that her books take place in the "continuous present.") All these changes brought the abolition of linear causality in the portrayal of character and activity; and this enabled Stein to introduce an event at one point of *Americans* and then postpone further consideration of it for several hundred pages. Stein was among the first imaginative writers to represent the modern awareness of discontinuous experience. In the nineteenth century, as Donald Sutherland put it, "Something belongs to everything automatically. But nothing now is really convincingly a part of anything else; anything stands by itself if at all and its connections are chance encounters." In *Americans*, I find a sense of indefinite space in which characters are distant from their surroundings and each other, where environment is not a formative factor, where the sense of time is more spatial than sequential. In her *Lectures in America* (1935), Stein justifies not only her own penchant for fragmentary perception but that of others as a distinctly American style of literary representation: "A disembodied way of disconnecting something from anything and anything from something."

All these experiments in style progressively freed Stein from the restrictions of conventional syntax (and the Aristotelian logic informing it); so that in future works she was able to explore the possibilities of not just one but several kinds of alternative language. Having worked with accretion and explicitness, as well as syntactical transposition, she then experimented with ellipses and economy; having written about experience with many more words than usual, she tried to write with far, far less. In *Tender Buttons*, which was initially drafted around 1911, her aim was the creation of texts that described a thing without mentioning it by name (the book's title, for instance, suggesting women's nipples?). The prose passages filling this book each have a sub-title or opening words that provide a context for otherwise unexplicit language. This passage is prefaced by the sub-title of "A Box":

> Out of kindness comes redness and out of rudeness comes rapid same question, out of an eye comes research, out of selection comes painful cattle. So then the order is that a white way of being round is something

> suggesting a pin and is it disappointing, it is not, it is so rudimentary to
> be analysed and see a fine substance strangely, it is so earnest to have a
> green point not to red but to point again.

What distinguishes this passage is a scrupulous disregard for everyday
linguistic functions — not only conventional transitions but any definitions
of extrinsic experience; and the language could be called "poetic" simply
because it is not prosaic.

   Though critics commonly suggest that the words in *Tender Buttons* have
some implicit relation to one's experience of the ostensible subject, the prose
often is (and can be) perceived apart from any content. In reviewing Stein's
book for the *Harvard Advocate*, E.E. Cummings, then an undergraduate,
recognized that, "Gertrude Stein subordinates the meaning of words to the
beauty of the words themselves." In the following pasage of "Susie Asado,"
which opens *Geography and Plays* (1922), Carl Van Vechten finds "an attempt
to recapture the rhythm of [a] flamenco dancer":

> Sweet sweet sweet sweet sweet tea
>   Susie Asado.
> Sweet sweet sweet sweet sweet sweet tea
>   Susie Asado.
> Susie Asado which is a told try sure.
> A lean on the shoe this means slip slips hers.

I personally find that this passage lacks the blatant percussiveness of
flamenco dancing; but whether or not Van Vechten's impression is correct,
it is surely astonishing, unprecedented prose that has particular charms and
effects. It also "makes poetic sense" apart from any subject or content. As
Sherwood Anderson put it, "She is laying word against word, relating
sound to sound, feeling for the taste, the smell, the rhythm of the individual
word." Her writings represent, at base, an extended celebration of human
language.

II

> One may, and Gertrude Stein did, write as if every instant
> of writing were complete in itself, as if in the act of writing
> something were continually coming true and completing
> itself, not as if it were leading to something. — Donald
> Sutherland, *Gertrude Stein* (1951).

   Certain other prose pieces, composed mostly in the post–World War
I decade, are yet more extraordinary, having no apparent subject or other
semantic content at all, because their real theme — their major concern — is
the kinds of coherences established within language itself:

> Able there to ball bawl able to call and seat a tin a tin whip with a collar.
> The least license is in the eyes which make strange the less sighed hole
> which is nodded and leaves the bent tender.

This comes from "A Sweet Tale (Gypsies)," where another passage reads:

> Appeal, a peal, laugh, hurry merry, good in night, rest stole. Rest stole
> to bestow candle electricity in surface. The best header is nearly peek.

Here and elsewhere in Stein, words become autonomous objects, rather
than symbols of something else. Their unifying forces are stressed sounds,
rhythms, alliterations, rhymes, textures and consistencies in diction —
linguistic qualities other than subject and syntax; and even when divorced
from semantics, these dimensions of prose can affect readers. Especially in
the articulation of these qualities, Stein's language approaches the density
of *Finnegans Wake*. She also discovered that disconnection enhances
language, precisely because it transcends mundane sentences: "You use
the glasses as a magnifying glass and so read word by word reading word
by word makes the writing that is not anything be something."

Elsewhere she explains how this discovery was exploited: "I took individual words and thought about them until I got their weight and volume
complete and put them next to another word and at this same time I found
out very soon that there is no such thing as putting them together without
sense."

Having abandoned prolix paragraphs, she then made fictions out of
abbreviated notations, such as these from "The King or Something" in
Geography and Plays:

PAGE XV.

We didn't.
Allow me to differ.

PAGE XVI.

Did you say it did.

PAGE XVIII.

Very likely I missed it.

PAGE XIX.

Turn turn.

PAGE XX.

You must never hurry yourself.
No indeed
Now I understand.

PAGE XXI.

Think a minute think a minute there.

Not only does such compression (along with the omission of page XVII)
represent a radical revision of fictional scale, but writings like these also
realize, in Sutherland's judgment, "the first uncompromising attempt to

create [in literature] a thing existing in itself." Though working apart from the French symbolists, she realized their theoretical ideal of a completely autonomous language — creating a verbal reality apart from extrinsic reality. However, whereas the symbolists regarded language as the top of the iceberg, revealing only part of the underlying meaning, Stein was primarily concerned with literature's surfaces, asking her readers to pay particular attention to words, rather than the content and motives that might lie behind them. What you read is most of what there is.

Such prose is frequently called "musical," because of its distance from expository language; but since words divorced from the demands of syntax and semantics are still words, that metaphor is inaccurate. Nonetheless, such writing serves as an accurate analogy for atonality in music. Whereas composers such as Debussy and Schoenberg were abandoning the tonality of tonics and dominants — the standard musical syntax since the Renaissance — in order to emphasize the cohering capability of other dimensions of musical material, Stein had similarly eschewed conventional syntax for alternative emphases. By neglecting semantics as well, she was free to emphasize strictly indigenous elements. What initially attracted the composer Virgil Thomson to Stein's texts was this absence of extrinsic referents. "There was no temptation toward tonal illustration," he explained. "If a text were set correctly for the sound of it, the meaning will take care of itself." A contemporary reader can scarcely believe that these passages were written over fifty years ago.

Stein also recapitulated the evolution of modernist painting. Her earliest works could be considered "cubist" in their syntactical radicalism, the redistribution of traditional emphases, and the distortion of space-time representation, in addition to the twofold attempts not only to abstract the most important elements from a mass of detail but also to depict an underlying reality that was beyond exterior surfaces. Her later, post–WWI works strike me, by contrast, as decidedly non-representational, lacking even the suggestion of anything outside themselves. To put it differently, as purely abstract paintings represented nothing more than color and shape on two-dimensional canvases, so abstract writing consists purely of materials indigenous to the medium of language — words which are unified by elements other than syntax and semantics. Thus, just as each new abstract painting is largely indebted to previous paintings, so Stein's prose refers largely to previous works of language. At these formal levels, painting-as-painting resembles writing-as-writing. Passages like those quoted before could also be characterized as "acoherent" with respect to traditional kinds of linguistic coherence, much as the epithet "atonal music" has been used to distinguish the new ways of organizing sound from earlier tonalities. As the "meaning" of such passages lies wholly within language, rather than beyond it, this prose need not be "interpreted" in terms of other meanings. What you read is all there is.

Abandoning certain constraints upon language, she looked for other rules to guide her propensities for linguistic invention. By regarding language as a technology that exists apart from herself, she could subject it to various experimental modifications. Viewing herself as a disciplined intermediary, she would write passages with words of only one syllable and others with consistently abrupt sentences. An entire book was written in the voice of her lifetime companion, Alice B. Toklas. Attuned to the linguistic possibilities of non-verbal experience, she wrote non-syntactical prose whose rhythms echoed those made by her dog's lapping and other passages that imitated the sounds made on a Parisian street; she drafted a whole novel in close proximity to a waterfall (*Lucy Church Amiably*). Stylistic ideas, rather than any worldly subjects, were the root inspiration of her most extraordinary works. "Language as a real thing," she wrote in *Lectures in America*, "is not imitation either of sounds or colors or emotions it is an intellectual recreation." All this experimenting with the technology of language produced not merely one original style but several, some of which were quite different from the others, all of which seem, nonetheless, to be distinctly Steinian.

Although Stein initially regarded herself as a novelist, descending not only from Henry James and Gustave Flaubert, but also from the classic tradition of English fiction, she must have recognized that her emphasis upon verbal style was applicable to other genres as well. In sharp contrast to those modernist poets who dabbled in other genres, producing mostly conventional work (e.g., T.S. Eliot's plays, Pound's essays), Stein let her artistic predilections transcend the demands of genre, rather than the reverse. Her plays, for instance, consist primarily of a series of prose passages, which are sometimes connected to characters (and other times not). Characters are only occasionally identified at the beginning, while the customarily concise texts rarely include stage directions of any kind. There is typically nothing about tone, pace, costumes, decor or any other specifics, all of which are thus left to the interpretation of the plays' directors. Instead of explicitly bothering with these dimensions, Stein created verbal texts that are so distinctive that their style, their sounds, their images inform every aspect of a theatrical production. Since scripts like these were simply not conducive to conventional realistic staging, most directors have favored highly spectacular, sensorily abundant productions that incorporate music and dance, in sum exemplifying not only Stein's idea of theater as an art of sight and sound but also the most valid kind of "opera" America has yet produced.

These texts are verbal settings for generating a performance, and in crucial stylistic respects they are clearly unlike anything ever written for earlier theater. They should be considered plays, rather than stories or poems, because, as Donald Sutherland perceives, they portray "movement in space, or in a landscape. . . . A number of people or things or even ideas

presenting themselves together, as existences in space constituted a play."
Many of these plays are non-representational, because they do not refer to
any world outside of language and the performers speaking it. Lacking any
attempt at illusionism, they "take place" in a second nature that exists apart
from mundane nature. As Van Vechten perceived, their aim was "without
telling what happened to make a play the essence of what happened." What
you see is most, if not all, of what there is.

Another dimension that separates them from traditional plays is the
emphasis upon each line, or upon each moment, primarily for itself, rather
than its contribution to any larger temporal structures; and as in Stein's
fiction, this redistribution of emphasis brings an elimination not only of
climaxes but also of sharp beginnings and decisive ends — in sum, a general
flattening of theatrical form. Sutherland suggested in 1951 that those "plays"
written before 1920 were not intended to be performed, but even by the sixties abstruse texts such as *What Happened* (1913) and *In Circles* (1920) were
successfully staged. What is most remarkable about Stein's plays is that they
were written at a time when varieties of realism dominated the American
stage. Her more prominent contemporaries included such forgotten names
as Percy MacKaye (1875–1956) and Eugene Walter (1875–1911); Eugene
O'Neill (1888–1953) was fourteen years her junior. Stein survived them all
in that her notions about what constitutes a theatrical text continue to influence contemporary playwrighting.

Her essays were also unlike anything written in that vein before. In
discussing a particular subject, she avoided the conventions of exposition,
such as example and elaboration, in favor of accumulating disconnected
details and miscellaneous insights, which were invariably subjected to her
pet device of repetition. As in her plays and prose, the result is an overall
flattening of expository form, so that an essay's themes are not concentrated
at the beginning and at the end but scattered throughout the piece. The
absence of linear focus accounts for the penchants for digression and *non-
sequitur*. Like the cubist painters, she endeavored, as she put it, "to describe
the inside as seen from the outside." Because her essays are structured as
a succession of detached moments, they are remembered not in terms
of their opening sentences or even their choicest aphorisms but by
what is repeated, whether words or phrases (e.g., Matisse is "strug-
gling").

In doing a portrait of "Monsieur Vollard et Cézanne" (1912), she
learned that perceptions could be organized vertically as well:

>   This is truth.
>   Trust
>   Thrust to be
>   Actually.

In an essay entitled "We Came: A History" (1930), she used equal signs as internal punctuation, suggesting that each part of a single paragraph is as important as any other. The mechanical device of a mathematical symbol becomes a means toward qualitative ends:

> History there = Is no disaster because = Those who make history = Cannot be overtaken = As they will make = History which they do = Because it is necessary = That every one will = Begin to know that = They must know that = History is what is it = Which it is as they do = . . .

She frequently boasted that in writing she was "telling what she knew," but most of her knowledge concerned writing. It is probably significant that the principal theme of her essays, reiterated as much by example as by explanation, is the autonomy of language.

Works that Stein meant to publish as poems, such as *Before the Flowers of Friendship Faded Friendship Faded* (1931) and the pieces posthumously collected in *Stanzas in Meditation* (1956), resemble her most abstract writing in eschewing subjects entirely in order to explore alternative linguistic coherence — diction, alliteration, rhythm, rhyme, timbre, repetition and other similarly non-semantic qualities:

> A clock in the eyes ticks in the eye a clock ticks in the eye.
> A number with that and large as a hat which makes rims think quicker than I.
> A lock in the eye ticks in the eye a clock ticks ticks in the eye.

Another passage from *Flowers* is yet more exemplary:

> It is always just as well
> That there is a better bell
> Than that with which a half is a whole
> Than that with which they went away to stay
> Than that with which after any way,
> Needed to be gay to-day.

A poem like "One or Two. I've Finished" (1914) pioneered the format of horizontal minimalism — one word to a line for its entirety — in addition to eschewing conventional linear syntax:

> There
> Why
> There
> Why
> There
> Able
> Idle

That Stein's poems are in English seems merely a convenience, perhaps testifying to her abiding love for her native language; for she did not follow Lewis Carroll's "Jabberwocky" (or precede Joyce's *Finnegans Wake*) in creating an artificial language. Not until recently have critics begun to examine Stein's characteristic poetic styles, and no dimension of her *oeuvre* illustrates as well Sutherland's suggestion, back in 1951, that, "Sooner or later criticism will have to get used to thinking in terms of forces, tensions, movements, speeds, attractions, etc."

Largely because Stein's writings were so unconventional, even in terms of literary modernism, it took her far, far too long to get them into public print. She subsidized the publication of two of her first three American books, and she sold a Picasso in order to finance Plain Editions that published four more volumes in the early thirties (one of which contained texts that had *all* been written more than two decades before). Her will included a provision for subsidizing the publication of her previously "unpublished writings," which ran to eight large volumes. Though she had been writing steadily from the age of twenty-nine, she was thirty-eight before any editor, on his own volition, accepted her work for publication (and that was Alfred Stieglitz of *Camera World*); not until she was fifty-nine (and one of the most respected writers in the English language) did any major U.S. publisher invest its own name and money in a book of hers. Though other publishers wanted to capitalize on the success of *The Autobiography of Alice B. Toklas* (1933), the books they issued were pale echoes of her previous achievements. (The best explanation for this decline is Thomson's contention that around 1926 she became attracted to a neoromanticism that fired her incipient egotism, as well as deleteriously repudiating the anti-expressionistic premises of her earlier writing.) Typically, nearly all her poetry first appeared in print after her death, and its excellences are still rarely acknowledged by poetry critics and anthologists. Since many of her greatest books were unavailable for more than twenty years after her death — the unabridged edition of *Americans* and *Geography and Plays*, for two — their active life with literate readers has been, to say the least, belated.

The enterprise of American literary criticism has scarcely noticed Stein's work, and too many critics honor and teach the simpler books, such as *Three Lives* and *Toklas*, to the complete neglect of the more extraordinary ones — those whose special qualities have never been exceeded. (Even Edmund Wilson preferred *Three Lives*, which he praised for its mimeticism: "caught the very rhythms and accents of the minds of her heroines.") Though her work as a whole is uneven and repetitious, no other twentieth-century American author has had as much influence as Stein; and none influenced his or her successors in as many ways. (It is significant that, until recently, her best "critics" were other writers.) There are echoes of Stein's writings in her friends Sherwood Anderson, Thornton Wilder and Ernest

Hemingway, as well as in William Faulkner's interminable sentences, E.E. Cummings' syntactical playfulness, John Dos Passos' ellipses and any narrative that is structurally uninflected. Because of her influence on Hemingway, Stein's preference for denotative language had an indirect effect upon American newspaper writing and upon crime fiction.

In his imperceptive biography of Stein, *The Third Rose*, John Malcolm Brinnin declares, "If Gertrude Stein had never lived, sooner or later works very much like those she produced would have been written by someone else." However, quite the opposite is more likely true, precisely because most of her innovations went against the grain of literary modernism, and her originality was so multifarious. Had she not existed — or had she not pursued her experimental proclivities — subsequent literature would have been quite different. What is more extraordinary is that this influence continues, not only through her imitators but directly through her own works — not only with her experiments in linguistic acoherence but in her general attitudes toward language and literary art.

Jack Kerouac (1980)

Not many prose writers alive (Celine, Genet, a few others) would dare the freedom and intelligence to trust their own minds, remember they made that jump, not censor it but write it down and discover its beauty. That's what I look for in K's prose. He's gone very far out in discovering (or remembering, or transcribing) the perfect patterns that his own mind makes, and trusting them, and seeing their importance — to rhythm, to imagery, to the very structure of the "novel." — Allen Ginsberg, *Village Voice* (1958).

Jack Kerouac's works might be better appreciated today, were not the man so deprecated and his books so misunderstood in his own lifetime; for we can see by now that no other major modern American writer suffered from such malicious, erroneous, foolish "criticism." Some of the remarks made about Kerouac two decades ago were so askew that quoting them now embarrasses his detractors more than Kerouac. One of the prepublication readers at Viking Press reported that *On the Road* (1957) contained "everything that is bad and horrible about this otherwise wonderful age we live in." On May 3, 1959, a New York *Times* reviewer dismissed his novel *Doctor Sax* as "largely psychopathic" and a "pretentious and unreadable far-rago of childhood fantasy-play." Earlier that year, the discreetly anonymous *Time* reviewer characterized Kerouac as "a cut-rate Thomas Wolfe"; on David Susskind's television interview program in September, Truman Capote cruelly dismissed Kerouac's books as "not writing but typewriting." In the *New York Times Book Review*, Nov. 29, of the same year, Kenneth Rexroth, once a Kerouac friend, resorted to an *ad hominem* attack: "Someone once said of Mr. Kerouac that he was a Columbia freshman who went to a party in the Village twenty years ago and got lost. How true."

Only the year before, Alfred Kazin paused, in an essay ostensibly about Sigmund Freud, to rate Kerouac as "a far less gifted and intelligent writer than [Norman] Mailer." In 1958 as well, Norman Podhoretz, soon to become the principal editor of *Commentary*, published in *Partisan Review* an essay entitled "The Know-Nothing Bohemians" in which he spoke of Kerouac's "simple inability to say anything in words" and demoted both *On the Road* and *The Subterraneans* to sub-art "so patently autobiographical in content that they become almost impossible to discuss as novels." Podhoretz continued, "The Beat Generation's worship of primitivism and spontaneity is more than a cover for hostility to intelligence; it arises from a pathetic poverty of feeling as well." Six years later, Podhoretz reprinted these insults, word for word, in his book *Doings and Undoings* (and one naturally wonders whether he would reprint them now). As late as 1964, John W. Aldridge, in his introduction to his book *Time to Murder and Create*, disparaged "writers like Jack Kerouac who continue to practice an extinct provincialism and to exult depressingly in experience that the rest of us have long since had." In truth, Kerouac's literary reputation was almost destroyed, not by critical neglect — the usual bane of innovative American writers — but by concerted critical attack.

Even Kerouac's closest friends often misunderstood what he was doing. It was, after all, Allen Ginsberg, not a philistine publisher, who, in April, 1952, wrote their mutual friend Neal Cassady (a.k.a. "Dean Moriarty"):

> [The manuscript that became *Visions of Cody*] is a holy mess — it's great all-right but he did everything he could to fuck it up with a lot of meaningless bullshit I think, page after page of surrealist free association that don't make sense to anybody except someone who has blown Jack. I don't think it can be published anywhere, in its present state. . . . Jack is an ignu and I all bow down to him, but he done fuck up his writing money-wise, and also writing-wise. He was not experimenting and exploring in new deep form, he was purposely just screwing around as if anything he did no matter what he did, was O.K. no bones attached. Not purposely, I guess, just drug out and driven to it and in a hold in his own head — but he was in a hole.

(Even someone as notoriously sympathetic to "advanced" writing as myself was slow to acknowledge Kerouac's excellence. Had I been as aware of his work as I am now, I would have included the second part of "Old Angel Midnight" [1964] in my anthology of short fiction, *Twelve from the Sixties* [1967], and the first part [1959] in my *Breakthrough Fictioneers* [1973]. Both collections, I now think, suffer from his absence. My only rationalization, admittedly inadequate, is that the malicious press deceived me too.)

Another cause for misunderstanding Kerouac is mistaking the man for his work. Since he wrote fiction that seems autobiographical (and, indeed, much of it is), readers make the common error of thinking that the books are the man, rather than his creations. In fact, he was a sadder, much sadder and less confident figure than, say, Sal Paradise. It is true that he often behaved badly; he drank compulsively without ever taking an alcoholic cure; he depended too much upon amphetamines to write; he wrote quickly; he interviewed badly; he invariably insulted the literary powermen who could have advanced his career; he left behind stories of outrageous behavior; and every place in which he lived he ultimately found disquieting. His relationship with his widowed mother was at once touching and pathological, for she both supported and infantilized him. From the wake of his fame, in his own mid-thirties, to his death, he lived primarily with her, migrating around the U.S., eventually settling in St. Petersburg, Florida (!), where in 1969 he died of alcoholic excesses, at the age of 47. However, the works are separate from the man; and only by overcoming certain impressions about his life can we get a surer sense of his extraordinary writings.

Further jeopardizing the processes of literary comprehension, his publishers served him badly. In part because of the unfavorable notices, a publisher doing one of his books precipitously lost courage when offered a successor; and when Kerouac's publishers urged him to repeat his commercial success (*On the Road*), rather than accepting something different, they revealed a limited sense of his literary talent. Not only were his manuscripts distributed among a dozen different publishers, but his single most extraordinary book, *Visions of Cody*, did not appear in print until 1973, four years after his death and more than two decades after it was written.

What has been lost in all these misunderstandings of Kerouac are certain irrefutable truths. First, he had an elaborate literary education, not only in schools but on his own; and from an early age, he seized literature passionately and read omnivorously. Shakespeare, Melville, Joyce, Thomas Wolfe, Rimbaud, Dostoevsky and Proust were among the authors to whom he returned. Secondly, even as a high-school football player, he wanted to be a writer; and once his athletic career ended, much of the ambition and disciplined energy he developed on the playing fields were channeled into writing. In prep school, he wrote fiction and contributed feature pieces to the student newspaper; and by the time he started to publish, in the late forties, he had already written, it is said, over a million apprentice words. He reportedly kept a separate journal for each of his creations, which were, in fact, far more conscious than they seem. Third, not only did he have a phenomenally evocative and precise memory — "Memory Babe" was a nickname from childhood — but as an adult he mastered the ability to exploit this talent in language. In his writings are a wealth of details, which are incorporated not clumsily and exhaustively, like Dreiser's, but in an impressionistic and efficient style.

Even when his literary reputation was at its nadir, he always had the kind of stubbornly faithful following that inevitably survives and expands in time. At its base were Allen Ginsberg, John Clellon Holmes, Donald Allen, Seymour Krim, Warren Tallman and the editors and publishers of those magazines sympathetic to that literature called "beat." (The enthusiasm of this nucleus of support was one reason why Kerouac was so vehemently attacked, for no one bothers deprecating a writer no one likes.) It seems to me that anyone sensitive to the peculiar processes of literary reputation-making could have predicted twenty years ago that by today, a decade after his death, every book Kerouac published in his lifetime — even the formerly scarce *Tristessa* (1959) would be in print and, yes, he would be widely regarded as a major American author. Although he may not have had the effect on prose-writing that Ginsberg, say, has had on poetry, he helped change American literature from what it was in 1950 to what it is now. Had he not come and done, American writing today would not be the same.

His literary intelligence had an experimental cast, so that most of his important novels began with a particular creative idea. *On the Road*, for instance, was originally written as a single paragraph, single-spaced, with no margins, on 250 feet of continuous drawing paper (which had to be transcribed onto rectangular sheets, paragraphed and punctuated to produce the text we know). Because this format was in part responsible for its forward-rushing style, it would be appropriate, by now, to publish a paper-roll edition of *On the Road*—even as a facsimile of the original manuscript—if only so we can see what the book would be like to read in the form that its author wrote it. (Isn't the National Endowment for the Humanities charged with the production of "definitive editions" of the major American authors?)

The last forgotten truth is that the life he led was, in fact, far less spectacular than the lives he wrote about (or some of the publicity about him portrayed). Born in 1922, in Lowell, Massachusetts, the son of a printer, he grew up in a working-class French Canadian household, speaking French before he learned English. As a high school sprinter and halfback, with short thick legs, he was recruited by Columbia University, which sent him to Horace Mann for a preparatory year. Quitting the Columbia football team, in the wake of a leg injury, he lost his scholarship and dropped out of college. After a hitch in the Merchant Marine, he hung around Manhattan with a group of incipient writers, including Allen Ginsberg, John Clellon Holmes and William Burroughs, while living mostly in Queens with his parents. After his father's death, he assumed responsibility for the care of his mother and, except for occasional wanderings, lived with her on Queens, in Lowell, on Long Island, briefly in Berkeley, on Cape Cod and then in Florida. He married thrice, the first two times for less than a year apiece, and the last time to a childhood friend, Stella Stampas, who joined both mother and son. Outside the house, he worked briefly as a railroad brakeman, a factory worker and a script synopsizer for Twentieth Century–Fox. When he was home, his mother became his patron, feeding him from wages she earned largely in shoe factories. He tended to write at night, after she had gone to sleep, setting his typewriter on the kitchen table and taking Benzedrines to keep himself going. Once he became a recognized author, they occupied houses that had a separate workroom, where he spent much of his sober time writing the books and articles that were their principal source of income. In 1956, Upton Sinclair published *A Cup of Fury*, documenting the deleterious effects of alcohol upon prominent American writers; and in this context, Kerouac becomes yet another major figure in a recurring tragic tendency. On the other hand, perhaps his penchant for self-destruction preceded his involvement with alcohol.

The tragedy of his professional life was that he did not know how to live as a controversial literary man. He lacked the cultural background, the creative imagination and the psychological resilience necessary to survive the hostile reviews, the snide remarks, the personal attacks and the erroneous publicity. So he cut himself off from his professional friends to join his mother, who supervised not only his finances but his personal life. In this respect, he differs strikingly from his colleague Allen Ginsberg, the son of a poet, who charmed his antagonists, answered all criticisms, patiently cajoled the literary powermen and thus survived the professional scattershot that contributed to Kerouac's undoing.

Not until he died, it seems, could readers separate their stereotypes of the man from both the facts of his life and the quality of his work; not until the seventies could respectful books about Kerouac begin to appear. The first of note was Ann Charters' *Jack Kerouac* (1973), a basically intelligent biography that was rushed into print and then distorted in production. (Because permission to quote from Kerouac's letters was withheld, while the author returned to her home in Sweden to bear a child, a secretary in the publisher's office reportedly rewrote numerous paragraphs. Though the author asserts that mistakes were corrected in the paperback edition, the "third printing" in my possession still misspells the names of Bern Porter and *Finnegans Wake*.) A more elaborate biography is Dennis McNally's *Desolate Angel* (1979), written intially as a doctoral thesis in the *history* department at the University of Massachusetts. The product of superior research, *Desolate Angel* is particularly good at placing Kerouac in his immediate milieu. Typically, McNally knows precisely where Kerouac was and with whom he was corresponding in every phase of his life; he knows what books Kerouac read (and when) and what music he favored while he wrote each book. In between these two biographies appeared *The Beat Diary* (1974) and *The Beat Journal* (1976), two anthologies of previously unpublished interviews and memorabilia, and *Jack's Book* (1978), a collection of his friends' memoirs, transcribed from tape and unified by a modest, circumspect commentary. In reviewing this last volume for the *New York Times Book Review*, I suggested that it was "neither criticism nor scholarship, but a labor of love, perhaps even hagiography."

The principal work in the critical reassessment of Kerouac is John Tytell's *Naked Angels* (1976), a sensitive and sensible study of the three major "beats"—Kerouac, Ginsberg, and Burroughs—it makes a strong case for Kerouac as the richest, most innovative figure. Tytell has an illuminating appreciation of *Visions of Cody*, and among other shrewd perceptions is his ingenious documentation of the likely stylistic influence of the long clauses of *Visions of Cody* upon the long lines of Ginsberg's classic poems. In my opinion, future Kerouac criticism will need to start from here. Perhaps the most unusual of the recent Kerouac books is *Jack Kerouac: essay-poulet* (1972), by the Quebecois novelist Victor-Lévy Beaulieu. Reprinted in English as *Jack Kerouac: a Chicken Essay* (1975), it regards the writer as the epitome of French-Canadian culture. Charles Jarvis's *Visions of Kerouac* (1974) is a yet more peculiar book, whose invaluable information about Kerouac's life in his hometown (Lowell) is nearly smothered by idiosyncratic prejudices and Jarvis's embarrassing self-aggrandizement. Other books are no doubt on the way, and the expectation now is that most, if not all, of them will be sympathetic.

A further fact is that by now nearly everyone literate has read Kerouac, much as two decades ago everyone literate had read Henry Miller, their mutually controversial reputations notwithstanding. Indeed, by now we can see that different people enjoy different Kerouac for different reasons. Those who have read only a little Kerouac tend to identify *On the Road* as their favorite book; it has sold over two million copies since its publication over two decades ago, and even Ann Charters considers it "probably the best." Undergraduates tend to prefer *The Dharma Bums* (1958), mostly because the portrait of Japhy Ryder (a.k.a. Gary Snyder) is so appealing. Sentimentalists tend to like *Maggie Cassady* (1959) and Kerouac's other nostalgic memoirs of childhood. Science fiction buffs remember Kerouac for "cityCityCITY" (1959), which otherwise seems an untypical work. Those inclined to abstraction (and perhaps psychedelic drugs) often prefer *Mexico City Blues* (1959). Victor-Lévy Beaulieu identifies *Doctor Sax* (1959) as "the best documentation we possess on Franco-American life in the 20s and 30s." Kerouac connoisseurs used to praise *Tristessa*, perhaps because, until recently, copies of it were so scarce. Those sympathetic to the experimental tradition of modernism, like Tytell and myself, prefer *Visions of Cody*, which contains much of his very best prose. Like all such schemes, this one is imperfect; however, it does suggest that Kerouac's works are richly various enough to inspire various enthusiasms. By no account should Kerouac be considered a "one-book author."

An essentially expressionistic artist, who worked quickly to comb his mind for literary material, Kerouac developed a different, profoundly experimental way of writing. These innovative methods are roughly outlined in his "Essentials for Spontaneous Prose," but perhaps the richest description appears in Seymour Krim's brilliant introduction to *Desolation Angels* (1965) — an essay subsequently reprinted in Krim's *Shake It for the World, Smartass* (1970), but lamentably not included in the current paperback reprint of the Kerouac book.

> Kerouac would 'sketch from memory' a 'definite image-object' more or less
> as a painter would work on a still-life; this 'sketching' necessitated an 'undisturbed flow from the mind of idea-words,' comparable to a jazz soloist

blowing freely; there would be 'no periods separating sentence-structures already arbitrarily riddled by false colons and timid commas'; in place of the conventional period would be 'vigorous space dashes separating rhetor-ical breathing,' again just as a jazzman draws breath between phrases; there would be no 'selectivity of expression' but instead the free association of the mind into 'limitless seas' of thought; the writer has to 'satisfy himself first,' after which the 'reader can't fail to receive a telepathic shock' by vir-tue of the same psychological 'laws' operating on his own mind; there would be 'no pause' in composition, 'no revisions' (except for errors of fact) since nothing is ultimately incomprehensible or 'muddy' that 'runs in time'; the motto of this kind of prose was to be 'speak now or forever hold your peace' — putting the writer on a true existentialist spot; and finally the writing was to be done 'without consciousness,' in a Yeatsian semitrance if possible and 'admit' in uninhibited and therefore 'necessarily modern language' what overly conscious art would normally censor.

This theory of the artist as a recording consciousness produces an art of in-corporation, rather than an art made by removal and refinement; and the run-on sentence, which offends grammarians, was perfectly appropriate to Kerouac's needs. Thus, his books have an uneven, improvisatory, unfin-ished quality that no doubt reflects their method of composition. However, when most of us write impulsively, we tend to repeat ourselves excessively, not only in style but in content; one sign of Kerouac's genuine genius is the fact that he did not.

One extreme result of this compositional method is "Old Angel Mid-night," to my mind his single most extraordinary piece of prose. As Ann Charters tells it, Kerouac had spent the evening of 28 May, 1965, boasting that he was "Shakespeare or Joyce reincarnated. . . . Jack returned to [Gary Snyder's] Mill Valley cabin and tried to prove his boast by writing a long exercise in spontaneous prose as his friends slept off the wine. The piece was titled 'Old Angel Midnight.' The prose was supposed to be Shakespearean, but Jack coasted on his personal currents of sweet wine associations and floating perceptions. In different sections, Jack ranged in his thought of friends and places, his form fluid as jello." McNally adds, "In fact, Jack's trance was so deep that much of 'Old Angel Midnight' was written in an il-legible scribble most unlike his usual neat printing."

"Old Angel Midnight" was scheduled to appear in the *Chicago Review*, Winter, 1959. However, in response to a Chicago newspaper columnist's attack upon the University of Chicago literary magazine for "filthy writing," the deans asked to see the new issue before it went to the printer and subse-quently ruled that two works should not appear. With the infallible taste of dismissive academics, they selected the very best. One, by William Bur-roughs, was an excerpt from a novel that would soon be internationally famous — *Naked Lunch* (1958); the other was Kerouac's prose piece. Not unreasonably, six of the seven editors of the *Chicago Review* resigned; and two of them, Irving Rosenthal and Paul Carroll, started an alternative magazine, called, after Kerouac's suggestion, *Big Table*. Once this new publication appeared, however, the United States Post Office banned its circulation through the mails. With characteristic determination, the publishers of *Big Table* lodged an appeal.

After five months, a verdict came down from Judge Julius Hoffman, the same federal judge who a decade later became the goat of the Chicago Seven trial. The anonymous editor introducing the fifth issue of *Big Table* remembers, "He found it unnecessary to rule on the constitutionality of the Post Office ban. Instead, Judge Hoffman held that *Big Table #1* was not 'obscene.' Commenting on the two articles in *Big Table #1* singled out by the Post Office as such [as well as by the University administration], Judge Hoffman ruled that both were in the broad field of serious literature. The Kerouac article was described by Judge Hoffman as 'a wild prose picnic. . . which seems to be some sort of dialogue, broadly, between God and Man.' "

It was unfortunate that "Old Angel Midnight" had gotten billed as obscene, because it scarcely is; but there is no question that it would disturb most readers. The principal problem is that the work does not appear to be about anything in particular. The numbered sections, into which the work is divided, do not ostensibly relate to each other, for adjacent sections are invariably leagues apart, not only in subject but in style. The only public clue to his purposes that Kerouac ever gave appeared at the end of sections 50–67, which initially appeared in *Evergreen Review* (Sept., 1964), where he speaks of "my idea of how to make a try at a 'spontaneous *Finnegans Wake*' with the Sounds of the Universe itself as the plot and all the neologisms, mental associations, puns, word mixes from various languages and non-languages scribbled out in the strictly intuitional discipline at breakneck speed."

The sole critic to acknowledge "Old Angel Midnight" at its initial publication, aside from Judge Hoffman, was the *Saturday Review*'s John Ciardi who, in the course of a sarcastic attack on recent censorship, described the work as "a series of Joycean improvisations (no less!) on the nature of irreality as created by a slangy and polyglot god once named Old Angel Midnight. . . . The writing, moreover, goes by something like musical principle, with basic themes recurring and being varied." It is scarcely surprising that most of Kerouac's critics have been reluctant to deal with "Old Angel Midnight"; indeed, only a few even mention it.

In my judgment, it is principally about the possibilities of both memory and language and especially about the limitless *intensities* of each. In form, the work is a series of pieces, mostly of prose, prefaced only by sequential numbers, and each incorporates moments of memory, not only from Kerouac's own life but also of literature, sports and other domains. Realizing qualities unique to prose, Kerouac works with conventional syntax and then without it; at one point, he even inserts punctuation marks to disrupt the flow. ("Why, hell, should, heaven, interfere, words, waiting, flesh, sure, I, know, write poems. . . .") He writes in various tones and style, as well as various languages; he makes puns and casts his words in pictorial shapes. In addition to the large definite changes from section to section, he makes swift shifts, often quite subtle, within a section or even within a single passage, much as the remembering mind jumps from realm to realm, amidst and over distracting flashes.

> Stump — all on a stump the stump — accord yourself with a sweet declining woman one night — I mean by declining that she lays back & declines to say no — accuerdo ud. con una merveillosa — accordde tue, Ti Pousse, avec une belle femme folle pi vas' t'councer — if ya don't understand s t t and tish, that language, it's because the langue just bubbles & in the babbling void I Lowsy Me I'se tihed. . . .

The suggestion is that Kerouac is stringing words together for their sound, rather than their syntactical necessities or semantic meanings; and in this respect he most resembles Dylan Thomas, of all contemporaries. There was nothing like this before in American prose, and scarcely anything like it since. (A second suggestion of this polylingual passage is that Kerouac could have written an entire book in French-English, much as Anthony Burgess developed Russian-English for *A Clockwork Orange* [1962].) What Kerouac is implying in "Old Angel Midnight" is a theme quite different from what most of his admirers think; his greatest truth is that literature is not about the representation of "experience" but about the possibilities of words creatively placed together.

In part because he could write so quickly, Kerouac had the temperament of a journalist, and perhaps the greatest misfortune of his professional life was that he never had a loyal periodical patron. It is true that, after dropping out of college, he worked as a sportswriter in Lowell; but he did not stay long enough for anything to appear under his by-line. The only journalistic opportunity he ever had was a back-page column, beginning in 1959, for the sub-*Playboy* "girlie" magazine, *Escapade*, published and edited in Derby, Connecticut. In these columns, Kerouac ranged freely in subject, writing at different times about baseball, politics, literature and jazz; but perhaps the most interesting subcurrent of this series is that his prose becomes progressively stronger and more expressionistic until, by the final columns, we read that flowing, rushing style that we have come to associate with Kerouac at his best. It is hard to think of any other American writer whose magazine columns are as profoundly literary as these; in a better America, he would have had national syndication every week.

Finally, it is not surprising that such a master of personal expression should also be one of the greatest letter-writers of the twentieth century. Perhaps because he was not assured of publication for most of his life, some of his best writing appears in letters, which contain not only drafts of poems and prose, but also descriptions of his professional ambitions and purposes. A few of them have been reprinted; but until everything he wrote is available — not only these letters, but the unpublished poems and stories (including those initially written in French), his journals for each book, and the thousand-page "Some of the Dharma" — we will never know completely what an extraordinary American writer Kerouac was.

Innovations in Fiction (1973)

So I believe that the next book form will be plastic-
representational. We can say that
1.) the hieroglyph-book is international (at least in its
potentiality).
2.) the letter-book is national, and
3.) the coming book will be a-national; for in order to
understand it, one must at least learn. — El Lissitzky, *Our
Book* (1926).

Fiction has currently been the literary art least obliged to experiment,
as those works commonly called "new" rarely leap as far beyond nineteenth-
century conventions as, say, contemporary music or sculpture have; and
the second, post–WWII revolution in modernist art that we call "contemporary" has scarcely affected the fiction published and publicized today.
The novels passing before one's eyes are invariably so familiar in language
and structure — so unproblematic as reading experiences, so conceptually
close to middle-class best-sellers — that this truth is clear: No literary form
today has a greater need for artistic resuscitation; for without stylistic
breakthroughs, need one say, there can be no future for fiction.

One reason that fictional art has not felt any obligation to change is that
most standards currently used by established "fiction critics" were just as applicable a century ago. The fact that they should be so responsive to familiar
formulas, and so backwards in their principles of selection for public notice,
is nearly incredible; but the unannounced, perhaps suppressed truth is that
no reviewer predisposed to avant-garde writing contributes regularly to
any periodical in America. Consider, by analogy, how unquestionably
laughable would seem an art critic who praised only representational art
and dismissed all abstract work for betraying "reality" — a charge so often
leveled in current reviews of fiction. (And if such backward art-criticism
were taken seriously, consider how different recent art would probably
be!) It is indicative that the honorific epithets "new" or "breakthrough" are
more often used, nowadays, not to characterize innovative achievement
but writing whose subject-matter was previously exempt from literature
(e.g., sex, madness, esoteric milieus), even if the work's style and form are
indubitably archaic. As every practitioner knows, the recent novels that

win the prizes and the lead reviews, that get discussed in the survey courses, are never those that make a step-ahead contribution to the art. Criticism is scarcely omnipotent, thankfully; but since reviewing is ultimately less powerful in its advocacies (or its rejections) than its outright omissions, the pervasive neglect of a whole body of art can contribute, senselessly, to its premature death.

It is also common knowledge that nothing, but nothing, will do more to keep an otherwise excellent fiction unpublished than an unfamiliar form: for the kind of difficult originality that would strike an editor or reader as "puzzling" in a short poem generally goes unread in a longer manuscript. Prudity alone can no longer effectively censor imaginative writing, but "editorial discretion" can, especially if certain taboos are pervasive in the business — for instance, that currently proscribing pronounced stylistic originality, especially in its more difficult forms, and those prohibiting predominantly visual fiction. Were James Joyce's *Ulysses* to come un- solicited into a New York publishing house today, there is no doubt that it would be rejected after a cursory perusal; and *Finnegans Wake*, that multi- lingual masterpiece of the century, would just as certainly be returned, all but unexamined, as "totally unpublishable [if not "unreadable"] in its pres- ent form, not just because of its turgid and obscure style, which ought to be cleaned up, but because its eccentric format makes production- typesetting costs prohibitive."

The polemical aim of my editing of *Breakthrough Fictioneers* (1973) is nothing less than a drastic enlargement of our sense of fictional possibility; for the individual selections were made with one elementary criterion in mind — their distance, as hypothetical positions, beyond what we have often read before. No particular deductions about fiction's future exclusive- ly shaped my choices — not even this needlessly conservative conclusion I drew four years ago: "What will, I think, primarily distinguish fiction of the future from the other arts will be an emphasis upon words as such, selected and arranged out of an evident taste for language, a measure of human significance, a sense of potential linguistic articulations, and an awareness of the viable traditions of literature." As the ensuing variety of stylistic alter- natives would suggest, however, there exists not one but several possible futures for fiction, and language is not necessarily prerequisite.

Innovative fictions move decisively beyond the five post-realist, post- symbolist "avant-gardes" having, in my observation, the greatest current influence on fictional creations: William Burroughs' collage, along with "cut-ups" and slicker pastiche; the mixing of physically separated words and images pioneered in America by Kenneth Patchen and extended by Donald Barthelme (in some recent works), R. Crumb, and other counter-cultural comix; the flat, scrupulously uninflected, absurdity-haunted prose of Samuel Beckett and his artistic successors; deranged and or picaresque first-person narrators obsessed by idiosyncratic perspectives and peculiar language, epitomized by Faulkner and lesser Southerners and, more recently, by John Hawkes and most of Barthelme; and the ironic pseudo-scholarship of John Barth, Jorge Luis Borges and Vladimir Nabokov. The inevitable debasement of all these successful (and, thus, much-imitated) artistic forms, along with the concomitant decline of their most prominent exponents, makes the forging of new directions more necessary and more likely. For that reason, there is a polemical spine to this book, notwithstanding the detached serenity of the selections, all implicitly supporting a battle for the sake of Art that needs desperately to be won. The revolution fundamental to artistic modernism is, and must be, permanent.

These innovative works suggest that "fiction" can be most generally defined as a frame filled with a circumscribed world of cohesively self-relating activity. This fictional material may be primarily human, naturalistic, or stylistic, which is to say that the fiction may predominantly deal with people, or things, or merely a certain linguistic style and or formal device; but within fictional art is usually some kind of movement from one point to another. In these respects of diversity and change within an acknowledged frame does fiction particularly differ from poetry, which emphasizes concise, static, generally formalized statement. Fictions tend toward fullness, while poetry is spare; fictions encompass, while poetry concentrates; fictions go, while poetry stops.

Fictions thus favor sequential forms (and yet remain distinct from film), as the difference between the material on one page and its successors (and predecessors) often generates the work's internal event. For instance, a single page of Raymond Federman's richly inventive *Double or Nothing* (1971) might succeed, in isolation, as a graphic picture or "word-image," where visualizations of various kinds complement the marvelous language; but Federman's frames in sequence, abetted by sustained preoccupations, begin to weave a *fictional* action not evident in one alone. More specifically, just as one page can facilely follow from another, so can it drastically contradict its predecessors — an esthetic interface also possible in the similarly *edited* arts of film and video-tape, but not in live performance, whether on stage or television, or in a lecture. That is, the act of turning pages, which is conducive to sequence, can introduce non-sequential material that is nonetheless artistically related, and in this respect can the interfacial forms of certain fictions resemble this entire anthology. On the other hand, even within a single page can sometimes be compressed a world of artistic activity that is ultimately more fictional than poetic, as well as yet more reduced than Beckett's *Nouvelles textes pour rien* (1958), to mention one prior milestone of literary minimalism.

What is new in contemporary art often deals inventively with the essentials of the medium; in fiction's case, the possibilities of language and narrative form, as well as the potentialities of both a rectangular printed page and the rhythmic process of turning pages; and "freedom" in any art means the uncompromised opportunity to use or fill these basic materials without restraint — without deference, to be more specific, to either literary conventions or worldly realities. Therefore, just as some new fictions depend upon unfamiliar linguistic signs, others eschew language completely in the telling of stories (thereby echoing Tristan Tzara's declaration for a Dada literature: "No More Words"). Once the old-fashioned, extraneous, needlessly restrictive criteria for "fiction" are phased out, it becomes readily clear that many alternatives are possible, which is to say that the fictional medium's components can still be artistically deployed in innumerable unprecedented ways. The "novel" may be dead, along with other historically mortal forms; but fictionalizing, as a creative impulse, is not.

Keeping such opportunities in mind, fiction's artists may, for instance, regard pictures as usefully as words, or mix one element with the other; and the vocabulary of mediumistic possibilities obviously includes both the blank page and the totally blackened one. As Robert Frost once defined the essence of poetry as what could not be successfully translated, so might the essence of many of these new fictions be characterized as what would remain unchanged in translation. (Another strain of new writing, however, favors radically special forms of language, which often resist adequate translation.) Nothing in my anthology finally qualifies, in my judgment, as "poetry," although a few selections nearly overlap these distinctions and several authors are primarily known as "poets." It should also be noted that though some fictions are more "true" than others, a lack of empirical specificity separates that literary art from journalism or history; and verifiable veracity is, needless to say, not a measure of fictional, or poetic, success.

New fictions selectively echo particular examples (usually neglected) in the consequential canon of literary modernism, as well as reflecting in diverse ways the recent avant-garde revolutions in recent visual and aural arts. Indeed, an operational truth is that advanced artists are likely to find their most productive inspirations in sources outside their own medium, and certain works reprinted here reflect, for instance, the abstractness of modernist painting, or the minimalism current in all visual arts, or the spatial predilections of recent choreography, or the permutational forms of music. Like the best new work in other arts, innovative fictions tend to be much more, or much less — in terms of quantity of information (words and or events in space) — than fiction used to be. Not only do the latter, much-less sort of fictions generally suggest more with less, but even the single-page stories, which at first appear to be much less, often encompass much more fictional material into such a limited space, especially in comparison to pages of old fiction.

Many of these selections will probably seem opaque, if not inscrutable, at first, not just because their fundamental conceptions are so complex, but also because their forms are unusual enough to befuddle before they entice.

They are not "formless," however, subjective preliminary impressions not-withstanding, because any created work with any semblance of perceptible coherence — whether stylistic or structural, and which may not be perceptible until rereading — has an ultimately definable form that is verifiable and or, more crucially, reapplicable. The point for now is this: How can anyone acknowledging the continuing metamorphoses of modern art dare dismiss or classify any radical work, such as those collected here, as "not fiction"?

Many new fictions eschew lines of horizontal type — the fundamental convention of literature since Gutenberg — for other ways of populating the available arena of a page; and many examples, as well as *Breakthrough Fictioneers* as a whole, mix words and images for effects impossible in either word or image alone. The format of the book offers, as noted before, a potential for the sequential development of images, with or without words — a structure resembling, of course, that of film; and if printed pages can likewise be considered a machine, so to speak, for effectively exposing experience, then one collective aim of innovative literature is developing our bookish technology. Resemblance to film notwithstanding, the exposition in these printed fictions is far more selective and concentrated — as is the audience's perceptual experience. It is true that some innovative literary forms reflect the new communications media of the age; but whereas certain examples of post-twenties fiction have reflected film by fracturing both sequential time and constant point of view, stories that are primarily, or exclusively, visual emulate the desire to implant an "after-image" — a sense of the whole visually embedded in the viewer's mind long after he has experienced the work. (Here too is the medium of printed pages both more selective and more concentrated than film.) This represents just one example of the two-fold attempt, implicit in much new fiction, to make the reading of sequential pages unlike anything experienced before and to reshape the history of printed books. Certain pieces reprinted here also aim to foment radically unusual states of mind.

The primary "meaning" in most truly new writing is the demarcation of yet another alternative possible in literary form, and any book criticism truly attuned to Art should regard such strictly mediumistic contributions as sufficient and germane. Nonetheless, as a representational mode, literature customarily deals with matters outside of art, and new fiction can often incorporate traditional themes and subjects. In innovative writing, however, such extrinsic resonances often go unperceived by befuddled readers. Those stories totally without words, or even any representational image, deal often with physical processes analogous to the action portrayed, so that a sequence depicting, say, a progressive growth of many small blocks into a single larger block epitomizes the constructive process in its many forms. In this sort of fiction, "form *is* content, content *is* form," to quote Samuel Beckett's classic remark about *Finnegans Wake.* Certain other works suggest that a particularly propitious subject for innovative fiction is advanced ideas, whose recent vintage and or futuristic relevance place them beyond mundane discourse; and when such a radical idea is successfully embodied in a fiction, the result is not only a new insight but a quality of intellectual realism that is invaluable.

Especially since movies, television and magazines have effectively assumed certain traditionally novelistic functions (e.g., the representation and or interpretation of immediate realities), new fiction aims to eschew the typical simplifications and redundancies of the modern media in order to provide experiences and perceptions that are simply not available in other technologies of communication. Unprecedented forms of art also serve to sensitize the intelligence for the unending contemporary task of making sense of unfamiliar forms in everyday experience. Readers thus learn from new fiction in ways that the old literature, or other media, cannot teach; and by this means in particular does innovative writing provide, in Kenneth Burke's classic phrase, "equipment for living." In all these respects do new fictions collectively represent researches into alternative modes of communication, in addition to the efforts of a new literary generation to forge its own styles of printed communication.

New Fiction in America (1974)

In reply, I should like to point out that in dealing with *new*
things there is a question that precedes that of good or bad.
I refer to the question, "What is it?" — the question of identity. To answer this question in such a way as to
distinguish between a real novelty and a fake one *is itself an*
evaluation, perhaps the primary one for criticism in this
revolutionary epoch when art, ideas, mass movements,
keep changing their nature, so that their most familiar
features are often the most misleading. — Harold
Rosenberg, *The Tradition of the New* (1959).

Literature often becomes superficially or inorganically conventional. This usually happens when it follows the narrow-
ing dialectic of a cultural elite belonging to a class which is
culturally ascendant but is losing its social effectiveness. . . .
The original writer in such a situation is likely to do
something that will be decried by this elite as vulgar, and
hailed by a later generation as turning from literary convention to experience. . . . It is difficult to think of any new
and startling development in literature that has not be-
stowed glass slippers and pumpkin coaches on some
subliterary Cinderella. — Northrop Frye, "Nature and
Homer" (1958).

A myth dominant in the fifties and taught as well to its "creative"
children said that everything imaginative had already been done — that Art
had come to an end through the exhaustion of intrinsic possibilities; but the
great truth of artistic modernism, especially reaffirmed in the late sixties,
is that there need be no end to experiment and innovation in any of the arts.
Genuine stylistic leaps in literature continue to be made, representing imaginative possibilities that no one has seen before, for creative motives as
old as man will always generate radically unprecedented forms. Just as
James Joyce's elaborately detailed portrait of one man in a metropolis — a
subject typical of naturalism — eventually took a counter-naturalistic style,
so the innovative fictions discussed in this essay echo traditional fictional
concerns and yet, in crucial respects, scarcely resemble ninety-nine percent
of the fictions we have already known.

Not all that is new is automatically good, of course; and just as some alternative developments will prove more fertile than others, now as well as in retrospect, so certain examples of a new artistic direction are better than most, and some new styles will inevitably have a more commanding influence upon artists and discriminating audiences than others. Nonetheless, the crucial rule in the serious appraisal or analysis of any new art is, to repeat, that only the best examples count, for anything less than first-rate work will be as surely forgotten as the bulk of Elizabethan theater.

One measure of contemporary excellence is the capacity to inspire in the reader, especially an experienced one, that rare and humbling awe that here before one's eyes is something that is quite different from what has gone before, and yet intrinsically successful and fine. Since the aim of creation in our time is to make a crucial contribution that extends an established artistic concern, nearly all attempts to create a "masterpiece for all time" succumb to those academic rules which are honored only between snickers of embarrassment. In truth, the dynamics of artistic change undermine the masterpiece-mentality.

Literary innovations not only expand the vocabulary of human communication, but they also inspire controversy that revives what might otherwise be moribund, thus making artists aware of neglected byways in their respective traditions. In practice, distinctly new fictions usually reject or ignore the recently dominant preoccupations of literature to draw selectively upon unmined or unfashionable strains of earlier work, recording an esthetic indebtedness that may not be immediately apparent. Thanks to innovative fiction, otherwise neglected precedents such as those forged by Gertrude Stein or Lewis Carroll are revived in literature's collective memory. Furthermore, new works tend to draw upon materials and structures previously considered beneath or beyond fiction, in addition to new developments in the other arts. Many of them articulate fresh social and scientific understandings, in addition to levels of consciousness that reflect, say, the influence of hallucinogenic drugs. Some of this new work is apt to be dismissed as "not-fiction," but once again it is necessary to point out that "fiction" includes any work of man that descends from fictional concerns or resembles previous fiction more than anything else. Its authors are "fictioners," to coin a necessary generic term for writers of both novels and stories (or works in between). This stylistically new literature suffers at its beginnings from a miniscule audience and critical neglect, for it is unlikely that even ten percent of the works discussed in the following pages are familiar to readers (and perhaps the editors) of the esthetically conservative reviewing media — the *New York Times Book Review*, *The Saturday Review* or *The New York Review of Books*.

The milestones in contemporary fiction are those stylistic positions that, though puzzling at first, now seem increasingly easy to understand and even imitate. One is the creation of an unusual narrative voice or voices, a technique spectacularly realized in the classic fictions of William Faulkner and Ford Madox Ford, but also informing the more recent novelistic monologues of Saul Bellow, John Hawkes, and Philip Roth, as well as most of Donald Barthelme's shorter stories (nearly all of these works take as their subject the madness or "vision" of their protagonists). However, since first-person narrators no longer provide problematic reading experiences, novels conceived in this form can become best-sellers. (Indeed, creating a fictitious voice nowadays is a favorite exercise in sophisticated fiction workshops which typically teach not "how to write," but how literature has recently been written.) A second milestone appropriates the poetic-painterly technique of collage-composition and applies it to fiction either as shrewdly placed juxtapositions, as in Michel Butor's magnificent *Mobile* (1963), or through the more random "cut-up" technique of William Burroughs. Successful examples of both methods display a narrative line more various and jagged than previous fictions and, at times, a realized multiple perspective, in addition to a continuity of style and vision that transcends the sharply discontinuous surface.

The stories of Jorge Luis Borges and Vladimir Nabokov's *Pale Fire* epitomize a third position, defined by turning the forms and trappings of literary scholarship into ironic fiction — a style that has influenced John Barth and Ronald Sukenick, among others. Physically separate words and images constitute a fourth fictional milestone whose tradition dates back at least as far as Kenneth Patchen's *The Journal of Albion Moonlight* (1944); and both Donald Barthelme's captioned prints and R. Crumb's beloved anti-comix are still, in form as well as contents, essentially funny books, differences in motives and imagery notwithstanding. Fiction's principal new structure in the early sixties was the scrupulously flat work in which the standard inflections of narrative are eschewed as the story simply goes on and on, all of its parts, whether paragraphs or just sentences, contributing equally to the whole. Generally dealing with social absurdity, these works come to conclusions that seem intrinsically arbitrary. The major influence here was Samuel Beckett's novels, though an earlier precursor, actually concerned with something else (ostinato repetition), was Gertrude Stein's *The Making of Americans* (originally written in 1906–12). A more recent gem in this mode, Kenneth Gangemi's *Olt* (1969), portrays a certain psychopathology; yet by the seventies, this strictly flat narrative form seems more past than present, as, incidentally, are the French "new novel" explorations in phenomenal perception.

Another early classic, Joyce's *Finnegans Wake*, holds a singular position because its multi-lingual techniques continue to be widely misunderstood, rarely imitated, and never exceeded — the closest approximation being *Fa!m'Abniesgwow* (1959), a neglected and unexported polyglottal book-plus-record by the German polymathic critic Hans G. Helms; and for these reasons, among others, the *Wake* still seems the great unsurpassable achievement of literary modernism. In short, the greatest fictions of recent decades establish several definite, post-realist positions that can in turn successfully classify most other prominent works of lesser rank. When Philip Roth charged, in the early sixties, that fiction could scarcely compete as imaginative experience with far-fetched "realities" found in American newspapers, he was really judging, it is now clear, the prosaic quality of fictional ideas and fiction-reading at that time.

The past decade also witnessed numerous experiments with alternative forms of literary coherence such as ellipses analogous to the associational form of post–Poundian poetry. Here is a passage from "Idaho" (1962), a short fiction by the poet John Ashbery:

> Carol laughed. Among other things,
>   till I've finished it. It's the reason of
> dropped into Brentano's.
>   get some of the
> a pile of these. I just grabbed one . . .
>   —Oh, by the way, there's a tele-
> "See?" She pointed to the table.

Between the rather crystalline fragments is implied much of the fiction's unclear action. This elliptical technique is extended to novelistic length in Willard Bain's *Informed Sources* (1969) and G.S. Gravenson's far superior fiction, *The Sweetmeat Saga* (1971), in which the fragments are splayed rectilinearly across the manuscript page. (Both books, curiously, draw heavily upon the elliptical language of wire services, and both depend so much upon the typography of typewriters that their manuscripts were photographed rather than typeset for final publication — their typing incidentally revealing far more of the authorial hand than normal typography.) Other examples of recent prose that seem acoherent represent attempts to use words to transcend language largely for unusual perceptual effects; but the master of this fictional motive, as well as so much other formal invention, remains Gertrude Stein — not only in the unabridged *The Making of Americans*, which is considerably different from the short paperback edition, but also in *Geography and Plays* (1922) and her posthumously published *Mrs. Reynolds* (1952), all of which serve contemporary fiction much as Pound's *Cantos* inadvertently stands to poetry today — as a compendium of pioneering techniques that need no longer be done. In practice, the acknowledgment of definite milestones makes the forging of new art not only more necessary but also more possible, for only by knowing exactly what has already been done can the fictionalizing artist create, or the critical reader discern, something radically new.

Whereas poetry usually strives for concentration and stasis, fiction, by contrast, creates a universe of circumscribed activity which may be human or naturalistic, imagistic or merely linguistic; within fictional art there is generally some kind of movement from one place to another. Precisely by containing diversity and change within an encompassing frame does fiction differ from poetry; for, as Marvin Mudrick noted, "In the beginning of poetry is the word; in the beginning of fiction is the event." For this reason, fiction has favored sequential forms, as the difference between the material on one page and its successors (and predecessors) generates the work's internal life. For instance, a single page of visual poetry might stand as a picture or a "word-image," but such frames in sequence begin to evoke a fictional world not evident in one alone. Nonetheless, a linear reading experience is not a necessary characteristic of fiction, as many innovative books like the *Wake* are best dipped into, rather than read from beginning to end. Also, certain examples of new fiction are very short, some just a single page in length, others just a single line, such as this by Toby MacLennan:

> He existed as a perfect sphere and rolled
> from room to room.

For even within an isolated space can sometimes be compressed a comprehensive world of artistic activity that is ultimately more fictional than poetic. (Many of these very short stories are unfortunately published and even anthologized as "prose poems," inadvertently blurring the necessary distinction between fictional fabrication and essentially poetic expression.) By and large, these general distinctions separate nearly all literary creations, though I can think of several, such as Armand Schwerner's *The Tablets* (1969, 1971), that straddle my categories, largely by mixing poetic forms with aspirations more typical of fiction.

II

The real technical question seems to be how to succeed not
even Joyce and Kafka, but those who've succeeded Joyce
and Kafka and are now in the evenings of their own
careers. —John Barth, "The Literature of Exhaustion"
(1967).

New fictions like new poetries can be divided into those that deal only with the traditional materials of the medium and those that intermingle with other arts. As the roots of fiction have been non-metered language and ways of structuring it into narrative forms, one sure measure of originality in fiction is luminous prose that is genuinely unlike anything written before such as the elliptical writing of bp Nichol in his *Two Novels* (1969):

> lay on his bed and gazed at the desk ties below the level he'd existed on
> body becoming his falling into her river joining every motion she made
> merely his own body entering himself loving noone but himself hating
> himself because his body wasn't his tho she had made her body his alive
> inside himself blobby mass of her breasts swaying against his chest
> choking mamma mamma steam rising

Or this inventive pornography from Ed Sanders's *Shards of God* (1970):

> He prayed over the sexual lubricant in the alabaster jar and swirled his
> cock directly into it, signaling to one of the air corps volunteers to grab
> her ankles as he oiled himself up like a hustler chalking a pool cue. He
> fucked this way, in the anklegrab position, until he heard the starter's gun,
> at which point he whirled about, faced the bed, and leaped up into the air
> toward it, executing a forward one-and-a-half somersault with a full twist
> and landed on all fours on the mattress, ready to grope.

Whereas Nichol and Sanders generally favor familiar vocabularies, a more
obvious stylistic originality comes from the simulated Africanisms of
William Melvin Kelley's *Dunford Travels Everywhere* (1970):

> They ramparded, that reimberserking evolutionary band, toring tend,
> detiring waygone, until that foolephant (every litre having a flow)
> humpened to pass Misory Shutchill's open wide oh to be, and glanzing in,
> unpocked his trunk, GONG to D-chel (musically)

Or by the Joycean overlappings of Kenneth King's "Print-Out" (1967):

> meanWHYle the JESTurer, danSING the E of e-MOTION, ex-
> SKULLclAIMed that ba(SICK)ly the d-REAMS are ex-
> CELLcenterIC, CRYPTOprogrammethODDical paraBABBLES
> and that the germMANIC traDICTION is RE:sPONDERsibyl for his
> being pHAZY on hiSTORYical phoneOMENona. It SEAMS HE
> FOUND doc(CURED)meants which TESTEfy that the QUEEN HAD
> A HISTORY (ECHO)TOMY, and PERSONA-ally sHEHE'HEds
> HESSEtant and not very optimimiMYSITC a-BOUT the FEWture.

Critical praise of inventive language needs no more support than an extended citation; but discussions of structural innovation in fiction are more
problematic in an essay this short.

Innovative art nowadays tends to be either much more or much less,
in terms of quantity of information (words and or events in space), than art
has previously been; and if *Finnegans Wake* represents an epitome of
linguistic abundance, creating so many words out of a rather hackneyed
subject (familial conflict), the contrary motive, analogous to minimalism
in painting and sculpture, endeavors to tell a story with far fewer words than
before as well as avoiding the familiar perils of standard paragraphs. Sections of Gangemi's two-page "Change" (1969), initially published in his collection of "poetry," make huge leaps with every new line (if not, at times,
with every new word), typically compressing great hunks of narrative experience into succinct notations:

> White face and red whiskers
> Red face and white whiskers

Or:

Prophase
Metaphase
Anaphase
Telophase

All of his short, uninflected lists vividly illustrate the fiction's title. Bill Knott's "No-Act Play" (1971) tells a less definable story in a few physically separate lines, while my own "Milestones in a Life" (1971) uses one word (or occasionally two) to define the important events in the life of a fictitious successful American:

    0 birth
    1 teeth
    2 walk

It begins on the left side of the page, continuing through columns that creep to the right to:

76 measles
77 death

Certain pieces superficially similar to "suggestive poetry" are closer to fiction because in only a few words they suggest a narrative action rather than a static event. An example is Steve Kaltenbach's

Perpetuate a hoax

which was first published in 1969. The pages of Emmett Williams' pioneering novel, *Sweethearts* (1967), represent another kind of minimalism, consisting only of that title word which is subject to sequential typographic variations that evoke a heterosexual relationship. Reduced fictions are not synonymous with very short stories, for example Russell Edson's very fine miniatures or the anecdotes comprising John Cage's "Indeterminacy" (1958), both of which contain conventionally structured sentences and paragraphs.

Some new fictional forms depend upon material or structures taken from sources outside of literature. In a witty pastiche that successfully masks its collage-composition, Frederic Tuten's *The Adventures of Mao on the Long March* (1971) mixes paragraphs of conventional historical narrative with fictitious incidents such as Greta Garbo propositioning Mao, and such extrinsic material as verbatim (but unidentified) quotations from a variety of literary sources (Hawthorne, Melville, Wilde, Jack London, Marx-Engels). Exploiting not only nonfictional materials but a nonliterary structure, Jan Herman's brilliant *General Municipal Election* (1969) takes the format of an elaborate election ballot which fills the 12" by 24" space with fictional (and sometimes satirical) choices, while John Barth's "Frame-Tale" (1968) must be cut from the book and then folded and pasted into a Moebius strip (an endless geometrical surface) that reads, "Once upon a time there was story that began" in an interminable circle. An extended masterwork in this mode is Richard Horn's novel, *Encyclopedia* (1969), in which alphabetized notations (filled with cross-references worth following) weave an ambiguous fiction about human interrelationships, paradoxically disordering by reordering; and this novel, like many other examples of new fiction, deliberately frustrates the bourgeois habit of continuous reading. One might say that both the rectangular page and the process of turning pages are as essential to fiction as prose and narrative form; but if the reader must skip around so much, how can he tell whether he has "finished the book"?

Several writers have considered the richly suggestive idea of an imaginative work whose parts can be interchangeably ordered like cards in a pack; however, the masterpiece in this mode has yet to arrive. *Composition No. 1* (1962) by the Frenchman Marc Saporta suffers from the semblance of a linear plot that must be pieced together; and the more pages one reads, the fuller becomes one's sense of Saporta's characters. It would seem that the form of interchangeable parts is more conducive to an absolutely uninflected work, all of whose discrete sections would have equal weight within the whole. Although the materials of *Shufflebook* (1971), a juvenile by Richard Hefter and Martin Stephen Moskof, are structurally more appropriate—one side of the cards containing "and the [name of an animal]" and the other side just verbs—the combinations are invariably slick and trivial. (Like other card fictions, this one can be played by oneself or in conjunction with others.) The only recent novel I know whose parts, mostly a page or two in length, can be read in any order is Marvin Cohen's *A Self-Devoted Friend* (1967) which was inappropriately published as a hardbound book. Henry James Korn's "The Pontoon Manifesto" (1970), published in conventional form in the third issue of *US*, consists of thirty-six fictional beginnings which can theoretically be read in any order (and were, appropriately, later printed on cards that can be shuffled).

Another of the supremely inventive recent novels, Madeline Gins' *Word Rain* (1969), also ranks among the most difficult, dealing with the epistemological opacity of language itself. The first sign of the book's unusual concerns and its equally special humor is its extended subtitle: "(or A Discursive Introduction to the Philosophical Investigations to G,R,E,T,A,G,A,R,B,O, It Says)"; a second is the incorporation of several concerns of new fiction—special languages, expressive design, extrinsically imposed form. Perhaps the surest indication of this novel's originality was the nearly total neglect of reviewers with the exception of Hayden Carruth who sneered in *New American Review* at fictioners' "fooling away their talents in endless novelistic puzzles, a pastime which seems to have reached an ultimate reduction—I hope it's ultimate—in *Word Rain* by Madeline Gins."

"The saddest thing is that I have to use words," announces Gins's narrator, not only echoing the opening sentence of Ford Madox Ford's fictional study of human opacity, *The Good Soldier* (1915), but also exemplifying that Gertrude Steinian paradox of using language to reveal the limitations of both language and the reading process. This last theme of linguistic opacity is reiterated in every section of *Word Rain* rather than developed in a step-by-step way, suggesting that the indicatively unpaginated book is best read in snatches as opposed to straight through. That method (which is also the book's subject) is revealed through a variety of opaque styles; but some of the passages remain more illuminating, if not more definite, than others:

> Each word on the page seemed ossified. The word face was a stone. The word guess was a flint. The words a, the, in, by, up, it, were pebbles. The word laughter was marble. Run was cartilage. Shelf was bone. Talk was an oak board. See was made of quartz. The word refrigerator was enameled. The word afternoon was concrete. The word iron was iron. The word help was wrought-iron. The word old was crag. The word touch was brick. The word read was mica and I was granite.

The book's pages are also distinguished by numerous inventive displays of printed material—lists of unrelated words with dots between them, whole sides filled mostly with dashes where words might otherwise be, pseudo-logical proofs, passages in which the more mundane expressions are crossed out, an appendix of "some of the words (temporary definitions) not included," even a photographed hand holding both sides of a printed page, and a concluding page of print-over-print which reads at its bottom: "This page contains every word in the book." *Word Rain* suffers from the perils of its theme—a linguistic resistance that prevents most readers from discovering its purposes and from entering its imaginative world. That is also a principal fault of Frederick Barthelme's comparable, though lesser effort, *War and War* (1971); but for now, Gins's work, stands as a touchstone of innovative prose.

III

Literature seems to be intermediate between music and painting; its words form rhythms which approach a musical sequence of sounds at one of its boundaries, and form

patterns which approach the hieroglyphic or pictorial image
at the other. The attempts to get as near to these boundaries as possible form the main body of what is called experimental writing. — Northrop Frye, "The Archetypes of
Literature" (1951).

The other strain of new fiction resembles certain parts of *Word Rain* in
mixing fictional concerns with materials and techniques from the other arts.
Visualization is probably a more feasible kind of miscegenation than sound-
fiction which only a few writers, including Norman Henry Pritchard II and
W. Bliem Kern, have broached. In the other fictional intermedium, visual
dimensions are not auxiliary to language as in certain Wright Morris
photographic works, but entwined within the verbal material as in word-
image poetry. In Nancy Weber's "Dear Mother and Dad" (1970), a rather
prosaic tale of the narrator's breakdown is brilliantly enhanced by
photographically reproduced handwriting that expressively changes (and
thus interprets the language) in the course of the four-page story; so that
without this visual dimension the fiction would be unremarkable. In Pritchard's "Hoom" (1970), two-page spreads filled entirely with "sh" are punctuated by a progressively increasing number of spreads with other kinds of
wordless typographical arrangements. And "Oab," by Robert Zend, a
Canadian born in Hungary, brilliantly mixes poems and prose in various
typographies with even more various designs.

In Raymond Federman's masterpiece, *Double or Nothing* (1971), a form
is established for each page — usually a visual shape but sometimes a gram-
matical device such as omitting all the verbs — and the words of his fiction
fill the allotted structure. Over these individually defined pages, which
reveal an unfaltering capacity for formal invention, he weaves several sustained preoccupations, including the narrator's immigration to America,
his poverty, his obsessive memories, his parsimonious passion for noodles.
In *Double or Nothing*, as in much other visual fiction, the page itself is the
basic narrative unit, superseding the paragraph or the sentence, as the work
as a whole becomes a succession of extremely distinctive, interrelated
pages. No other "novel" looks like Federman's contemporary reworking of
Kafka's *Amerika*, which was written fifty years before; none of the other
visual fictions is quite so rich in traditional sorts of content. Reflecting this
new sense of fictional unit, several otherwise less substantial recent novels
incorporate reproductions of a typewritten manuscript (Earl Conrad's
Typoo [1969]); full-page graphics (Steve Katz's pioneering *The Exagggerations
of Peter Prince* [1967] and Eugene Wildman's *Nuclear Love* [1972]); and also
blank pages and totally black ones, the latter two usually signifying the
absence of action or an extended, otherwise undefinable pause.

Predominantly visual fictions emulate the structure of the film in the
sequential development of related images with or without words; but even
in totally visual stories, the narrative exposition is far more selective and

concentrated than in film and so is the audience's perceptual experience and subsequent memory of the work. Many stories that are primarily or exclusively pictorial strive to implant what artists call an "after-image" — a sense of the whole that is visually embedded in the viewer's mind long after he has experienced the work; for in this process the medium of printed pages can be more focused than film. However, since visual fictions, unlike film, cannot simulate the experience of time, much of the "story" and nearly all of its elapsed duration occurs *between* the fiction's frames.

The best of Duane Michals' wordless photographic *Sequences* (1970) is a set of six pictures collectively entitled "The Lost Shoe," the first showing a deserted urban street with the fuzzy backside of a man walking away from the camera and up the street. In the second frame he drops on the pavement a blurred object which in the third frame is seen to be a lady's shoe; and this frame, as well as the next two, suggests that he departs up the street in a great hurry. In the sixth frame the man is nowhere to be seen, while the shoe is mysteriously inflamed. The realism of all the photographs starkly contrasts with the mysteriousness of the plot, while the large changes between frames accent the absolute immobility of the camera. For this last reason, the authorial perspective is as Chekhovian as both the work's title and its passive acceptance of something inexplicably forbidding; and although "The Lost Shoe" could conventionally be classified as a photographic sequence, its ultimate impact is decidedly fictional and, as fiction, is very fine and clearly new.

M. Vaughn-James, an English artist living in Canada, has produced two book-length, line-drawn narratives that superficially resemble the comics but are far more profound and difficult, depending less upon language than pictures in sequence. The first, *Elephant* (1970), seems a prelude to *The Projector* (1971), a superior work, whose 8 ½ " by 11" pages contain rectangular images of various sizes — one, two, four, or six to a page, or one across two pages. These frames, usually devoid of words, articulate a horrifying, almost surreal vision that is finally more bookish than cinematic. *Crackers* (1969), by the Los Angeles painter Edward Ruscha, tells a story almost entirely in photographs which are set on every right-hand page, occasionally accompanied by captions on the left. Perhaps because the pictures all have the same size and each is rather closely related to both its predecessor and successor, while the textures of the photographs seem reminiscent of old movies (and the captions printed on the left echo the silents), *Crackers* seems far closer to film — one wants to flip the pages — yet it is still a book. Eleanor Antin's *100 Boots*, begun in 1970, is an epistolary serial whose parts are picture post cards which she mails once a fortnight. In each frame, 100 boots are seen in various settings, the herd of shoes assuming a life of their own in the course of an extended narrative that will, upon its completion, hopefully be bound into a book.

Other visual fictions differ from "The Lost Shoe" by compressing all of their material into a single page — those of Lee De Jasu and Norman Ogue Mustill — or by their total abstractness, presenting just a sequence of related shapes. In Marian Zazeela's "Lines" (1969) are five pages of related meditative shapes that become more complex for four pages prior to a delicate resolution on the fifth; Jesse Reichek's *etcetera* (1965) is an unpaginated succession of abstract black and white shapes, superficially resembling Rorschach blobs, that echo and complement each other for sixty frames, all presented without any preface or explanation. The progress seems at time symbolic of a descent, but the frames remain largely loyal to their own terms of abstract narration. In this and similar pieces, "Form *is* content, content *is* form," to quote Samuel Beckett's classic remark about *Finnegans Wake*, for both of these dimensions are by necessity experienced simultaneously. And visual fiction can articulate kinds of stories and perceptions — and offer kinds of "reading" experiences — simply unavailable to prose. This is not to say that one picture is worth a thousand words — that is usually nonsense — but that certain kinds of fictional statements can best be made in images alone. Though the old forms of story-telling may be "dead," the impulse to create something new remains doggedly alive, especially in those works that invent fiction twice over — not only its material but its form.

Most of the writers discussed here are still underground — disaffiliated and disorganized, rarely surfacing into public print, inhabiting a culture of little magazines and small press (or self-published) books, somewhat known to each other but unrecognized by more orthodox poets and novelists, all but totally invisible to the larger reading public and then totally excluded from nearly all anthologies except their own; so that their creative adventure is, for the while at least, doomed to isolation and frustration. There is no doubt that an intelligent audience exists for this work; the success of earlier kinds of avant-garde literature — Barth, Borges, Beckett, Barthelme — demonstrates that a large literary public does appreciate innovative writing, and that fact provides reason for hope.

Since established critics ignore this literature, reputations are primarily made among fellow avant-garde artists who, in spite of inevitable conflicts and jealousies, generally acknowledge genuine achievements and advances. As in other arts, stylistic imitation implicitly becomes the sincerest form of flattery and the most honest way of bestowing artistic honor. Despite all the pressures toward cultural alienation and literary hermeticism, most of this new literature is remarkably accessible once the open-minded reader overcomes the superficial difficulties posed by anything original.

If writers coming of age in the twenties thought poetry was king, while those in the thirties and forties were most awed by fiction (and those in the sixties by both personal journalism and poetry), it is my hunch that the next decade will be dominated by innovative literature — by writing in any genre that decidedly surpasses what has been written before.

Bibliography

Ashbery, John. "Idaho," *The Tennis-Court Oath*. Middletown, CT: Wesleyan Univ. Press, 1962.

Bain, Willard. *Informed Sources*. Garden City: Doubleday, 1969.

Barth, John. "Frame-Tale," *Lost in the Funhouse*. Garden City: Doubleday, 1968.

Barthelme, Frederick. *War and War*. Garden City: Doubleday, 1971.

Beckett, Samuel, et al. *Our Examination Around His Factification*. Paris: Shakespeare & Co., 1929.

Berne, Stanley. *The Dialogues*. N.Y.: Wittenborn, 1962.

————. *The Multiple Modern Gods*. N.Y.: Wittenborn, 1964.

————. *The Unconscious Victorious*. N.Y.: Wittenborn, 1969.

Bowles, Jerry, ed. *This Book Is a Movie*. N.Y.: Delta, 1971.

Carruth, Hayden. "The Writer's Situation," *New American Review*, 8 (April, 1970).

Conrad, Earl. *Typoo*. N.Y.: Paul S. Eriksson, 1969.

Depew, Wally. *Once*. Paradise, CA: Dustbooks, 1971.

Edson, Russell. *The Childhood of an Equestrian*. N.Y.: Harper & Row, 1973.

Federman, Raymond. *Double or Nothing*. Chicago: Swallow, 1971.

Fox, Hugh. *The Living Underground*. Troy, NY: Whitson, 1970.

Gangemi, Kenneth. *Lydia*. Los Angeles: Black Sparrow, 1970.

Gins, Madeline. *Word Rain*. N.Y.: Grossman, 1969.

Herman, Jan. *General Municipal Election*. San Francisco: Nova Broadcast, 1969.

Horn, Richard. *Encyclopedia*. N.Y.: Grove, 1969.

Katz, Steve. *The Exagggerations of Peter Prince*. N.Y.: Holt, 1967.

Kelley, William Melvin. *Dunfords Travels Everywheres*. Garden City: Doubleday, 1970.

King, Kenneth. "Print-Out," in Richard Kostelanetz, ed. *Future's Fictions*. Princeton, NJ: Panache, 1971.

Knott, Bill. "No-Act Play," *Auto-Necrophilia*. Chicago: Follett, 1971.

Kostelanetz, Richard. *In the Beginning*. Somerville, MA: Abyss, 1971.

————. *Accounting*. Sacramento, CA: Poetry Newsletter, 1973.

————. "Milestones in a Life," *In Youth*. N.Y.: Ballantine, 1972.

————, ed. *Breakthrough Fictioneers*. W. Glover, VT: Something Else, 1973.

MacLennan, Toby. *1 Walked Out of 2 and Forgot It*. Millerton, NY: Something Else, 1972.

Michals, Duane. *Sequences*. Garden City: Doubleday, 1970.

Nichol, bp. *Two Novels*. Toronto: Coach House, 1969.

Pritchard, Norman Henry II. "Hoom," in Ishmael Reed, ed. *19 Necromancers from Now*. Garden City: Doubleday, 1970.

Reichek, Jesse. *etcetera*. N.Y.: New Directions, 1965.

Ruscha, Edward. *Crackers*. Hollywood: Heavy Industry, 1969.

Sanders, Ed. *Shards of God*. N.Y.: Grove, 1970.

Saporta, Marc. *Composition No. 1*. N.Y.: Simon & Schuster, 1963.

Schwerner, Armand. *The Tablets, I–XV*. N.Y.: Grossman, 1971.

Shiomi, Chieko. *Events and Games*. N.Y.: Fluxus, 1964.

Stein, Gertrude. *The Making of Americans*. N.Y.: Something Else, 1966.

————. *Geography and Plays*. N.Y.: Something Else, 1968.

————. *Painted Lace*. New Haven: Yale Univ. Press, 1955.

Tuten, Frederic. *The Adventures of Mao on the Long March*. N.Y.: Kasak/Citadel, 1971.

Vaughn-James, M. *Elephant*. Toronto: New Press, 1970.

————. *The Projector*. Toronto: Coach House, 1971.

Weber, Nancy. "Dear Mother & Dad," in Richard Kostelanetz and Henry Korn, eds. *Assembling*. Brooklyn: Assembling, 1970.

Wildman, Eugene. *Nuclear Love*. Chicago: Swallow, 1972.

————, ed. *Experiments in Prose*. Chicago: Swallow, 1969.

Young, La Monte; and Marian Zazeela. *Selected Writings*. Munich: Heinar Friedrich, 1970.

Zekowski, Arlene. *Concentrations*. N.Y.: Wittenborn, 1962.

————. *Abraxas*. N.Y. Wittenborn, 1964.

————. *Seasons of the Mind*. N.Y.: Wittenborn, 1964.

Zend, Robert. "Oab," *Exile*, I/1 (1972).

Michel Butor (1963)

Before writing *Mobile* (1962), Michel Butor must have posed this problem to his imagination: How can I depict the entirety of America between a single set of covers? His answer is to describe our land as it would be seen through a binocular kaleidoscope, traveling suspended high above America. The eye of the instrument shifts from one side of America to the other, picking up details and suggestively juxtaposing them against other details. This technique is announced in the opening phrases: "pitch dark in/CORDOVA, ALABAMA, the Deep South,/pitch dark in//CORDOVA, ALASKA, the Far North closest to the dreadful, the abominable, the unimaginable country where it is already Monday when it is still Sunday here. . . ." The kaleidoscope's details, as well as the author's attitude toward them, weave a coherent mosaic which represents Butor's vision of America today.

The ways Butor reveals his vision and attitudes are shrewd and interesting. First, he selects factual details carefully, dwelling particularly on America's passion for the superfluous (the incomparable variety of automobiles and the incredible plethora of spare parts), our insane need for inessential possessions, the vivid irrevocable history of exploitation of both Negroes and Amerindians, and the incessant advertising that corrodes the sense of taste, among other native horrors. In these pages the only fount of sweetness is the exotically flavored ice creams at the local Howard Johnsons.

Against these facts of America, Butor juxtaposes paragraphs of quotation from our idealistic sages—Jefferson, William Penn, Ben Franklin, Louis Sullivan—to show that American dreams, so innocently espoused, have been betrayed by ghastly realities. For instance, in "discussing" American religion, Butor in alternate paragraphs mixes extracts from the blurbs of a Trappist travel folder with a narrative of the Salem witch trials. The tone of Butor's report, so heavily rooted in details, suggests that he wants less to accuse America of hypocrisy than to reveal the tragedy of American experience. For this reason, when he expresses anger, it is aimed at our refusal to accept that we have failed our aspirations—a refusal exemplified in the gall that prompts us to name a town "Eden." Although *Mobile* suffers from Butor's reluctance to confront many aspects of contemporary America—bureaucratic life and academia being two—no recent essay I know by a foreigner, imaginative or otherwise, so successfully comes to terms with the whole of contemporary America.

In picking up *Mobile*, one is immediately faced with the problem of how to read this 319-page collection of fragments. In my experience, one need not read it straight through, as one would a traditional narrative. As in all books of vision, the effects here are repetitious. Second, since the book's structure is thoroughly spatial (rather than linear-narrative), neither Butor's technique nor his basic attitude develops in the course of the book; his points are proved by example, not by developed argument. Therefore, *Mobile* should be dipped into from time to time. As one learns to assimilate the travelogue's technique, he finds himself reading more of it at each snatch.

Incidentally, it is lamentable that this most difficult of contemporary books was shamefully mistreated by the media of review. In a decision that betrayed its disinterestedly highbrow pretentions, *The New York Review* assigned *Mobile* to Truman Capote, who has declared in print (*Paris Review Interviews* No. 1) that he can spare no more than two hours to read a book. Capote, discovering that *Mobile*, of course, required more effort than his quota, snidely reported what his editors could have surely expected—that the book to him was unreadable. Since each of Butor's several works has been more difficult than its predecessor, the expectation is that the next ones will be even more complex. Must we similarly expect that they will just as surely get mishandled by the American reviewing press?

Jean-François Bory (1974)

I first noticed Jean-François Bory's work in the Summer 1967 issue of *Chicago Review*, which its editors had decided to devote to "concretism," for Bory's contribution, entitled "Spot," was clearly the most distinguished work in an otherwise disappointing anthology. What particularly struck me about Spot was Bory's sensitivity to the rhythm of turning printed pages, for the difference between one image of Spot and the next duplicated, to my senses at least, the time that the reader takes in moving from one page to another. I later wrote that "Spot" consists of "the same image progressively magnified over seven right-hand pages until the page is all but entirely blackened by just a portion of the middle letter; and this inundating image becomes an ironic inversion of the otherwise progressive process of magnification (a form similar to Eugene Ionesco's ironically linear, *The New Tenant*, where the room fills up with so many objects that the new occupant is smothered)." "Spot," like Bory's later work, was neat and clean (and thus graphic) rather than hand-made (or painterly).

As Bory included my own work in an anthology he compiled, *Once Again* (New Directions, 1968), we began to correspond, and I have since then always treasured his letters, which are written in an idiosyncratic pastiche of French and English. Though Bory's syntax is scrambled, the meaning behind his words is always clear. (Another Parisian visual poet, by contrast, writes me in grammatically proper English sentences, whose meaning I cannot comprehend.) I was also gratified to discover, in correspondence (as we still have not met), that Bory shared my own low opinion of most "concrete poetry." Our mutual judgment led in turn to my own subsequent questioning of the validity of that once-popular term.

By this time, I regarded Bory as not a "poet" but a "fictioner," which is to say a teller of stories. For me he discovered that the rectangular page, rather than the sentence or the paragraph, could be the basic unit of fictional discourse; and the key to his compositional style lay in combining comprehensible words with visual abstractions in essentially fictional sequences. As he wrote in *Once Again*, "The page itself can become a material, a statement, the information, the text, progressing or diminishing from page to page. The writer, thus becoming the layout artist of his book, will no longer write stories (or moments), but books."

In *Once Again*, Bory included a brilliant sequence that I have not seen reprinted elsewhere, "The worldWord is . . ." (It resembles his "Fouilles Anticipes," which was published in France; but the two are not identical.) In this concise gem, words progressively emerge from the image of a large black circle, which reduces in size, only to enlarge, progressively again, to its original size as the words pass back into the black ball. Over a succession of only ten images, this work tells a universal story about language and its relationship to man. (This theme reminds me of John Furnival's monumental panels, *Tours de Babel Changés en Ponts*, which tells a similarly synoptic story about language — over a series of six wooden doors, each six feet high, the whole being fourteen feet across.)

The next Bory work that awed me was "Saga," which initially appeared in the third number of *Approches* (1968), for Bory successfully extended his interest in sequential word-images into a longer fiction — a novella, if you will — which portrayed a descent followed by a re-emergence. Since "Saga" was the most successful example I had ever "read" of visual fiction, I acknowledged this excellence in an essay written early in 1969, but not published until Sept., 1970, in *Art International*. Here I described "Saga" as a "sequence of word-images [in which] the phrase *On Va*, or 'One Goes,' is superimposed over background photographs; and in turning the twenty-eight pages, the reader experiences a descent into a mysterious realm, where images are forbidding and unclear, and vaguely perceptible letters are scrambled. The reader then encounters surreal maps where places are renamed as parts of speech, only to emerge at the conclusion with an image identical to that at the beginning. Within less than thirty pages, in sum, is all the material and linear experience of a silent movie or, perhaps, a novel."

Soon after this essay appeared, Bory sent me *Post-Scriptum* (1970), which documents his creative evolution — away from exclusively verbal texts, set in horizontal lines of type (like conventional poetry) and into more experimental, mostly visual work. What distinguishes the book, in my judgment, is the variousness of both the imagery and the syntax — both the material on the page and the ways in which the pages relate to each other. The collection reaffirmed my earlier sense of Bory as a true master — not as just a poet or a story-teller but as a "literary artist" of the first rank. I gather that *Post-Scriptum* signals Bory's repudiation of printed media, not only as a predilection of his ironic intelligence but also as a reflection of his assertion that "the end purpose of the book is that there will be an end to books."

Bory has since devoted most of his energies to one-of-a-kind visual works, closer to paintings than books, which have been exhibited all over Europe. Since these unique works-to-display have not yet come to America (which remains unfortunately ignorant of certain developments in contemporary art), I have not been able to see them. One price of success within the world of visual art is a loss in public communication. The primary reason why this is lamentable is that Bory has been a pioneer in a continuing development — the art of international book-making, which is to say bound volumes that need not be translated because their material can be universally understood. It is as a book-artist that I particularly revere Bory.

Tom Phillips (1976)

My whole work is dominated by Coleridge's idea of keeping
the greatest number of things suspended in a unity, the
greatest diversity possible within a single thing.

Tom Phillips is a British artist known to us primarily as the author of
A Humument, an exemplary visual narrative whose parts have appeared in
several American anthologies. In brief, *A Humument* is a visual re-working
of a Victorian novel, *A Human Document* by W.H. Mallock. What Phillips
did is paint over parts of Mallock's pages, so that only certain of the original
words shine through, shrewdly extracting from each of Mallock's pages a
personal, Phillipsian text. (Typically, out of "A Hum(an Doc)ument"
comes "A Humument.") The result he describes as "an attempt to make a
Gesamtkunstwerk in small format, since it includes poems, music scores,
parodies, notes on aesthetics, autobiography, concrete texts, romance,
mild erotica, as well as the undertext of Mallock's original story." In Phillips'
hands, this technique is far more fertile than I for one imagined it to be. As
Phillips justly testifies, "I have so far extracted from it over six hundred
texts, and have yet to find a situation, statement or thought which its words
cannot comprehend or its phrases adapted to cover." Since the book is such
an obvious masterpiece, I have for years now been awaiting the complete
edition, ideally in the original colors (which get lost in the black-white
reproductions). This new Phillips book, alas, is not that.

Instead, Hansjörg Mayer, an otherwise first-rate German avant-
garde publisher, has recently issued a spectacular volume, entitled *Tom
Phillips. Works. Texts. To 1974*, that contains not only choice pages from *A
Humument* (too few, in my judgment) but also reproductions, often in full
color, of Phillips' works in other media — paintings, prints, drawings,
musical scores, etc. — in addition to Phillips' own running commentary on
these endeavors. This book portrays Phillips as a conscientious, hard-
working, intelligent, premeditated artist who works in various ways, for
various purposes, toward various ends, simultaneously. Whereas most
visual artists concentrate upon developing an instantly recognizable
idiosyncratic style, it is Phillips' heresy to cultivate diversity. His expository
commentaries reveal not the dominance of a single vision but a persistent

concern with materials — postcards, books, maps, canvas, paper, film, musical theater; so that he speaks mostly of the technical problems that were confronted (and resolved) in the making of each work.

Perhaps the sole identifying characteristic of his visual art is the incorporation of language into the face of most, though not all, of his works. This use of language, as well as his variousness, perhaps reflects the fact that he was initially educated in literature, rather than visual art; and one theme of his autobiographical introduction is how Phillips, in his twenties, transformed himself into a polyartist — someone whose serious creative work falls into and across several artistic domains. Surprisingly, *A Humument* is scarcely the core endeavor in Phillips' career. It began, instead, merely as "idle play" that, as he puts it, "has been done in the evenings so that I might not, had the thing become a folly, regret the waste of days." Fortunately, Mallock's *A Human Document* is such a rich source of suggestion that Phillips has completed a second, entirely different reworking of Mallock's pages, and is already beginning a third.

This new book, *Tom Phillips*, serves the function of bringing the artist's variousness together into a single package; it is a catalogue, so to speak, for an unheld exhibition — or, even better, a one-man retrospective by itself, in a compact portable package. I find it indicative that, like the premier modern polyartist Moholy-Nagy, Phillips should find that the spine-bound book is the best medium for exhibiting the sum of his interests, which is to say the totality of his artistic intelligence and achievements. [Moholy's exemplary polyartistic restrospective was *Vision in Motion* (1947)]. Indicatively again, *Tom Phillips*, with its commentaries, is also more coherent than the body of his disparate works; from reading it, I for one have a better sense of what his art is about — a better sense than the works by themselves can provide. (Not unlike other polyartists, Phillips is terribly uneven; some of his works strike me as much superior to others.) Phillips speaks of *A Humument* as "a paradoxical embodiment of Mallarmé's idea that everything in the world exists in order to end up as a book." That perception implicitly extends to *Tom Phillips*.

(1985)

Back in 1965, as he tells it, Tom Phillips, then a young British author-artist, discovered William Burroughs' experimental hypothesis of the literary "cut-up." Inspired by the idea of taking apart and reassembling another author's text, Phillips resolved to purchase the first fat book he could get for threepence (less than a dime). That book turned out to be a forgotten Victorian novel by W.H. Mallock, *A Human Document*. However, instead of cutting the book apart, Phillips decided to draw directly on its pages, so that only certain words showed through. Using this process of reduction through addition, or extraction by addition, Phillips literally authored his own book on Mallock's pages.

While Mallock's prose became raw material for Phillips' elliptical poetry, *A Human Document* became, with the elimination of a few letters, *A Humument*. What had been garbage fiction became a contemporary artist's feast. "I have never come across its equal in later and more conscious searchings," he writes in the afterword here. "Its vocabulary is rich and lush, and its range of reference and allusion large. I have so far extracted from it over one thousand texts [four hundred more than before], and have yet to find a situation, statement or thought which its words cannot be adapted to cover." As the 375 pages of *A Humument* are more than the 367 of the original book, Phillips has obviously done several Mallocks more than once.

The words on the Phillips opening page look like this:

```
The following
            sing
I
            a
book.      a      book
                of   art
                            of


                    mind
                     art
            and
            that
                which

                 he
                 hid
            reveal  I
```

In place of the missing Mallock words is a beige field punctuated by white space in the shape of an arrow; around the edge of the field is a gray border of cross-hatched lines that only partially mask the book's type. On other pages of *A Humument*, visible words are surrounded by a variety of images, both representational and abstract, in many colors and shapes.

Black and white pages from Phillips' project began appearing in literary and art magazines, in both England and America, in the late 1960s, and a selection of these pages, also in black and white, titled *Trailer* (as in movie trailers), appeared in 1971 under the imprint of Hansjörg Mayer, a German printer-poet who teaches graphic design in London. I remember that around that time I recommended *A Humument* to publishers here, but they all balked at the fact that the originals were not in the black and white of periodicals (and *Trailer*) but in color, whose reproduction would be prohibitively expensive. So some color reproductions appeared not within the structure of a spine-bound book but as small separate prints, more suitable for framing. Color reproductions of yet other pages also appeared in a book-length retrospective of Phillips' *Works. Texts. To 1974* (1975) that was likewise published by Hansjörg Mayer. These color selections from *A Humument* were so superior to the black-and-white that I remember wondering if this work, by then a genuine underground classic, would ever be publicly available in its original form of a spine-bound book with sequential colored pages. It was no pleasure crediting Phillips with innocently producing something that book publishers piously insist cannot exist: the masterpiece that no one, utterly no one, is able to publish.

To the rescue again came Hansjörg Mayer, whose family happens to own a large Stuttgart printing company; and it produced a color edition, in roughly the same size as Mallock's original novel and thus in the same size as Phillips' original pages. Copies of this definitive edition are distributed not by Mayer's firm, like earlier Phillips books, but by an Anglo-American art house at a price so incredibly low, given all the color work, that it (like the book itself) would be impossible, were someone not doing both the author and the public a great favor.

The beauty of *A Humument* lies not only in the designs for individual pages, but in the sequential rhythms that are established as the reader moves from page to page. This is the sort of esthetic experience indigenous to the book medium, especially when, as here, the means of enhancement are as often visual as verbal. Like William Blake before him, Phillips appears to be one of those rare artists who work best with word and image together. (Indeed, for all these similarities in this last respect, the two are quite different. That observation suggests, in turn, that visual-verbal terrain is still quite open.) *A Humument* must be seen to be believed; not even reproductions in magazines and, especially, newspapers can do justice to its hues.

Another sign of the book's weight is that other artists have imitated its additive/extractive form — among them Doris Cross in a recent issue of the American magazine *Kauldron* — but none have achieved the wit, the inventiveness or, most important, the scale of Phillips' work. In recent years, Phillips himself has concentrated more on his painting, which is perhaps better known outside the U.S. Like other adventurous artists nowadays, he has explored areas far beyond his initial terrain. His musical version of pages from *A Humument* and a similar work, *Irma*, have been released on two scarce records. But his principal project for the past few years has been another visual-verbal creation with Blakean echoes: an illustrated edition of his own translation of Dante's *Inferno*. Good as he may be at other arts, at book art Tom Phillips is a master.

Richard Grayson (1981)

Richard Grayson is a compulsive fictioner who, in addition to publishing over 150 stories before turning thirty, has a penchant for transforming everything he can into fiction. Two of the more unusual creations in his collection, *With Hitler in New York* (1979), appear on the dustjacket flap that encases the book and as a "Note on the Type" that concludes it.

The former in its entirety is also an introduction to the characteristic density of Grayson's style and the weight of his individual sentences:

> The anarchist bomb that killed Czar Alexander II in St. Petersburg in 1881 led to the Russian pogroms and to the anti–Semitic May laws of 1882. To these events we Americans owe countless things: the comedy of Woody Allen and Lenny Bruce; the popularity of psychoanalysis; the vaccine against polio; the radical movement on America's campuses; the novels of Nathanael West and Philip Roth; the entrance of the noun "chutzpah" into the *Random House Dictionary of the English Language*; Al Jolson's rendition of "mammy" in blackface; seven gold medals won by the United States Olympic swimming team in 1972 at Munich; the Ziegfeld Follies; a certain kind of suburban vulgarity typified by the town of Woodmere, Long Island; the establishment of the International Ladies' Garment Workers Union and that of Murder, Incorporated; Father Coughlin's radio broadcasts; Sunday brunches featuring bagels and lox; the condominium culture of southern Florida; the fact that it is no longer considered good form to use the word "Jew" as a verb meaning "to bargain."

> Furthermore and more importantly, these events in Russia a century ago led to my being here in these United States, to my becoming a fiction writer, to my writing of this book, and ultimately to your reading of it.

> So if you have any complaints about *With Hitler in New York*, address them to the anarchist whose bomb snuffed out the life of the Czar. I take no responsibility for this whatsoever.

In that fiction of two hundred-plus words is, by any measure, a lot of presentation, action and interpretation.

A principal character of Grayson's stories is someone named "Richard Grayson," for he has mastered the devices of Chekhov and Moravia for intimately relating to the reader, in addition to populating his stories with familiar names (Howard Cosell, Warren Burger, Pol Pot, et al.) and referring familiarly to his immediate relatives. So successful is he at making everything he writes seem real that one woman recently published a critical essay in which she tried to define Grayson the person by pulling together the pieces in his stories. "His stories sound so confessional," she testifies, "it is hard to separate the author from the character."

No, "Grayson" is Grayson's favorite character; and not unlike other ironists, he creates a fiction to give this ruse away. It tells of an actor named "Grayson Richards" who for twenty-seven years has played a television soap opera character named, you guessed it, "Richard Grayson." To compound the irony, this story is told in the breathless, methodical style of *TV Guide*. One quality that I especially like in this book is the strength of Grayson's fictionalizing intelligence, for its ultimate theme is the nature and variety of fictional artifice. Style is marbles; everything else is *schmutz*. At the end of one paragraph in this story is the revelatory tag: "Fiction won out."

Grayson publishes generously, and is generous in his publishing. The copyright page to this collection acknowledges, in sum, *"Shenandoah, Confrontation, Carleton Miscellany, Epoch, Writ, Junction, Zone, riverrun, Student Lawyer, Dark Horse, Boxspring, Statements 2: New Fiction, Tailings, Phantasm, Contrast, Calvert, Uroboros, Bellingham Review, Dragon Fire, Ataraxia, The Small Pond, Mikrokosmos, Star-Web Paper, Willmore City, Chouteau Review, Paris Voices."* A list so diversified indicates that Grayson is "making it" on the strength of his work, rather than the putative reputations of the places in which his fiction appears (or, by extension, the putative reputations of his fellow contributors). When, by contrast, the latest "discovery" of the literary-industrial complex appears only in *Esquire* and *The New Yorker*, you know not that this new writer is good but that some literary operator is working overtime. Whereas such hotshots may disappear with changes in management, Grayson will survive, because he has "made it" so far.

Grayson is good; and as he passes thirty, there is every reason to believe he will get better. He is funny and serious, inventive and competent, ambitious and abundant. (This I can deduce from the work, not from piecing together pseudo-biographical details.) There are more collections of his fictions to be published, and I look forward to reading them.

Twenty-Five Fictional Hypotheses
(1969)

All art, it seems, begins as a struggle to vanquish chaos
with the aid of the abstract or the holy; never does it begin
by representation of the individual. — André Malraux, *The
Imaginary Museum* (1953).

I.) *Fiction* n. 1.) a making up of imaginary happenings; feigning.
2.) anything made up or imagined, as a statement, story, etc. 3.) a) any
literary work portraying imaginary characters and events. b) such works
collectively; esp. novels and stories. — *Webster's New World Dictionary* (1966).

II.) *Fiction* 1.) The action or product of fashioning or imitating — 1784.
2.) Feigning; deceit, dissimulation, pretense — 1609. 3.) the action of
feigning or inventing imaginary existences, events, states of things, etc.
1605. b. That which is feigned or invented; invention as opposed to fact.
c. A statement proceding from mere invention; such statements collectively
1611. 4.) Fictitious composition. Now usually prose novels and stories collectively, or the composition of such works 1599. — *Oxford English Dictionary*
(1933).

III.) There are no definite limits upon the extrinsic materials available to
the teller of stories; the practical limits upon fictional possibility are intrinsic
in the creative imagination and one's chosen medium.

IV.) As the stuff of fiction is invention, so fiction comes from the invention
of stuff — this observation suggesting that writers so far have scarcely sam-
pled all the possible ways of stuffing "fiction."

V.) Words need not be the building blocks of fiction, or sentences the glue,
or paragraphs the frames, or human beings the "characters"; for realized
fiction, no matter now unusual, cannot but create its own subject, its own
style, its own "events," its own life.

VI.) The primary subject of the best printed literature has always been
capabilities indigenous to the medium — effects that come from special
language and or the turning of pages; but just as neither pages nor prose

182

are absolutely essential to fiction, so this mediumistic emphasis does not deny the possibility, or value, of extrinsic references.

VII.) Even the most innovative fictions embody at least *one* element of the classic literary art, whether that be heightened language, the semblance of narrative, credible detail, or developed characterizations; but it is highly unlikely, though not impossible, that a story containing all of these traditional elements will be unquestionably new.

VIII.) Perhaps the line will supersede the word, the page the sentence, the chapter the paragraph, and the binding the chapter as the basic fictional units — or vice versa, the word the line, the sentence the page, etc.; but these changes in scale notwithstanding, the crucial test of every new fiction will be whether it achieves a synthetic and yet self-consistent world.

IX.) Fiction created for sequential printed pages is likely to emulate in form the dominant communications vehicles of the age — in our time, newspapers, films, television; yet the best literary art necessarily eschews not only the contents but the forms already familiar to these new media.

X.) Fictions alone cannot change the world, though they are forever infiltrating, if not liberating, the imaginations of those who do and might; and though artists are clearly influenced by popular culture, in the end the mass media, and much else, remain far more indebted to elitist art.

XI.) The consequential fictions have always touched upon essential themes — history, nature, growth and decay, communication and relationships, reality and illusion, imagination, fate, etc.; but unfamiliar artifice often puts a surmountable block between such meanings and readers who are initially superficial or oblivious.

XII.) A passion for the medium itself and some visions of its possible uses are by now the primary reasons for creating fictions; everything else, such as narrative, say, or prose, is inevitably secondary.

XIII.) The use of imposed constraints, as in traditional poetic forms, forces the creating imagination to resist the easy outs, if not clichés as well; and they encourage problem-solving and other processes of playfulness, in addition to challenging the reader to discern sense and significance in what at first seems inscrutable.

XIV.) Certain new works are so original that at first they scarcely resemble any "fiction" we know; but since only a Philistine would dare dismiss an unfamiliar creation as "not-fiction," art once again prompts us to review our standards of literary convention and esthetic appropriateness.

XV.) Formal advances in a particular art often come from adapting the ideas and procedures developed in another field; and sometimes out of this process of cross-fertilization blossoms not just a new step in the art but a true hybrid, in this case between literature and something else.

XVI.) Can it be that presenting a painter's work in chronological succession tells the story of his creative life—the fictions he wrought—so definitively that nothing more need be written; in that case, doesn't everyone carry his "autobiography" snugly in his head?

XVII.) Specificity signals the end of art and the beginning of journalism, history, sociology, or some other form of non-fiction; fiction at its best is neither factual nor familiar but feigned.

XVIII.) Literary fiction could be characterized as the residue of the confrontation between a fictionalizing intelligence and the printed page; but the rectangular paper frame is so plainly the most indomitable constraint upon those imaginations that seem eager to burst through the page.

XIX.) There can be no end to fiction before the demise of imagination, which is to say that as long as man survives there will be new forms of fictionalizing—though that historical form called "the novel" may be judged "dead," fiction isn't.

XX.) A measure of artistry in fiction is personal touch, even though nothing about the author himself need be revealed; the crucial question is this: Could—even would—any other name sign this work?

XXI.) The canon of modernist fiction—Stein, Lissitzky, Faulkner, Joyce, Beckett, Borges—established a tradition of the new that must in turn be artistically surpassed in the present.

XXII.) The new fiction of today need be no more different from the old than, say, 1970 differs from 1960, whose automobiles, clothes, hair styles, advertisements, machines, etc. clearly belong, we know, in junk shops or museums.

XXIII.) The only evidence of true madness in creative art is a breakthrough, because much that pretends to originality is merely capricious eccentricity or exploitative faddishness; insanity itself, however, is generally counter-productive.

XXIV.) Modern art at its best deals not in the manipulation of conventions but their conspicuous neglect, because familiar forms are the most common counters of commerce; one test of genuine innovation in art, even today, is its resistance to an immediate sale.

XXV.) New fiction bears little superficial resemblance to old fiction, while the experience of "reading" radical work is also profoundly different; so too must the standards and perhaps the language of fiction's criticism radically change.

Constructivist Fictions (1974)

Constructivist fictions are built, rather than expressed; they originate, to a greater degree than other art, in those parts of the writer's mind that are, in Mondrian's phrase, "unconditioned by subjective feeling and conception."

Constructivist fictions exist in space and time — the space of a printed page and the time it takes a reader to turn from one page to the next.

Conceived before they are executed, such fictions customarily reflect premeditated principles that are articulated within the work itself; the relevance and meaning of each detail are initially intrinsic.

The materials within a particular fiction constitute its predominant language, and how they change within the space and time of printed pages is the principal method of "storytelling."

Constructivist fictions tend "to write themselves," once their initial premises are established; the process by which they are made could be called "generative."

They embody an intelligence that exists apart from their author, and this intelligence focuses upon matters of detail; constructivist fictions are intelligent in ways their authors might not be.

"Generative" is not the same as mechanical, for decisions of taste inform the genesis and operation of the work's construction.

One recurring theme is variation and development within a systemic constraint.

Constructivist fictions extend the modernist tradition of mediumistic purification, in which forms and materials within the work represent little, if anything, beyond themselves.

In their literalism, in contrast to "realism" or "symbolism," such narrative sequences could be characterized as "pure"; what the reader sees is most, if not all, of what there is.

The language of such fiction articulates height, width, shape, space, motion and perhaps depth, in addition to interrelations among these elements.

Titles in constructivist fiction tend to be descriptive, and this description is usually verifiable, the title suggesting a primary meaning without exhausting the reservoir of possible secondary significances.

Structure within constructivist fiction is usually more explicit than implicit; the lines of activity are elemental and unadorned.

Syntax in these pieces tends to be systemic, for how a certain page relates to its immediate predecessors will influence, if not determine, how that page relates to its immediate successors.

Not one page but two or at most three should indicate crucial characteristics of the system.

Since every part has a particular appropriate place in a system of signs that is intrinsically evolved, nothing but nothing is arbitrary.

In constructivist fiction, as in every rigorously conceived and executed art, "mistakes" can be verified and thus can also be corrected.

The most distinctive marks of this work, to some minds, are not what it contains but what is excluded — in terms not only of materials but of evocative qualities; however, critical interpretations that emphasize omissions (e.g., "anti-fiction") are invariably partial and obscure.

All literature represents transformations or reifications of the author's experience; but the constructivist writer differs from others in emphasizing kinds of human experience — kinds of information and perceptions — that were previously foreign to literature.

The constructivist artist finds order outside himself, rather than within himself.

Constructivist artists eschew the representation of an object or a scene that is familiar in order to create a meta-reality that they regard as "true" (which may or may not be true), but what is indisputable is the sense that the reality — the world of activity — of their creation stands first of all by itself.

Gabo and Pevsner suggested in 1920 that "art should stop being imitative and try instead to discover new forms."

II

Constructivist fiction differs from journalism (and most current fiction) in being more general than particular; in this respect, it resembles classic literature.

Constructivist fiction is primitive in its taste for elemental forms and sophisticated in its operative assumptions; it represents an extreme, perhaps ultimate, development of formalism in fiction.

The author superficially resembles the child who moves the blocks around, but here his compositional principles are ultimately more sophisticated.

The idea of constructivist fiction is indebted to the visual works and theoretical writings of van Doesburg, Mondrian, Moholy-Nagy, among others; it acknowledges esthetic biases that have had scarce impact upon literary creation, especially in America.

Esthetic assumptions that once seemed "heretical" in painting, say, still strike most writers as "unthinkable" in literature.

Constructivism resembles Dada in its nonpsychological outlook and its freedom with materials; it has little in common with "Surrealism."

I would like to think that Moholy-Nagy could have written stories like these, had he decided to write fiction, because these works, like his, draw upon modernist traditions in all the arts — not just literature but painting and music as well.

Perhaps the most prominent current practitioner of constructivist fiction is Sol LeWitt — not in his three-dimensional objects but in such printed books as *Arcs, Circles & Grids* (1972).

Constructivist literature does not express personality, however idiosyncratic its style; yet a body of work undoubtedly reveals, in indirect ways, deeply personal proclivities.

Constructivist fiction is impersonal in content but personal in style.

Reflecting neither nature nor personality, constructivist fiction exists in an autonomous realm, echoing nothing so much as itself.

Pattern articulates space in making not a single picture, but a narrative.

The work could be called "Structural Fiction," because of its emphasis upon structural development; but since it has no explicit relation to French "structuralism" in either philosophy or literature, that term would be deceptive.

Constructivist Fiction is very concrete (i.e., "characterized by or belonging to immediate experience of actual things or events" and or "formed by coalition of particles into one solid mass").

He who feels draws; he who thinks patterns.

Since the "content" of even the best literature tends to be simplistic by philosophical standards, it is for something else that we turn the page — primarily the experience of effects intrinsic to the medium itself.

Constructivist fictions exist within and outside the traditions of modernist literature, within and without the traditions of modernist visual art.

Much of my own earlier visual fiction could be characterized as not "constructivist" but merely abstract, as I wanted to tell a story entirely within its own terms, with minimal extrinsic reference, using verbal titles much as an abstract painter does — to function as an entrée to one of the ways in which the images might be understood.

III

As the processes of its creation differ from those of most fiction, so must constructivist fiction be perceived differently.

Most readers of fiction, to be frank, have been trained to look for elements that, in constructivist fiction, are not immediately apparent, but closer examination will reveal how some of these traditional elements are present here in other languages such as lines in visual space.

Reading constructivist fictions at a pace approximately similar to that demanded by a page of prose, one perceives the whole of a page and then the parts, which relate not only to the whole but also to the gestalts of the preceding pages.

Form is field is form is field.

Titles in these stories function much like this essay — to tell what the work is about, not what it is; there is no substitute for first-hand, unmediated experience of the work itself.

What might initially shock the experienced fiction-reader will become more accessible on second viewing or third; since the language of constructivist fiction inculcates the reader in itself, its mode of communication can eventually become more familiar.

Constructivist fiction is more spiritual than natural, more mental than material, more conceptual than perceptual, more empirical than ambiguous, more intellectual than emotional, more thoughtful than thoughtless, more biological than psychological, more synthetic than analytical, and more exterior than interior.

Constructivist fictions incorporate qualities indigenous to painting and music and yet remain narrative and thus literature; antiliterary in certain respects, they are pre-eminently literary in others.

One factor distinguishing constructivist fiction from a constructivist painting is the assumption that the former is, like the printed book, structurally sequential and infinitely reproducible.

Constructivist fictions differ from abstract animations primarily in their sense of pace: proceeding at a rate quite different from the automatic 24 frames a second of motion pictures, a visual narrative composed on printed pages acknowledges the time a reader takes to turn the page; the most appropriate mechanical analogue is slide projection.

Spatially, constructivist fictions acknowledge the framing functions of the printed page, resembling in this respect the appearance of traditional prose typography.

In constructivist fiction, circles and lines, say, can function as "characters"; their metamorphosis with its entanglements and denouements becomes the plot.

One aim of constructivist fiction is enlarging our capacities for narrative perception; the pleasures offered by this work are hopefully both sensual and intellectual.

Only by broaching a domain that initially strikes most readers as "not fiction" can a writer expand the possibilities of literature, for the mere consideration of unfamiliar materials allows both reader and writer to rediscover literary essentials.

Because this work is formally advanced, it is culturally progressive, teaching people how to perceive and assimilate something they have not experienced before; it also functions as an antidote to both artistic decadence and the literary-industrial complex.

These particular works embody such ethical ideals as purposefulness, constraint, purity and connectedness, in addition to the esthetic ideals of harmony, both visually and temporally, and complexity within simplicity.

In the chaos of human activity, one redeeming force is human constructive consciousness.

One critical issue in constructivist fiction is verisimilitude — the fidelity of every detail not to extrinsic reality, but to material that went before and material that follows, which is to say the fictional reality fabricated within the piece itself.

In systemic fiction, the scheme emerging from the whole is the principal theme — not only anterior but superior to any of its individual realizations; this generative content, though not evident on any particular page, is implicitly present throughout.

Constructivist fictions are susceptible to multiple interpretations but not to "ambiguous" ones.

The process of turning these pages ideally evokes sensations that must be defined as "esthetic," in part because they cannot be classified as anything else; partially because these feelings are inexplicable except in their own terms, they can be characterized as "pure."

One virtue of symmetrical organizations is purity; a second is verifiability; a third is impregnable stability; a fourth is the beauty of elemental, monumental forms.

"Mystery" is not a quality necessarily prerequisite to art; verification is not a process contrary to esthetic perception.

These fictions tell their stories in a language so universal that the works themselves need no translation; for non–English-speaking readers, only the titles need be glossed, ideally in a footnote.

The sculptor Naum Gabo said that he used the word "constructivist" to indicate that, "We want it to be known as a distinct form of art, different from other forms of art."

And So Forth (1978)

Initially conceived as an extension of my Constructivist Fictions, *And So Forth* is similarly concerned with telling a story entirely in the language of lines, with an intentionally limited vocabulary of shapes, and with "events" that are a single page in length and square in frame. This new work differs, however, from the Constructivist Fictions in two crucial qualities. These images are *not* perfect, four-sided symmetries, although the shapes within each drawing often echo each other geometrically. Secondly, in this work the progress from image to image, from page to page, from event to event, is not systematic but associational. Thus, one image does not necessarily lead to another, but each could precede or succeed any of the others. The loose pages can be shuffled and reshuffled to taste, or even hung along a wall so that they can all be seen at once, or deposited looseleaf in an envelope, or put into a spring binder. In certain structural respects, this new work is closer to my collection of single-sentence stories, *Openings & Closings* (1975) than to my previous visual fiction. By some measures, this new work represents an advance for me; by others, it is perhaps a step behind. In most respects, *And So Forth* is something new.

On *Symmetries*: My Visual Novel (1985)

The simple line and its development in purely geometrical regularity was bound to offer the greatest possibility of happiness to the man disquieted by the obscurity and entanglement of phenomena. — Wilhelm Worringer, *Abstraction and Empathy* (1908).

Two radical qualities distinguishing my artistic work are that I sometimes use symmetry, along with other rigorous systems (that are purportedly contrary to the spirit of Art), and that I write poems and fictions with materials other than syntactical sentences (that are purportedly the basis of Literature), which is to say that I have made both poems and fictions out of isolated words, nonsyntactic sequences, numbers and uninflected lines.

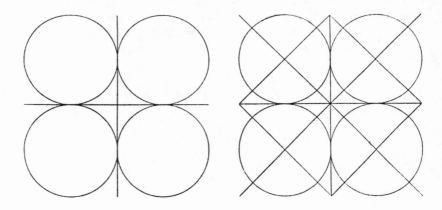

Symmetries is a novel, composed in the language of lines; it is divided into three chapters, each considerably longer than its immediate predecessor. Its "setting" is three generations of rectilinear grids that do not change; its three principal "characters" are a diagonal line that leans 45 degrees to the left, a diagonal line that leans 45 degrees to the right, and a circle. These figures in their various symmetrical arrangements enact not only a single sustained narrative but numerous subplots of varying length, all of which incorporate, among other motifs, antagonism and resolution. One structure distinguishing *Symmetries* from conventional fiction is that its sequences can be read in both directions; either cover can be considered its "front" or its "back."

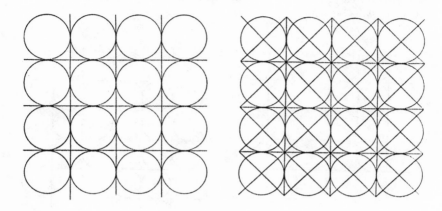

The principal theme of *Symmetries* is that system informing its composition; each part epitomizes a form that embodies the content. Just as each page is a component of the whole, which could be described as an exhaustive permutational exploration of a single general statement about four-sided geometrical symmetries, so each image, though visibly different from all the others, incorporates characteristics common to all parts of the entire work. Simple and skeletal in certain respects, *Symmetries* is quite complex and full in others; it is also perhaps the most complete realization of certain visionary principles that have informed my fiction for the past dozen years.

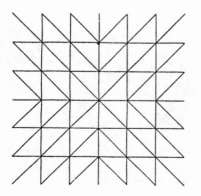
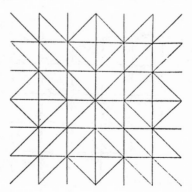

What makes symmetrical forms more attractive than asymmetrical is not only their balance and proportional harmony but their capacity for a precise narrative development that is eventually resolved. Exhaustibility — both visually, within a single image, and sequentially, from image to image — can be as esthetically satisfying as symmetry. A secondary theme of *Symmetries* is change and constancy — the enormous variousness of related scenes within a single encompassing idea; that is also a secondary theme of *War and Peace,* among other novels.

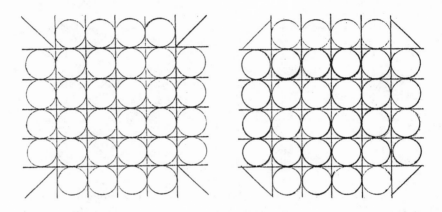

Symmetries is composed more strictly than a conventional novel, for every image has an empirically irreplaceable location in the entire work. Within terms of the whole, no single image can be considered superfluous. The system is at once a constraint that forbids both short cuts and arbitrary turns in the plot and yet a generative form that brings a narrative to an appropriate conclusion. As an extended example of my "Constructivist Fiction," *Symmetries* can be internationally understood. For publication elsewhere in the world, nothing more than its title need be translated.

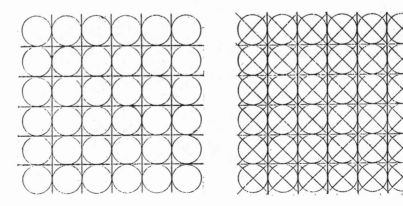

This novel should appear in a book whose format is 4" high and 14" wide, with four images running across its page; so when opened flat the book would reveal a 28" sequence of eight drawings stretched horizontally across the two-page spread. With 392 separate images, the narrative would begin (and end) with a sequence of four images on each of its covers and run for 96 pages.

Epiphanies (1983)

My principal creative project these past few years has been *Epiphanies*, which is a collection of over two thousand discrete single-sentence stories which I hope to "publish" in several unusual forms:

1.) a set of at least three thick pocket-sized volumes with one story on each page, printed not across its shorter dimension, as in conventional books, but parallel to the longer side of the page.

2.) a single large-format hardback book, with several stories on each page, in different typefaces, with plenty of white space between — much like newspaper headlines without accompanying texts.

3.) a series of audiotapes, of at least ten hours total duration, in which the stories would be individually articulated, each in a distinct acoustic setting.

4.) a theatrical version, in which the Epiphanies, typed on cards, are read by at least fifty performers distributed among the audience in a non-theatrical space (say, a ballroom or a gymnasium).

5.) a series of videotapes, likewise at least ten hours long, in which the texts of the stories would appear on the screen, one at a time, with letters produced by a video character-generator.

6.) a museum exhibition for which the stories would be typeset with headline-sized letters and individually mounted on 8" by 10" boards that would be distributed throughout a space.

7.) a film composed of Epiphanies found in other filmmakers' footage ("outtakes") — at least a thousand excerpts for a film of four hours duration. (The sound track for this film would come mostly from #3 above.)

8.) an operatic version, with additional musical material by Bruce Kushnick; here some Epiphanies would be of words alone, others of music alone and yet others of both words and music, all presented in the widest variety of complementary ways.

9.) a skywritten version, in which stories would appear and disintegrate in the wake of each other, all over a geographical area, in the course of a full Sunday.

10.) other realizations no doubt inspired by the first nine.

Retrospect on My Fictions (1985)

In seventeen years' exploration of fiction writing, I have produced

1.) a novella with no more than two words to a paragraph (and then, in one published form, no more than two words to a book page),

2.) a story with only single-word paragraphs,

3.) stories that are narrated through a series of shapes that are composed exclusively of words or letters,

4.) stories consisting exclusively of words whose meaning changes with the introduction not of other words but of different shapes or nonverbal imagery,

5.) stories composed entirely of nonrepresentational line-drawings that metamorphose so systemically that each image in the sequence belongs only to its particular place,

6.) stories composed of just cut-up photographs whose chips move symmetrically through narrative cycles,

7.) individual sentences that are either the openings or the closings of otherwise unwritten stories,

8.) separate modular fictions of photographs that can be read in any order, of line-drawings whose positions in a sequence are interchangeable (and thus can be shuffled), of sentences that are reordered in systemic ways to produce different emphases of the same words and gestures, if not radically different stories,

9.) circular stories that flow from point to point but lack beginnings or ends,

10.) narratives, one as long as a book, composed exclusively of numerals,

11.) a story composed of sixteen different (but complementary) stories interwoven in print in sixteen different typefaces and on audiotape told in sixteen purposefully different amplifications of a single voice,

12.) a modular fiction whose sentences are reordered in systemic ways to produce different emphases of the same words and gestures, if not radically different stories,

13.) over two thousand single-sentence fictions representing the epiphanies of over two thousand otherwise unwritten stories,

14.) manuscripts of stories (*Epiphanies*) that have been offered to periodical editors not to publish *in toto* but from which to make their own selections that can then be ordered and designed to their particular tastes,

15.) a film and a videotape whose imagery is nothing other than words telling stories,

16.) a film with symmetrical abstract fictions (described in #5 above) that metamorphose in systemic sequence,

17.) fictions that exist primarily on audiotape — that cannot be performed live, whose printed version is no more than a score for its realization,

18.) a film composed of verbal and visual epiphanies that have no connection to each other, either vertically or horizontally, other than common fictional structure,

19.) perhaps a few other departures whose character cannot yet, for better or worse, be neatly encapsulated,

20.) the purest *oeuvre* of fiction, as fiction, uncompromised by vulgar considerations, that anyone has ever done,

21.) no conventional fiction — absolutely none — which is to say nothing that could pass a university course/workshop in "fiction writing" (and get me a job teaching such), and no familiar milestone from which simpleminded critics could then measure my "departure."

Even though these fictions of mine have appeared in over three dozen literary magazines, and over a dozen volumes of these fictions have appeared in print, there have been few reviews of individual books, no commercial contracts, no offers from small presses to do a second book, no grants for fiction writing, no inclusion in surveys of contemporary fiction, no public acknowledgment of my alternative purposes in creating and publishing fiction; only one story was ever anthologized by someone else (Eugene Wildman, in his *Experiments in Prose* [1969]). Does anyone care? Should anyone care (other than me)? (Should I care? If so, how? Should I have written this?) What should be made of the fact that no one else — absolutely no one else visible to us — is making fiction in these ways?

Index

Abish, Walter 107, 109
Abrahams, William 73, 74
Adams, Glenda 109
Addison, Joseph 28, 54
Agee, James 22
Ahern, Tom 4
Albert, Mimi 109
Algren, Nelson: *Man with the Golden Arm* 22; *A Walk on the Wild Side* 47
Allen, Donald 143
Anderson, Sherwood 78, 139; *Winsburg, Ohio* 41
Antin, Eleanor 4; *100 Boots* 167
Apollinaire, Guillaume: *The Debauched Hospodar* 21; "Zone," 66
Arias-Mission, Alain 9
Arnheim, Rudolf 9
Ashbery, John 107; "Idaho" 160
Auchincloss, Louis 22
Auerbach, Erich 76

Babel, Isaac 25, 80; "The Sin of Jesus" 79
Bain, Willard 160
Baker, Elliott 25
Baldwin, James 70, 91; *Another Country* 23, 59; *Going to Meet the Man* 59
Ball, Hugo 119
Banks, Russell 107, 109
Barnes, Djuna 24
Barth, John 4, 27, 40, 42, 50, 51, 57, 66, 67, 70, 82, 89, 123, 153, 159, 168; *The End of the Road* 28, 32; *The Floating Opera* 28, 32, 33; *Giles Goat-Boy* 33, 62-65, 69; *The Sot-Weed Factor* 2, 28-34, 51-56, 58, 62-63, 65, 123; "Frame-Tale" 164;

"The Literature of Exhaustion" 124-25, 161; "Title" 123
Barthelme, Donald 52, 67, 68, 80, 83-85, 123, 152-53, 159, 168; *Come Back Dr. Caligari* 40; "Margins" 74; "To London and Rome" 40, 74, 79
Barthelme, Frederick 165
Baumbach, Jonathan 107, 109
Beaulieu, Victor-Levy 146
Beckett, Samuel 50, 52, 67, 68, 73, 78, 80, 82, 110-12, 122, 132, 152, 155, 159, 168; *Comment c'est* 27, 53, 110, 122; *Company* 110; *Nouvelles textes pour rien* 153; *Waiting for Godot* 53
Beigel, Uli 85
Bellow, Saul 3, 56, 69, 81, 159; *Herzog* 26, 59; *To Jerusalem and Back* 112; "Sono and Moso" 83
Berger, Thomas 25
Berne, Stanley 4, 26
Berryman, John 68
Bierce, Ambrose 80
Bingham, Sallie 74
Blattner, H.W. 46, 73, 83- 84
Blatty, William Peter 40
Blechman, Burt: *How Much?* 46; *The War at Camp Omongo* 46
Borges, Jorge Luis 67-68, 70, 80, 83, 122, 153, 159, 168; "Pierre Menard, Author of Don Quixote" 79, 122; "Tlön, Uqbar, Orbis Tertius" 122
Bory, Jean-François 3, 173-75; *Once Again* 173-74; *Post-Scriptum* 174
Bourjaily, Vance 23
Bowles, Paul 48
Breton, André 117
Brinnin, John Malcolm 140
Brown, Norman O. 67

Brownstein, Michael 107
Buahin, Peter Kwame 80
Buechner, Frederick 22
Bumpus, Jerry 107, 109
Burgess, Anthony 149
Burke, Kenneth 90, 156
Burnett, David 72
Burns, John Horne 22
Burroughs, William 27, 74, 80, 85,
    110, 123, 124, 144, 145, 152, 159;
    Cities of the Red Night 111; *The
    Exterminator* 47; *In Search of Yage* 48;
    Junkie 46; *Naked Lunch* 2, 46–47,
    58, 111, 127, 147; *The Nova
    Express* 47; *The Third Mind* 112; *The
    Ticket That Exploded* 47
Butor, Michel 125, 159, 171–72

Cacciatore, Vera 80
Cage, John 68, 70, 130; *Indeterminacy*
    163; *A Year from Monday* 117, 124;
    "Talk I" 124
Camus, Albert 32, 82
Capek, Milic 67
Capote, Truman 59, 141, 172
Carroll, Lewis 66, 139, 158
Carroll, Paul 147–48
Casares, Adolfo Bioy 80
Celine, Ferdinard-Louis 35, 141
Charters, Ann 145
Charyn, Jerome 107, 109; *The Man
    Who Grew Younger* 59; *Once Upon a
    Droshky* 25
Cheever, John 75
Chekhov, Anton 73, 77, 80
Ciardi, John 148
Codrescu, Andrei 107
Cohen, Marvin 127, 164
Cole, Tom 74
Connell, Evan S., Jr. 23
Connolly, Cyril 90
Conrad, Earl 166
Conrad, Joseph 89
Cooper, Clarnece L. 48
Coover, Robert 60
Cozzens, James Gould 69
Crane, Stephen 128
Cross, Doris 179
Crumb, Robert 152, 159
Cummings, E.E. 133, 140

Dagerman, Stig 80
Dante Alighieri 179
Davis, Christopher 74
Dawson, Fielding 107
DeJasu, Lee 168
DeMott, Benjamin 25
Dickens, Charles 77
Doctorow, E.L. 58, 68
Doesburg, Theo van 187
Donleavy, J.P. 22
Dos Passos, John 140
Dostoevsky, Fyodor 21, 27, 41, 83,
    91, 143
Dreiser, Theodore 74, 128, 143
Dryden, John 131
DuBois, W.E.B. 2

Edson, Russell 163
Eich, Gunter 80
Elevitch, M.D. 4, 107
Eliot, T.S. 41, 88, 91, 95–96, 101, 136
Elkin, Stanley 25
Elliott, George P. 23, 75, 77, 81
Ellison, Ralph 26, 31, 56, 59, 86–102;
    Invisible Man 2, 86, 90–92, 94–95,
    98, 101; *Shadow and Act* 88, 93, 97;
    "And Hickman Returns" 26
Empson, William 131
Emshwiller, Carol 4
Esslin, Martin 27, 118

Farina, Richard 60
Faulkner, William 27, 77, 78, 80, 131,
    140, 153, 159; *Absalom, Absalom* 47;
    As I Lay Dying 25; *The Sound and the
    Fury* 25, 27, 61, 122; "The
    Bear" 25, 73
Faust, Irvin 27, 50, 51, 67, 69, 75,
    81, 83; *Entering Angel's World* 45;
    The File on Stanley Patton Buchta 71;
    Roar, Lion Roar 2, 44, 58; *The
    Steagle* 60, 61–62, 71; *Willy
    Remembers* 71; "The Dalai Lama of
    Harlem" 74; "Jake Bluffstein and
    Adolf Hitler" 44–45, 60, 61; "Philco
    Baby" 74
Federman, Raymond 107, 153, 166
Ferlinghetti, Lawrence 40
Fiedler, Leslie A. 31, 51, 103–05; *Back*

to China 104; *Being Busted* 105; *An End to Innocence* 103; *The Last Jew in America* 59, 105; *No! in Thunder* 103; *Pull Down Vanity* 103; *The Second Stone* 25; "Nude Croquet" 25, 104, 105

Flaubert, Gustave 136

Foley, Martha 72–75

Ford, Ford Madox 159, 165

Foreman, Richard 11

Freud, Sigmund 21, 88, 117

Friedman, B.H. 107, 109

Friedman, Bruce Jay 27, 58, 85; *Black Angels* 59; *Far from the City of Class* 44; *A Mother's Kisses* 44; *Stern* 43–44, 58, 59

Frost, Robert 41, 154

Fruchter, Norman 25

Frye, Northrop 157, 165–66

Fuller, R. Buckminster 67, 70

Gabo, Naum 190

Gaddis, William 25, 47, 59

Gangemi, Kenneth 4; *Olt* 159; "Change" 162–63

Gàscar, Pierre 80

Gass, William 60

Gelber, Jack 25

Genet, Jean 21, 141

Gerz, Jochen 3

Gide, Andre 25, 77

Gilgun, John F. 25

Gins, Madeline 164–66

Ginsberg, Allen 48, 141–45

Glynn, Thomas 109

Gogol, Nikolai 23, 41

Gold, Herbert 22

Gold, Ivan 25, 85

Grass, Gunther 50

Gravenson, G.S. 160

Grayson, Richard 109, 180–81

Haldeman, Charles 25

Harrington, Alan: *The Revelations of Doctor Modesto* 26; *The Secret Swinger* 59

Hauser, Marianne 109

Hawkes, John 24, 75, 153, 159

Hawthorne, Nathaniel 74, 77, 163

Hefter, Richard 164

Heller, Joseph 27, 51, 66, 82, 123; *Catch-22* 2, 34–35, 49–53, 57, 58, 123; *Something Happened* 59

Helms, Hans G.: *Fa:m 'Ahniesgwow* 4, 159

Henry, O. 74, 78

Herman, Jan 163–64

Higgins, Dick 3

Highwater, Jamake (aka J Marks) 4

Holmes, John Clellon 143, 144

Homer 75

Horn, Richard 164

Horovitz, Israel 107

Howard, Maureen 107

Howe, Irving 93

Hughes, Langston 89

Hughes, Ted 80

Hulsenbeck, Richard 123

Huxley, Aldous 48

Hyman, Stanley Edgar 28, 31, 54, 90, 101

Ibsen, Henrik 41

Ionesco, Eugene 52, 121, 123; *The Chairs* 37, 52; *The Lesson* 43; *The New Tenant* 173

Irving, Washington 77

Jackson, Shirley 41, 81, 90

Jacobson, Dan 77

James, Henry 74, 80, 89, 101, 136

Jarry, Alfred 27; *The Exploits and Opinions of Doctor Faustroll, 'Pataphysician* 68, 120; "The Supermale" 80, 121, 123

Jarvis, Charles 146

Johnson, B.S. 80, 122, 126

Johnson, James Weldon 2, 95

Jones, James 22

Jones, LeRoi: *Dutchman* 98; *The Moderns* 26; *The System of Dante's Hell* 60

Joyce, James 27, 77, 79, 110, 124–25, 128, 131, 143, 147, 161; *Finnegans Wake* 6, 122, 127, 139, 145, 148, 152, 159, 162, 168; *Ulysses* 33, 122, 152; "The Dead" 79; "Ivy Day in the Committee Room" 79

Kafka, Franz 21, 80, 105, 124–25, 161; "The Penal Colony" 73, 79
Kahn, Herman 67
Kaltenbach, Steve 163
Karlen, Arno 25
Katz, Steve 107, 109, 166
Kazin, Alfred 141
Kelley, William Melvin: *A Different Drummer* 25; *Dunford Travels Everywhere* 162
Kenner, Hugh 129
Kern, W. Bliem 166
Kerouac, Jack 23, 141–50; *Desolation Angels* 146; *The Dharma Bums* 146; *Doctor Sax* 141, 146; *Maggie Cassady* 146; *Mexico City Blues* 146; *On the Road* 141, 142, 144, 146; *The Subterraneans* 141; *Tristessa* 144, 146; *Visions of Cody* 142, 143, 145, 146; "Essentials for Spontaneous Prose" 146; "Old Angel Midnight" 142, 147, 148; "Some of the Dharma" 150
Kesey, Ken 39–40
King, Alexander 48
King, Kenneth: "Super-Lecture" 123; "Print-Out" 162
Kleinman, Bruce 109
Klinkowitz, Jerome 4
Knott, Bill 163
Knowles, John 24
Koch, Kenneth 51, 52, 58, 67, 75, 80, 84; *Ko* 39; "The Postcard Collection" 39, 74, 83; "The Red Robins" 39
Korg, Jacob 118
Korn, Henry James 164
Kostelanetz, Richard: *And So Forth* 6, 7, 191; *Breakthrough Fictioneers* 4, 142, 152, 155; *Constructs* 6; *Constructs Two* 6; *Epiphanies* 9, 10, 196–98; *Exhaustive Parallel Intervals* 6; *Extrapolate* 7; *Foreshortenings & Other Stories* 7, 8; *In the Beginning* 5; *Inexistences* 7; *Metamorphosis in the Arts* 3; *Modulations* 7, 8; *More Short Fictions* 4; *The New American Arts* 58; *Numbers: Poems & Stories* 6; *Openings & Closings* 6, 8, 9, 191; *Reincarnations* 6; *Short Fictions* 5, 6; *Symmetries* 192–95; *Tabula Rasa* 7; *The Theatre of Mixed Means* 3;

Twelve from the Sixties 4, 67; *The Yale Gertrude Stein* 11; *The Young American Writers* 123, 124; "Dialogues" 3; "Excelsior" 5, 6, 9; "Goods" 5; "Innovations in Fiction" 4; "Milestones in a Life" 5, 8, 11, 163; "Plateaux" 9; "One Night Stood" 5, 7; "Times Perceived: A Working Day" 6; "Twenty-Five Fictional Hypotheses" 3
Kraf, Elaine 109
Kramer, Laura 109
Krauss, Ruth 4
Krim, Seymour 143, 146–47

Landolfi, Tommaso 80
Larner, Jeremy 60
Leavy, Timothy 70
Levin, Harry 79
Lewis, R.W.B. 31
Lewis, Sinclair 1, 67, 105
Lind, Jakov 80
Lindsay, Vachel 128
Lissitzky, El 151
Litwak, Leo E. 22
Locke, Alain 89
London, Jack 163
Lonider, Lynn 75
Lowry, Malcolm 46, 83
Ludwig, Jack 80; *Confusions* 40; "Thoreau in California" 83
Lytle, Andrew 22

McCarthy, Mary 22, 74, 77, 81, 127
Macauley, Robie 23
McClure, Michael 48
McCullers, Carson 22, 81
McElroy, Joseph 60
MacKaye, Percy 137
MacLennan, Toby 161
Mac Low, Jackson 4
McLuhan, Marshall 67, 70, 75
McNally, Dennis 145, 147
Mailer, Norman 69, 141; *The American Dream* 23, 59; *The Deer Park* 23; "The Time of Her Time" 23
Major, Clarence 107, 109

Malamud, Bernard 3, 25, 80, 81; *The Fixer* 59; *The Natural* 23, 56–57, 59
Mallock, W.H. 176
Malraux, Andre: *Days of Wrath* 89; *The Imaginary Museum* 115, 182; *Man's Fate* 89
Mann, Thomas 128
Manoff, Eva 74
Markfield, Wallace 24
Marks, J (aka Jamake Highwater) 4
Marshall, Paule 58, 75
Marx, Karl 21, 88, 163
Mathews, Harry 52, 123; *The Conversions* 40, 66, 123; *Tlooth* 66, 123
Maupassant, Guy de 80
Mella, John 4
Melville, Herman 74, 77, 91, 143, 163; *Billy Budd* 56; *Moby-Dick* 47; "Bartleby" 41, 83
Mencken, H.L. 103
Merrill, James 60
Michals, Duane 167
Michaux, Henri 48
Miller, Henry 2, 27, 31
Miller, Warren 24, 74
Mirsky, Mark 107
Moholy-Nagy, L. 118, 119, 177, 187–88
Molinaro, Ursule 107, 109
Mondrian, Piet 186–87
Moravia, Alberto 50
Morris, Richard 115
Morris, Wright 22, 166
Moskoff, Martin Stephen 164
Motherwell, Robert 118
Mudrick, Marvin 161
Murray, Albert 91, 94, 101
Mustill, Norman Ogue 168

Nabokov, Vladimir 27, 59, 153, 159; *The Gift* 41; *Lolita* 26, 41; *Pale Fire* 26, 41–43, 50, 51, 58, 122
Nemerov, Howard 59
Neugeboren, Jay 60
Nichol, bp 161, 162
Nietzsche, Friedrich 21
Nin, Anais 115

O'Connor, Flannery 22, 74, 81
O'Connor, Frank 75, 78
O'Hara, John 85
Ohmann, Richard 4
Oldenburg, Claes 70, 123
Olsen, Tillie 67, 75, 81, 85; "Tell Me a Riddle" 25, 73, 83
O'Neill, Eugene 137
Oppenheimer, J. Robert 125
Orwell, George 24, 63
Ozick, Cynthia 60

Paley, Grace 25, 75
Palinurus (aka Cyril Connolly) 86
Patchen, Kenneth 152, 159
Peden, William 75
Percy, Walker 27, 51, 60; *The Last Gentleman* 59; *The Moviegoer* 43, 49, 58
Perelman, S.J. 27
Phillips, Tom 3, 176–79; *A Humument* 176–79; *Irma* 179; *Works. Texts. To 1974* 176–77, 179
Plath, Sylvia 83
Podhoretz, Norman 141–42
Poe, Edgar Allen 21, 74, 77
Poirier, Richard 73, 74
Pollini, Francis 59
Pope, Alexander 41
Porter, Katherine Anne 80
Pound, Ezra 88, 131, 136, 160
Powers, J.F. 22, 81
Pritchard, Norman Henry, II 166
Proust, Marcel 77, 128, 143
Purdy, James 3, 51, 58, 80; *Malcolm* 38, 50, 83; *The Nephew* 38; "Don't Call Me by My Right Name" 38, 84; "Goodnight Sweetheart" 38, 84; "63: Dream Palace" 84
Pushkin, Alexander 59
Pynchon, Thomas 3, 27, 50, 51, 57, 58, 66, 80, 123; *The Crying of Lot 49* 64–66; *V.* 35–38, 52–54, 58, 64, 65, 84; "Entropy" 37, 65, 82, 84; "Morality and Mercy in Vienna" 38, 65; "Under the Rose" 65

Queneau 52, 121

Rabelais, François 56
Raglan, Lord 90
Rahv, Philip 64
Rechy, John 24
Reed, Ishmael 107
Reichek, Jesse 168
Rexroth, Kenneth 130, 141
Richler, Mordecai 27; *The Appren-
  ticeship of Duddy Kravitz* 38; *Stick
  Out Your Neck* 38-39
Richter, Hans 118
Rimbaud, Arthur 143
Robbe-Grillet, Alain 25, 80, 120,
  122, 132
Roehler, Klaus 80
Rooke, Leon 109
Rosenberg, Harold 157
Rosenfeld, Isaac 22
Rosenthal, Irving 147-48
Rot, Dieter 4
Roth, Philip 24, 67, 85, 159, 160
Roussel, Raymond 66
Rubin, William S. 118
Rumaker, Michael 27, 45, 75, 83
Ruscha, Edward 167

Sade, Marquis de 21
Salinger, J.D. 59, 81; *Catcher in the
  Rye* 41; *Seymour: An Introduction* 22
Sanders, Ed 162
Saporta, Marc 126, 164
Sarraute, Nathalie 27, 50
Sartre, Jean-Paul 1, 60, 80, 82
Schapiro, Meyer 115
Schuyler, James 74
Schwartz, Delmore 22, 81
Schwerner, Armand 161
Schwitters, Kurt 119, 124
Scott, Nathan A. 101
Selby, Hubert, Jr. 26, 49, 58, 59,
  74, 80, 85
Shakespeare, William 143, 144
Sigal, Clancy 24
Sinclair, Upton 77, 144
Singer, Isaac Bashevis 23, 59, 80
Skillings, R.D. 107, 109
Smithson, Robert 4

Smollett, Tobias 33
Sondheim, Alan 4
Sontag, Susan 24, 75, 85
Sourian, Peter 25
Southern, Terry 24
Spielberg, Peter 107, 109
Spoerri, Daniel 121
Stein, Gertrude 88, 128-40, 158, 165;
  *The Autobiography of Alice B.
  Toklas* 139; *Before the Flowers of
  Friendship Faded Friendship
  Faded* 138; *Geography and Plays* 133,
  134, 139, 160; *In Circles* 137; *Lectures
  in America* 132, 136; *Lucy Church
  Amiably* 136; *Mrs. Reynolds* 160; *The
  Making of Americans* 129, 131-32,
  139, 159, 160; *Tender Buttons* 132-
  33; *Three Lives* 129, 139; *What
  Happened* 137; "The King or
  Something" 134; "One or Two. I've
  Finished" 138; "Monsieur Vollard
  et Cezanne" 137; "Susie
  Asado" 133; "We Care: A History"
  138
Stern, Richard 26
Sterne, Laurence 56
Strand, Mark 107
Styron, William 59; *Lie Down in
  Darkness* 22, 41; *Set This House on
  Fire* 22, 46
Sukenick, Ronald 106-09, 159
Sutherland, Donald 128, 132-37, 139
Swados, Harvey 75

Tallman, Warren 143
Taube, Myron 85
Taylor, Peter 75
Taylor, Simon Watson 120
Tertz, Abram 80
Thomas, Dylan 80, 149
Tolstoy, Leo 77
Trilling, Lionel 81
Trocchi, Alexander 48
Tuten, Frederic 107, 163
Twain, Mark 50, 54, 104
Tytell, John 145-46
Tzara, Tristan 118, 119, 154

Uchimura, Naoya 8
Updike, John 69, 74, 85
Uris, Leon 22

Vaughn-James, M. 4, 167
Vechten, Carl Van 133, 137
Veitch, Tom 123, 124
Verne, Jules 1
Voltaire, F.M.A. de 91
Vonnegut, Kurt, Jr. 40

Walter, Eugene 137
Warhol, Andy 70, 126
Warren, Robert Penn 22, 101
Weber, Max 21
Weber, Nancy 166
Weinstein, Norman 129
West, John Anthony 24
West, Nathanael: *The Day of the
    Locust* 2, 24, 103; *The Dream Life of
    Balso Snell* 27
Wharton, Edith 80
Whitman, Walt 131

Wilde, Oscar 4, 163
Wilder, Thornton 139
Wildman, Eugene 107; *Experiments in
    Prose* 198; *Nuclear Love* 166
Williams, Emmett 4, 163
Wittgenstein, Ludwig 119
Wolfe, Thomas 24, 141, 143
Wolfe, Tom 59, 67
Woolf, Douglas 26
Wordsworth, William 41
Wouk, Herman 22
Wright, Richard 2, 89

Yates, Richard 24
Young, Philip 31
Yount, John 25, 74, 85

Zahn, Curtis 49, 58, 59, 74, 80, 85
Zazeela, Marian 168
Zekowski, Arlene 4, 26
Zend, Robert 166
Zola, Emile 21